Task-Based Instruction for Teaching Russian as a Foreign Language

Task-Based Instruction for Teaching Russian as a Foreign Language presents the most recent developments in the field of task-based language teaching (TBLT) and highlights impactful research-based instructional practices of applying TBLT for the teaching of Russian.

This comprehensive volume extends the current understanding of the nature and role of tasks in course development, authenticity in task design, the role of the instructor in TBLT, teaching culture through TBLT, the intersection of complex morphology and explicit grammar instruction with task-based approaches, collaborative interaction within TBLT, and technology-mediated tasks. This resource focuses on the unique set of factors and challenges that arise when applying TBLT in the instruction of Russian and other morphologically rich languages.

This edited volume will be of interest to teachers of Russian as well as researchers in Russian language acquisition, language pedagogy, and Slavic applied linguistics.

Svetlana Nuss is a Language Acquisition Instructional Consultant and Coach, University of Alaska Fairbanks, U.S.A.

Wendy Whitehead Martelle is Assistant Professor of Applied Linguistics, ESL, and Russian at the University of Alaska Fairbanks, U.S.A.

Routledge Russian Language Pedagogy and Research
Series Editor: Svetlana V. Nuss
University of Alaska, USA

Routledge Russian Language Pedagogy and Research series publishes academic resources on research and pedagogy of teaching the Russian language. Written by experts from across the world, the series brings together diverse schools of thought and serves as an inclusive discussion forum showcasing state-of-the-art advances in teaching and researching Russian. All chapters in the edited volumes of **Routledge Russian Language Pedagogy and Research** undergo a rigorous double-blind peer review process to ensure the highest academic standard.

Task-Based Instruction for Teaching Russian as a Foreign Language
Edited by Svetlana V. Nuss and Wendy Whitehead Martelle

For more information about this series please visit: www.routledge.com/Routledge-Russian-Language-Pedagogy-and-Research/book-series/RLPR

Task-Based Instruction for Teaching Russian as a Foreign Language

Edited by Svetlana V. Nuss and
Wendy Whitehead Martelle

LONDON AND NEW YORK

First published 2022
by Routledge
4 Park Square, Milton Park, Abingdon, Oxon OX14 4RN

and by Routledge
605 Third Avenue, New York, NY 10158

Routledge is an imprint of the Taylor & Francis Group, an informa business

© 2022 selection and editorial matter, Svetlana V. Nuss and Wendy Whitehead Martelle; individual chapters, the contributors

The right of Svetlana V. Nuss and Wendy Whitehead Martelle to be identified as the authors of the editorial material, and of the authors for their individual chapters, has been asserted in accordance with sections 77 and 78 of the Copyright, Designs and Patents Act 1988.

All rights reserved. No part of this book may be reprinted or reproduced or utilised in any form or by any electronic, mechanical, or other means, now known or hereafter invented, including photocopying and recording, or in any information storage or retrieval system, without permission in writing from the publishers.

Trademark notice: Product or corporate names may be trademarks or registered trademarks, and are used only for identification and explanation without intent to infringe.

British Library Cataloguing-in-Publication Data
A catalogue record for this book is available from the British Library

Library of Congress Cataloging-in-Publication Data
A catalog record for this book has been requested

ISBN: 978-0-367-70441-4 (hbk)
ISBN: 978-0-367-70443-8 (pbk)
ISBN: 978-1-003-14634-6 (ebk)

DOI: 10.4324/9781003146346

Typeset in Times New Roman
by Apex CoVantage, LLC

Contents

List of contributors vii
Preface viii
SVETLANA V. NUSS
Acknowledgements x

1 **Task-based instruction for teaching Russian as a foreign language: perspectives and practice** 1
SVETLANA V. NUSS AND WENDY WHITEHEAD MARTELLE

2 **Morphology acquisition research meets instruction of L2 Russian: a contextualized literature review** 15
SVETLANA V. NUSS

3 **Cracking the Cyrillic code through tasks: implications for instruction and foreign language teacher education** 36
NINA KOSITSKY

4 **Learner corpus as a medium for tasks** 47
ALEKSEY NOVIKOV AND VALENTINA VINOKUROVA

5 **Task-based vlogs in an elementary Russian classroom** 65
KATIE ESSER

6 **Russian and Russia through tasks for beginners: applying task-based language teaching at a low proficiency level** 77
VITA V. KOGAN AND MARIA BONDARENKO

7 **Teaching Russian in Brazil: learner-centered task design and TORFL connection** 98
ANNA SMIRNOVA HENRIQUES, NADEZHDA DUBININA,
YULIA MIKHEEVA, AND VOLHA YERMALAYEVA FRANCO

8 Task-based learning in the "grand simulation" context: six
principles for success from isolated immersion programs 121
SARA NIMIS, NATALIA V. KRYLOVA, AND IULIIA FEDOSEEVA

9 Использование целевого задания в краткосрочных курсах
РКИ для иностранных студентов-нефилологов 135
EKATERINA BURVIKOVA AND YEVGENIYA STREMOVA

10 Task-based peer interaction in Russian as a second/foreign
language classes 152
DMITRII PASTUSHENKOV

11 Kommunalka: virtual space as a platform
for task-based learning 171
EVELINA MENDELEVICH

12 Developing global competence in an advanced Russian course 190
SNEZHANA ZHELTOUKHOVA

13 TBLT in Russian classrooms: reflections on practice
and future directions 206
WENDY WHITEHEAD MARTELLE AND SVETLANA V. NUSS

References 218
Index 242

Contributors

Maria Bondarenko, Heidelberg University, Germany; University of Montreal, Canada

Ekaterina Burvikova, University of New Hampshire, U.S.A.

Nadezhda Dubinina, Saint Petersburg State University, Saint Petersburg, Russia

Katie Esser, University of Vermont, U.S.A.

Iuliia Fedoseeva, Concordia Language Villages, U.S.A.

Vita V. Kogan, Queen Mary University of London, U.K.

Nina Kositsky, University of Maryland, U.S.A.

Natalia V. Krylova, Concordia Language Villages, U.S.A.

Evelina Mendelevich, New York University, U.S.A.

Yulia Mikheeva, Language School Yu Cursos de Idiomas, Brasília, Brazil

Sara Nimis, Concordia Language Villages, U.S.A.

Aleksey Novikov, University of Arizona, U.S.A.

Svetlana V. Nuss, University of Alaska, U.S.A.

Dmitrii Pastushenkov, Michigan State University, U.S.A.

Anna Smirnova Henriques, Pontifícia Universidade Católica de São Paulo; Language School Clube Russo Priviet, São Paulo, Brazil

Yevgeniya Stremova, Language Link, Moscow, Russia

Valentina Vinokurova, University of Arizona, U.S.A.

Wendy Whitehead Martelle, University of Alaska Fairbanks, U.S.A.

Volha Yermalayeva Franco, Universidade Federal da Bahia, Salvador; Language School Clube Eslavo, São Paulo, Brazil

Snezhana Zheltoukhova, Stetson University, U.S.A.

Preface

Svetlana V. Nuss

Task-based instruction for teaching Russian as a foreign language (RFL) is a collection of task-based practices for teaching Russian as a second and foreign language (L2 Russian). The cases described here offer a rich sample of instructional practices set within a broadly conceived task-based language teaching (TBLT) movement to include task-supported instruction (TSI). The featured cases are diverse in their instructional forms: from an overarching framework of a task-based syllabus and course development to incidental instructional episodes of various lengths and complexity, providing a comfortable starting point for instructors who would like to give TBLT a try in their practice on a smaller scale. The chapters are organized by learner proficiency and represent levels from complete beginner to advanced. The chapters include nuanced reflections from both experienced and novice practitioners on the challenges morphologically rich languages present for instruction along with possible solutions. The compilation is preceded by a chapter on Russian morphology, research developments in its L2 processing, and how they inform the instruction of L2 Russian. The chapter sets the context for the volume's deeper discussion of L2 Russian instruction by providing a comprehensive overview of recent research advances in L2 Russian morphology acquisition.

The volume responds to the needs of the language teaching professionals and researchers beyond instruction of RFL, as it helps inform the instruction of other Slavic languages with morphological systems similar to Russian that may have a smaller L2 learner- and research base to draw from. It concludes with the chapter outlining practitioners' perspectives on what research they consider most useful for teaching L2 Russian along with the questions they raise and provides the field possible directions for relevant classroom research.

The chapters of the volume have the following features: first, structured introductions are included in English and in Russian to provide a succinct overview of the instructional case at hand and to make the volume more accessible to those of our readers who are mostly Russian-speaking, affording them a fast preview option. Second, each chapter features a task overview table with the essential task information available at a glance: title and type of task, its brief description, the level of proficiency and learner needs analysis, and the type(s) of assessment used. Third, each chapter offers authors' reflections on the lessons they learned in implementing task-based instruction and their perspectives on the challenges of teaching Russian as a Foreign Language. Furthermore, each chapter includes a literature review of the particular aspect of instruction it details while broader issues of TBLT as an instructional approach in general and the development of TBLT in the teaching of L2 Russian are addressed by the editors in Chapter 1.

Several factors influenced the creation of this volume. First, Leaver and Willis (2004) laid the groundwork for L2 Russian pedagogical narration in their *Task-based instruction in foreign language education*. It contained a chapter based on U.S. government Slavic language programs, including Russian (Leaver & Kaplan, 2004). Leaver and Willis's (2004) compilation spanned ten languages and created the precedent for this volume as it featured practitioner accounts of TBLT instruction, introduced and contextualized in the preface. Our main inspiration, however, comes from personal experiences gained in teaching L2 Russian. With both editors teaching bilingual education and applied linguistics graduate courses, we gained a strong theoretical grounding in second language research and instruction. We also had the freedom, professional curiosity, and courage to explore new instructional strategies with each new cohort of L2 Russian students in our own classrooms. This created the perfect conditions for us to pursue the search of our own L2 Russian methodological "gold," and we did find some pedagogical nuggets along the way. The creation of this volume is fueled by our desire to provide the kind of instructional support for teachers of L2 Russian that our L2 English and L2 Spanish colleagues enjoy globally. The volume is published with the understanding that the diverse learners of L2 Russian stand to gain from it the most.

Acknowledgements

The editors express their deep gratitude to everyone involved in the production of this book. First and foremost, we are eternally grateful to Routledge, Taylor and Francis Group, for its vision in establishing a series on the pedagogy of Russian, a less commonly taught morphologically rich language, in support of its teachers and to the benefit of its learners. We are especially indebted to Samantha Vale Noya, Commissioning Editor at Routledge: her wise foresight, persistent professional curiosity, and thorough expertise helped bring this volume to life. We also thank Rosie McEwan, Editorial Assistant, for incredible attention to detail and overall competence.

The editors wish to thank a distinguished panel of expert reviewers for their invaluable help in providing thoughtful comments on the chapters and asking challenging questions: your expertise and service to the profession are no short of admirable!

> Lyudmyla A'Beckett, Thomas Beyer, Nadezda Christopher, Seetha Jayaraman, Sviatlana Karpava, Olesya Kisselev, Natalia Krylova, Jonathan Ludwig, Cynthia Martin, Daniel Martín-González, Jennifer Morris, Jill Neuendorf, Oksana Polyakova, Sabine Siekmann, Wolfgang Stadler.

We express sincere appreciation to Betty Lou Leaver and William Comer for their valuable knowledge, enthusiastic encouragement, and collegial support in the initial stages of volume creation.

It is only appropriate to mention the name of someone whose heart and soul had been vested in Task-Based Language Teaching and who passed away a few short months prior publication of this volume: Michael H. Long had been an inspiration to many and a powerful agent of change in the way languages are taught. His legacy lives on.

Our sincerest gratitude goes to all the authors who have contributed to this book. Their innovative work, quality scholarship, and enthusiasm for teaching the Russian language are truly inspirational. We publish this volume with hopes to support teachers in diversifying their choices of instructional strategies to the greater benefit of learners of the Russian language all around the globe.

Chapter 1

Task-based instruction for teaching Russian as a foreign language
Perspectives and practice

Svetlana V. Nuss and Wendy Whitehead Martelle

Chapter summary

The chapter opens with a discussion of the cyclic nature of pedagogy and a brief overview of TBLT-related publications of the last decade. It then presents a comprehensive review of TBLT literature in the context of teaching L2 Russian beginning with Leaver and Kaplan (2004). The terms *systemic mode* (when an entire syllabus or institutional program is built and sequenced using task-based approach) and *incremental mode* (when teachers use tasks as an increment of instruction, more or less cohesively integrating them in an otherwise non-task-oriented course work, to include the use of tasks for assessment) are proposed to conceptualize and distinguish between the two ways tasks are used in teaching languages. Three instruments of task design are offered as potentially impactful for instructional design of task-based teaching of L2 Russian. The first instrument addresses Russian morphology and accounts for linguistic demands entailed in the task structure (based on Pallotti, 2019). The second instrument is the list of linguistic features that learners of L2 Russian should have command of, organized by proficiency levels (based on Long et al., 2012). The third instrument is the growing bank of pedagogical narrations of incremental and systemic models of task-based instruction of L2 Russian developed to date with a brief recap of the list. The chapter includes a comprehensive thematic analysis of the present volume's contributions and their treatment of TBLT and its practice in L2 Russian classroom: (a) all tasks, whether used in systemic or incremental modes, involve a needs analysis before the task design; (b) the intention behind task design has a focus on meaning with a clear outcome other than the use of language; (c) the tasks involve authenticity in some form (either situational or interactional); (d) the tasks reflect a learner-centered approach that promotes learner agency and learner autonomy; (e) the tasks foster interaction. In addition, all contributions contain a cultural component, many authors emphasize proficiency development, feature technology-mediated tasks, address task sequencing, and reflect on the role of teacher and teacher agency in task-based instruction.

Краткое содержание главы

В главе рассматривается цикличность педагогики как общественного процесса, место целевого задания в обучении русскому как иностранному (РКИ) и достижения текущего десятилетия в развитии методики целевого задания. Подробно освещаются публикации, посвященные развитию метода целевого задания в обучении РКИ, начиная со статьи в соавторстве Leaver и Kaplan (2004). Вводятся термины *системное* (уровень программы или общего подхода в организации образовательного поля) и *эпизодическое* (использование целевого задания как отдельного эпизода в образовательном процессе, более или менее органично встроенного в курс, в том числе в целях выявления языковых компетенций обучающихся) употребление целевого задания в педагогической практике обучения иностранным языкам. Определены и описаны три инструмента для разработки целевых заданий в курсе РКИ. Первый инструмент выявлен у Pallotti (2019) и представляет собой систему определения лингвистической нагрузки целевого задания с учетом богатой морфологии русского языка. Второй потенциально действенный инструмент – Long et al. (2012), где статистически обоснованы и распределены по уровням компетенций языковые структуры русского языка, характеризующие уровень обучающегося. Третьим инструментом признана растущая база практических разработок и описаний вариантов воплощения целевого задания на практике; приводится подробный список рекомендуемых публикаций, освещающих и эпизодическое, и системное применение целевого задания в практике РКИ. Глава содержит синтез практических рекомендаций авторов сборника, использованные авторами определения целевого задания и интерпретации определений в практике РКИ. Так, (a) все без исключения авторы данного сборника выстраивают обучение, исходя из идентификации потребностей обучающихся в каждом конкретном случае как эпизодического, так и системного применения целевого задания; (b) целевое задание выходит за рамки языковой практики; смысловая нагрузка целевого задания имеет приложение в действительности; (c) целевое задание предполагает интерактивную или ситуативную аутентичность; (d) целевое задание личностно ориентировано, сосредоточено на обучающемся и его целях, предполагая наличие и способствуя формированию активного личностного начала обучающегося; (e) целевое задание порождает и развивает общение. Более того, все целевые задания имеют культурную составляющую; многие делают акцент на продвижении и развитии общей языковой компетенции; целевые задания задействуют современные компьютерные технологии; целевые задания структурированы и упорядочены в систему, выстраивая программу всего курса обучения; анализируется роль учителя/преподавателя в практике использования целевого задания при обучении РКИ.

Cyclic nature of pedagogy: task-based instruction and its use in teaching of Russian as a foreign language

In post–civil war Russia of 1930, its people devastated by famine and organized crime, in a country with ruined infrastructure and a nation entangled in societal tensions beyond any measure, a book was published. The book was titled *Task-based instruction in a soviet preschool ~ Метод целевых заданий в советском детском саду*: an earnest search for better ways to raise youth and a powerful testimony to the good of human spirit. Allow yourself to get past the politically charged language, and you will discover a rich source of task-based instruction that sounds surprisingly modern in its nature. Considering the number of orphans in Russia in the 1930s, the publication of this resource was a commendable event: dissemination of best practices in working with children who experienced severe adversity and trauma early in their young lives was the next best thing to not having such experiences enter the life of a child in the first place.

The book was published by the *Институт повышения квалификации педагогов народного комиссариата просвещения* [Institute of Continuous Teacher Education, Department of Education], in partnership with the *Подотдел социального воспитания Московского отдела народного образования* [Social Education Program of Moscow School District], and boasts an impressive 250 pages. In its opening chapter, the authors debate the nature of task-based learning with American colleagues and offer their own perspective on it. Many of the tasks described in the rest of its chapters, with small adjustments, would make meaningful units of instruction in a modern classroom: From starting a home library to finding out how pencils are made; from learning what firefighters do to arranging a dove's nest (dove-keeping still exists as a hobby in Russia today); from discovering the wisdom of sustainable life in planning and planting a garden to raising a chicken – authentic, student-centered, and hands-on meaningful learning by any standards.

This long-forgotten volume of early childhood and youth pedagogy is living evidence of how cyclical the nature of society and pedagogy really is, and how often distance – time or miles – transforms *new* and *old*, thereby helping the next cycle to begin. It is difficult to tell with certainty when task-based instruction first came to be used in education; the field of foreign language teaching has employed it and formally researched and written about it since at least the 1980s (Breen, 1989; Crookes, 1986; Long, 1983, 1985; Prabhu, 1987; Richards et al., 1985).

Today TBLT is a widely practiced and researched approach to second language teaching (Plonsky & Kim, 2016). TBLT is adopted in various educational contexts (Schurz & Coumel, 2020) with a proven record of its effectiveness in facilitating language acquisition (Bryfonski & McKay, 2017). TBLT gained significant ground as an approach to practice in the last decade alone with new research advances summarized in Long (2015, 2016), Ellis (2017), Mackey (2020), *inter alia*; its own international association with a biannual conference (IATBLT – International

Association of Task-Based Language Teaching), and a series of peer-reviewed publications. Some recent publications are setting-specific, such as TBLT in Asia (Thomas & Reinders, 2021); many volumes focus on the connection between TBLT and other theoretical concepts such as pragmatics, interactions, repetition, focus on form, and more (Ellis et al., 2020; Taguchi & Kim, 2018; Bygate, 2018; Willis & Willis, 2007; Nunan, 2004). In the most recent edited volumes related to TBLT, scholars have explored connections between tasks/TBLT and a variety of pedagogical concepts. For example, an early volume on technology-mediated TBLT (González-Lloret & Ortega, 2014) investigated the interface between tasks and the affordances of technology, with contributions focusing on L2 English, L2 Spanish, and L2 Chinese. In a more recent qualitative meta-analysis (Chong & Reinders, 2020) of 16 studies on technology-mediated TBLT, 14 highlighted English as an additional language, with the other two on L2 Chinese and L2 German. Bygate (2018) highlighted empirical studies on the effects of task repetition, all of which were in ESL or EFL contexts. In order to conceptualize TBLT as a research pedagogy, Samuda et al. (2018) brought together contributions by practitioner-researchers, the majority focusing on L2 English and some sample tasks in L2 French, L2 Spanish, L2 Chinese, L2 Japanese, and L2 Dutch. Volumes edited by Lambert and Oliver (2020) and Ellis et al. (2020) examine TBLT in a number of practice- and research-oriented chapters in various settings primarily in the context of L2 English (with some discussion of other languages) in theoretical and pedagogical perspectives, as well as weighing in on the issues of assessment of learning with tasks and of TBLT as an approach to instruction. In a volume on task-based approaches to teaching and assessing pragmatics (Taguchi & Kim, 2018), most of the contributions were carried out in an ESL/EFL context, with some studies focusing on L2 Spanish, L2 Dutch, L2 Italian, and Korean as an L2 and heritage language. To date, the great majority of volumes related to TBLT focus on the relationship between TBLT and pedagogical or theoretical concepts, while very few explore TBLT in language-specific settings other than ESL/EFL.

Contributor showcase

Continuing the well-established scholarship of teaching language through task, *Task-based instruction for teaching Russian* imparts a new cycle in RFL pedagogy with its collection of individual task-based instructional episodes and syllabus design exemplars. As such, it is the first representative collection of pedagogical narratives devoted entirely to task-based instruction of Russian as a foreign language. These pedagogical narratives come from a variety of voices and language-learning settings – the contributors range from novice practitioners to instructors with many years of experience. The settings encompass undergraduate university courses, a graduate-level teacher education class, language immersion or intensive programs, a community-based private school, and a study abroad short course. Some cases presented in this volume may impress the reader as extraordinary and cutting-edge, while others look more like daily instruction; every teacher needs both kinds in their professional repertoire. However, the fact that TBLT is successfully used in a RFL classroom is a feat in itself: the inner work and professional skill of someone who creates all or parts of course instruction for each cohort of their learners anew is no short of admirable. Teaching entirely without a textbook and even implementing tasks as increments requires time, creative energy, and a great deal of planning and foresight. It comes as no surprise that the most frequent instructor questions to experts are practice-related (Groothuijsen et al., 2020; Jefferson Education Exchange, 2019). Leaver and Kaplan (2004) report on the teaching conditions of the Defence Language Institute, where the instruction is often orchestrated *в четыре руки* – with two instructors teaching one cohort of students. Such environment is conducive to cooperative teaching and lends itself to common planning time and continuous collegiate reflection on instruction: a position of privilege not characteristic to the field of teaching RFL in the U.S. Having two instructors in an L2 Russian classroom is certainly far from norm in the realities of everyday foreign language teaching practice in the U.S. today.

One of the fundamental questions capable of informing instructional practices and shifting them to better meet the needs of learners of L2 Russian is the question of how acquisition of L2 morphology occurs and develops. Applied linguistics is still in search of the definite answer with two distinct approaches dominating the field: representational difficulties and processing difficulties (Montrul et al., 2008; Polinsky, 1997, 2008). The rich tapestry of Russian morphology has been a specific focus in a number of empirical SLA studies of the last two decades, marking this topic as particularly interesting to teachers of L2 Russian. To their benefit, this volume opens with an overview of recent research on the acquisition of L2 Russian as a morphologically rich language and the insight it provides for L2 Russian pedagogy (Nuss, Chapter 2).

The contributing authors have learned about TBLT from a variety of sources and share the definitions they have chosen as they developed tasks in their particular contexts. Within TBLT, defining the term *task* has been a point of discussion among scholars who have researched and used tasks in the language classroom. For example, Ellis (2003) compares various definitions of a task from a number of researchers (Breen, 1989; Bygate et al., 2001; Crookes, 1986; Lee, 2000; Long, 1985; Nunan, 1989; Prabhu, 1987; Richards et al., 1985; Skehan, 1996). Acknowledging its deeply nuanced nature, the discussion of what does and does not constitute a task, therefore, is largely kept out of this volume concentrating the focus of this volume on the aspects of specific relevance to L2 Russian. In addition to some of the definitions from the aforementioned scholars, this volume's contributors have drawn on various descriptions of a task within the context of Russian as a Foreign Language: from Comer (2007, 2012a), deBenedette (2020), Markina (2018), and Gilabert and Castellví (2019). Although the contributors have chosen different definitions of task and task-based instruction, we notice a number of shared principles:

1   ***All tasks involve a needs analysis before the task design,*** that is, all instructors took into account their learners' needs, interests, proficiency levels and abilities to inform the design of the task(s).

2. ***The intention behind the task design has a focus on meaning with a clear outcome other than the use of language.*** For Kositsky (Chapter 3), the learners needed to "break the code" of the Cyrillic alphabet; Kogan and Bondarenko's contribution (Chapter 6) highlights the necessity of reading and interpreting real-world data like demographic charts or economic statistics. For Burvikova and Stremova's participants (Chapter 9), asking for directions and researching/preparing for a train trip were the specific outcomes, while for Smirnova Henriques et al. (Chapter 7) the learners ordered food, bought souvenirs at a cultural fair, and learned how to write appropriate emails/texts in a variety of situations (such as a student explaining to an instructor why s/he would be late to class). Some of the outcomes relate specifically to the use of technology: in Esser's contribution (Chapter 5), students created vlogs, Mendelevich (Chapter 11) highlights how students created an identity and interacted in virtual space, and Novikov and Vinokurova's contribution (Chapter 4) showcase the use of an online corpus to aid in student essay writing. Additionally, some chapters focus on developing interview skills (Pastushenkov, Chapter 10; Zheltoukhova, Chapter 12), as well as debating skills (Zheltoukhova, Chapter 12; Nimis et al., Chapter 8), and participating in role-playing games (Pastushenkov, Chapter 10; Nimis, Krylova, & Fedoseeva, Chapter 8).

3. ***The tasks involve authenticity in some form (either situational or interactional).*** For instance, Zheltoukhova (Chapter 12); Novikov and Vinokurova (Chapter 4); Kogan and Bondarenko (Chapter 6); Nimis et al. (Chapter 8) each highlight the use of authentic materials such as a travelogue or demographic data (in other words, created by native speakers for native speakers to convey a "real" message – for discussion on how authenticity can be defined in foreign language learning, refer to Gilmore, 2007). Some contributors mention authenticity in terms of "situational authenticity" (Ellis, 2009), that is, activities that are done in the "real world" such as researching a trip (Burvikova & Stremova, Chapter 9); Nimis, Krylova, and Fedoseeva, Chapter 8), ordering food in a restaurant (Smirnova Henriques et al., Chapter 7), interacting in a virtual space (Mendelevich, Chapter 11), creating vlogs (Esser, Chapter 5), conducting interviews outside the classroom (Zheltoukhova, Chapter 12). Other contributors focus on "interactional authenticity" (Ellis, 2009), where the activities were done predominantly in the classroom, but resulted in the types of language use that occur naturally outside of the classroom – namely, negotiating for meaning during classroom interactions (Pastushenkov, Chapter 10; Kositsky, Chapter 3; Burvikova & Stremova, Chapter 9).

4. ***The tasks reflect a learner-centered approach that promotes learner agency and learner autonomy.*** Nunan (2012) highlights that "proponents of learner-centered curricula are less interested in learners acquiring the totality of the language than in assisting them gain the communicative and linguistic skills they need to carry out real-world tasks" (p. 16). All tasks highlighted in this

volume adopt a learner-centered approach and follow several of the principles highlighted in Benson (2012), some of which include being "sensitive to individual needs and preferences," "encourag[ing] construction of knowledge and meaning," "draw[ing] on and integrat[ing] language learning with students' life experiences," and "encourag[ing] authentic communication" (p. 32). Additionally, some chapters (Nuss, Chapter 2; Kositsky, Chapter 3; Novikov & Vinokurova, Chapter 4) emphasize *discovery learning* and *pattern recognition.* Learner-centeredness is further manifested in *how tasks assess student learning.* Assessment takes various forms in both formative and summative modes; student self-reflection is attended to and promoted.

5 *The tasks foster interaction.* Some chapters emphasize interaction with technology (Esser, Chapter 5; Novikov & Vinokurova, Chapter 4; Mendelevich, Chapter 11), other contributions focus on peer interaction (Zheltoukhova, Chapter 12; Kogan & Bondarenko, Chapter 6; Kositsky, Chapter 3; Pastushenkov, Chapter 10; Mendelevich, Chapter 11; Nimis et al., Chapter 8), while Smirnova Henriques et al. (Chapter 7); Burvikova and Stremova (Chapter 9); and Zheltoukhova (Chapter 12) promote interaction with the outside community.

Several themes emerged in the tasks that are highlighted in this volume. Notably, all contributions contain a *cultural component*, and several bring it to the forefront (Zheltoukhova, Chapter 12; Kogan & Bondarenko, Chapter 6; Mendelevich, Chapter 11; Smirnova Henriques et al., Chapter 7; Burvikova & Stremova, Chapter 9; and Nimis et al., Chapter 8). Some chapters emphasize *proficiency* development: a connection to the Test of Russian as a Foreign Language (TORFL) is highlighted in Smirnova Henriques et al. (Chapter 7) and the ACTFL World Readiness Standards in Zheltoukhova (Chapter 12). Several chapters feature *technology-mediated tasks*: Esser (Chapter 5: task-based video), Mendelevich (Chapter 11: Kommunalka, a virtual space), Novikov and Vinokurova (Chapter 4: online learner corpus). Lastly, several chapters (Kogan & Bondarenko, Chapter 6; Pastushenkov, Chapter 10; Kositsky, Chapter 3; Nuss, Chapter 2), address *task sequencing* in TBLT and reflect on the *role of the teacher* as well as teacher agency in the field of teaching and researching of L2 Russian.

TBLT in L2 Russian pedagogy

Svetlana V. Nuss

The following presents a brief overview of the research and pedagogy of task-based instruction in the context of L2 Russian. Based on how tasks are used in classroom practice, I suggest a frame to help refine ways of looking at TBLT's structure consisting of two main modes of design in facilitating L2 instruction: (1) incremental mode, when teachers use tasks as an increment of instruction, more or less cohesively integrating them in an otherwise non-task-oriented course work, to include the use of tasks as assessment episodes; and (2) systemic mode, when an entire syllabus or institutional program is built and sequenced using task-based approach. The two terms, *incremental mode* and *systemic mode* of task-based instruction, will be used to contextualize the following review of pedagogical narrations and research in the context of L2 Russian.

Leaver and Kaplan's (2004) work stands out as the first pedagogical account describing implementation of TBLT in an L2 Russian classroom. It documents the use of tasks in an advanced Russian course within a U.S. government language program. With the syllabus adjusted for each student individually, the tasks were used extramurally as a part of community outreach, where the students interacted with native speakers of Russian. Both experienced teachers and administrators, Leaver and Kaplan detail the administrative side of running a task-based program and reflect on the challenges therein. The authors identify the amount of time it takes for teachers to plan instruction, curate and create resources, and develop assessment as one of the persisting encounters in organizing systemic TBLT instruction. Leaver and Kaplan document and bring forward examples when – even with an added benefit of team-teaching and the combined resources two or more educators bring to the planning table – class preparation took dyads and teams of teachers five hours for each hour they taught. At the very best, preparation equaled the instruction time, when teachers spent four hours preparing to instruct four hours of class time.

Leaver and Kaplan offer the insight gained in government language-teaching institutions on overcoming the challenge of time-consuming planning and preparation in TBLT and, based on their combined experiences, propose that teachers (1) increase their experience in task-based teaching, (2) employ direct assistance of the administration and others, (3) get paid development time, and (4) make use of an archive. Interestingly, they note that as the program unfolded and the teachers gained more experience working with tasks, the amount of preparation time decreased significantly; however, the teachers who elected to retain textbook-based instruction supplementing it along the way with their own materials continued to drain their resource of time. In addition to (1) overcoming the challenge of time required for implementation, Leaver and Kaplan point out that task-based instructional programs (2) must devise ways to deal with the lack of predictability, (3) need to attend to faculty development, (4) foresee obstacles related to student expectations of teaching and testing, and (5) must address paucity of materials, possibly by developing and sharing an archive of authentic language materials and successful lessons.

Among the benefits task-based instruction affords students and teachers, the authors identify greater student and teacher motivation, opportunity for repetition without boredom, greater curricular flexibility, promotion of learning how to learn, opportunity for natural error correction, higher proficiency results, increased student satisfaction and greater risk taking, and better overall program evaluation results. In their summary, Leaver and Kaplan highlight that in the described context, task-based instruction was introduced alongside content-based instruction and underscore winning points of such combination, as well as the versatility of task-based instruction as evidenced by its effectiveness in various program types.

The authors note that in addition to its positive pragmatic attributes, task-based instruction is simply fun for both students and teachers.

Moving in chronological order, the next contribution in advancing task-based instruction of L2 Russian comes from Comer's (2007) pedagogical narration, where he briefly introduces TBLT as a concept and reflects on its features in the context of communicative teaching of L2 Russian. In the conclusion of his literature review, Comer states that TBLT in the context of teaching L2 Russian is mostly being explored in theory, citing Leaver and Kaplan's 2004 article as the one and only example of previous publications on task-based instruction of Russian as a foreign language (RFL) to date (Comer, 2007). The author suggests that the theoretical construct of TBLT is yet to be embodied into the practice of L2 Russian by developing its own entourage of supports for teachers and learners in the form of lesson plans and case studies. Comer goes on to offer a case study of his own, detailing a task-based lesson of L2 Russian in a tertiary setting that was conducted as an increment of instruction in a second semester textbook-based course.

The instructional segment analyzed by Comer (2007) contained four pedagogical tasks, designed and sequenced in accordance with Nunan's seven principles for planning task-based lesson (Nunan, 2004): scaffolding, task dependency, recycling, active learning, integration, reproduction to creation, and reflection. In Comer's lesson, (1) student work was scaffolded by previous instruction, since students had acquired the vocabulary and language forms they needed for successful task completion beforehand; (2) the tasks were interdependent: an outcome was necessary to proceed to the next stage; (3) tasks were set within one theme, providing students opportunities to repeatedly employ target language features; (4) students were producing units of work to ensure active learning: they were engaged in gathering and evaluating information; (5) mapping of form and meaning was facilitated by the instructor's corrective feedback in the form of recasts and restatements; (6) the reproduction to creation principle was implemented only partially due to time constraints; a solution was offered for further development; (7) instructors reflected on the lesson and provided their analysis in the form of the article. The final task served as an assessment of student performance, albeit not labeled as such neither in the lesson plan nor in its analysis. No account of formalized student reflection (other than the explicit grammar question-answer student-teacher exchange with a spotlight on one verb conjugation pattern at the end of the lesson) is provided either in the body of the article (Comer, 2007, pp. 181–194) or in the Appendix outlining the activities that took place during the class in chronological order (pp. 197–199), although it could be argued that formative assessment was taking place throughout the lesson, prompting student reflection. Nevertheless, the role of student reflection should not be underestimated as it not only informs future instruction, but also helps facilitate learner agency and autonomy (Leaver & Campbell, 2020) as well as set realistic expectations of level of achievement and progress rate (Martin, 2020). More attention to student reflection would also help alleviate the instructor's doubts and answer the teacher's question Comer reports as unanswered, "whether the students had attended enough to the language content of the class" (Comer, 2007, p. 190).

Comer (2007) notes several issues that make TBLT difficult to implement for teachers. In relation to general L2 teaching, the overall instructional frame of TBLT is too wide: the author points out the lack of specific instructional methodology combined with the absence of an agreed upon definition of task. This notion is supported by other voices of teachers of L2 Russian (Kogan & Bondarenko, Chapter 6, this volume; Whitehead Martelle & Nuss, Chapter 13, this volume; Nuss et al., 2021), who speak of challenges involved in conceptualizing, planning for and committing to the task-based instruction caused by the vague definition of task.

Based on Comer's (2007) conclusions, teaching L2 Russian via a task-based approach meets three additional barriers specific to this setting: (1) lack of defined instructional strategies that would bring forward the salient features of Russian morphology and help learners map form and meaning; (2) a broad needs analysis has yet to be conducted in order to determine a set of real-world tasks in which organized groups of learners of L2 Russian would potentially engage; (3) the inner syllabus of the L2 Russian learner has not been determined, therefore, the order of presentation of language features and structures is not defined. Moreover, (4) it is not clear what features need to be scaffolded by negative feedback, which ones can be acquired through input implicitly, and which ones should be explicitly addressed. The four challenges outlined by Comer (2007) are still present today. While some headway has been made in the area of case acquisition (e.g., Magnani & Artoni, 2015), the L2 Russian learner inner syllabus is yet to be defined. The present volume contains some ideas on meeting the challenges identified in Comer (2007): that of L2 Russian instructional strategies, articulating needs analyses and explicit vs. implicit scaffolding of morphology acquisition.

Comer's (2012a) overview of communicative language teaching (CLT) of L2 Russian positions task-based instruction as one of the directions of CLT. The author claims verifiable outcome to be the essential quality that sets task-based teaching apart from information gap activities, structured input activities, and processing instruction activities.

A proof of concept study dealing with the notion of proficiency in L2 was conducted in the context of L2 Russian by Long et al. (2012) and aimed to determine the linguistic correlates of proficiency. The study used tasks to identify what linguistic features L2 learners of Russian had command of, to what degree, and at what proficiency level. The study was framed within the Interagency Linguistic Roundtable (ILR) proficiency scale; the researchers were concerned with levels of proficiency 2, 2+, and 3. The research resulted in a compiled list of linguistic features distributed by proficiency levels. The 33 tasks used in the study were originally developed in an earlier study (Long et al., 2006) and are available as a technical report.

Mezhdu nami, an online textbook of Russian for beginners by deBenedette et al. (2015). www.MezhduNami.org is positioned by its authors as the first internet-based textbook for the instruction of L2 Russian to systematically implement principles of a TBLT syllabus. Per its authors, the textbook "incorporates principles of communicative and task-based language teaching" (deBenedette et al., 2015, n.p.).

Spasova (2017) advocates for bringing real-life scenarios into the L2 Russian classroom from the very beginning stages of instruction. The author presents scenarios of online instruction for beginner learners of L2 Russian, where students put to use linguistic skills they have learned in the lesson. For example, the learners review the Russian alphabet through a series of interactive real-life-based experiences as they make breakfast choices in the hotel, shop for the ticket to the theater, or navigate the metro. The projects feature H5P and Adobe Captivate software that allows for scaffolding and targeted feedback. As the course unfolds, the students communicate with their Russian bosses (real estate agents, developers, and store owners) as they negotiate for a time and date of a meeting, respond to emails, arrange consultations, analyze properties and markets, or take care of merchandise. The author points out that as the students complete the tasks, also labeled by the author as *projects*, they are inspired and motivated by the real-life nature of their experience. It is worth noting that, although the author does not mention it, Spasova (2017) exemplifies instruction which effortlessly integrates language learning and culture as the author introduces language features already embedded in everyday life experiences of people in Russia.

Markina (2018) further shapes the narrative of task-based instruction of L2 Russian by introducing empirical evidence regarding task-based and task-supported instruction in the context of L2 Russian. The overall results of her research extend into theoretical, methodological, and pedagogical areas of applied linguistics. The study sets out to determine whether task-based or task-supported instruction would be more impactful in the acquisition of case forms of nouns and verbs of motion. It also looks at learners' language in terms of accuracy, syntactic and lexical diversity, and fluency. It features a systematic overview of TBLT as an approach to second language instruction and its place in a larger discourse within applied linguistics, detailing concepts of syllabus design, task assessment and sequencing, focus on form vs. focus on forms, and the effectiveness of task-based teaching. One of the conclusions the author makes is that, in addition to cognitive complexity, linguistic demands must be accounted for in task design when working with L2 Russian and, by theoretical extension, with other morphologically rich languages. The study supplies new empirical evidence confirming that Russian can be learned when it is instructed in a communicative language teaching stream framed by task-based approach. The results are also interpreted as lending new evidence to the theory of input processing (VanPatten, 1996) in the context of L2 Russian. The study carries pedagogical value as it presents a model of task-based syllabus for teaching case and verbs of motion.

Task design and sequencing in L2 context of morphologically rich languages merits special consideration of their linguistic qualities (Gilabert & Castellví, 2019). Highlighting the fact that most research on task features has primarily been based on English, a morphologically impoverished language, Gilabert and Castellví state that linguistic difficulty (for a comprehensive literature review and discussion of the terms linguistic complexity and difficulty, code complexity and difficulty see Markina, 2018) should be attended to in task design. The authors substantialize their main argument by drawing on Robinson's Cognition Hypothesis (Robinson, 2001b, 2003) when they claim a more central role for the linguistic code in task design and sequencing, since – in the case of Russian – the linguistic code profoundly influences learner's cognitive processes and affects language learning. Gilabert and Castellví (2019) also point out the possible reasons why linguistic features remain largely outside of the TBLT research agenda and state that an overwhelming number of studies on tasks (1) investigate outcome and not the process of language learning; (2) focus on cognitive and conceptual complexity as independent variables; and (3) have been conducted in the context of morphologically poor languages (Gilabert & Castellví, 2019). The authors unambiguously argue that linguistic difficulty should be measured and accounted for in empirical studies of task-based instruction as an independent variable or as a task design factor, as it is clear that linguistic difficulty (1) competes with conceptual demands; (2) interferes with successful task completion by increasing cognitive load; and (3) should be measured in terms of the number of language features as well as their relative difficulty (Gilabert & Castellví, 2019; Markina, 2018).

Employing the term *task* in its title, deBenedette's (2020) article presents a content-based syllabus for advanced Russian that makes use of pedagogical tasks to facilitate student language learning. In terms of TBLT, its pedagogical value comes in the author's exemplars of information gap, focus on form, structured input, and vocabulary-building activities. A task-based instructional exemplar offered by the author is a reflection essay the students have to write about whether or not a song fits the film's narrative.

Nuss (2020) compares features of task-based learning in general education and some elements of design that come into play in language learning, discusses textbook and other materials development for teaching RFL from the TBLT perspective, and explores possible reasons for the growing popularity of task-based instruction in teaching foreign languages in general and Russian in particular. The author argues that the largely elective nature of foreign language learning, rarely mandated by educational authorities and therefore not systemically institutionalized in K–16 settings in the United States, is primarily responsible for the advances in L2 instructional strategies. These instructional advances are largely caused by the need for language teachers, as opposed to institutions and general policy, to attract and retain the numbers of learners necessary to keep the programs running and the educators employed in the workplace. The elective nature of foreign language instruction is both a blessing and a curse: in order to stay afloat and attract learners, foreign language educators in the United States must be creative in their delivery of the subject (Nuss, 2020). In other contexts, where foreign language and culture competency is valued as a core educational concept and therefore mandated as a graduation requirement in K–16 educational settings, foreign language classes, just like classes for mathematics or English language arts, are filled without having to entice and allure the learners.

Three instruments of task design for teaching L2 Russian

Svetlana V. Nuss

In the field of instruction of morphologically rich languages, three instruments stand out as positive developments potentially impactful in instructional design for teaching L2 Russian. As teachers design their task-based incremental or systemic instruction (see the previous section of this chapter for a definition of terms), in addition to their professional intuition and experience, they can now turn to the following three resources developed by the field in the last fifteen years. The first one, although not Russian- or TBLT-specific, is a Morphological Complexity Index (MCI; measures morphological complexity of a text) substantialized in Brezina and Pallotti (2019) and in a broader linguistic task complexity discussion by Pallotti (2019) where he speaks of *linguistic difficulty* or *code complexity* as not only contributing to the task's global difficulty, but also having impact on sequencing of a task-based syllabus. In addition to MCI, Pallotti (2019) considers lexical diversity and sophistication and length of syntax constructions. The discussion of linguistic demands of task-based language learning that MCI helps to substantiate stands out as a possible concrete way leading to a more holistic and comprehensive discourse about the nature of tasks within the space of L2 Russian. At the very minimum, it arms the field with an empirically based procedure (albeit too complex to use on a daily basis) of establishing the level of linguistic difficulty of a task, taking the field a step ahead in the present largely theory-based discussion in the context of L2 Russian (Comer, 2007). Pallotti's study (2019) is positioned as an illustration of how the linguistic demands of a task could be empirically measured and makes no claims of generalizability of its results. Nevertheless, it operationalizes MCI in task design, which is particularly valuable for instruction of morphologically rich languages, as it takes into account linguistic demands entailed in the task structure.

The second instrument teachers can employ in task design when working with L2 Russian is the list of linguistic features that learners of L2 Russian should have command of, organized by proficiency levels. The list was established in the Long et al. (2012) study on the linguistic correlates of second language proficiency. Additional insight can be gained from the technical report by Long et al. (2006), which describes the tasks that informed Long et al.'s (2012) study design.

The third instrument is the growing bank of pedagogical narrations of incremental and systemic models of task-based instruction of L2 Russian developed to date. The following is a brief list of its main contributions to date: Leaver and Kaplan (2004), Comer (2007, 2012a), deBenedette et al. (2015), Markina (2018), Gilabert and Castellví (2019), deBenedette (2020), Spasova (2017), Nuss (2020),

Nuss et al. (2021). A conversation on using tasks with heritage learners of Russian has its own dimensions that should also be considered here (Kisselev et al., 2020). While the detailed overview of using tasks with heritage learners is outside of this volume's scope, one article in this volume (Zheltoukhova) provides an example of differentiating instruction for heritage speakers in task-based settings. We also include here ACTFL's World-readiness standards for Russian (National Standards in Foreign Language Education Project, 2015) as it provides task-based learning scenarios, the largely task-based STARTALK initiative of the National Security Agency for the critical-need foreign languages – including Russian – with its curriculum units of instruction in open access, and the present volume's contributions.

Chapter 2

Morphology acquisition research meets instruction of L2 Russian

A contextualized literature review

Svetlana V. Nuss

Chapter summary

This chapter presents a review of the research on the acquisition of Russian morphology and discusses how it informs the practice of teaching Russian as a foreign or second language (L2 Russian). Influential publications from the current decade are reviewed, particularly research that directly addresses classroom instruction of L2 Russian or where instructional strategies can be unambiguously extrapolated. First, I analyze the gap between research and teaching practice. Then, I discuss why Russian morphology should be regarded as a central element of L2 Russian instruction based on the qualities of the Russian language and the latest research regarding the acquisition of L2 morphology. I provide a brief overview of the distinct features of the Russian language, followed by a literature review on the acquisition of inflection, derivation, and compounding and address their relevance to the instruction of L2 Russian. Finally, I highlight the necessity of magnifying the voices of practitioners who work with learners of L2 Russian in diverse settings. The overall result presents a picture of recent theoretical and research advances in teaching Russian as a morphologically rich language through the lens of classroom application. The chapter contributes to balancing research and practice fields of L2 Russian by contextualizing research findings in the practice of teaching Russian as a foreign language (RFL) and encourages self-reflection for both teachers and researchers of L2 Russian.

Краткое содержание главы

В главе анализируется состояние научного знания в области освоения русской морфологии инофонами и представляются возможные варианты влияния особенностей русской морфологии на организацию образовательного процесса изучения русского языка как иностранного (РКИ), унаследованного в иноязычной среде или второго. Анализируются результаты исследований, проведенных в этой области, в основном, в текущем десятилетии, с особым акцентом на работы, из которых возможно недвусмысленное экстраполирование методологических приемов обучения.

Обсуждается разрыв тематики в теоретических наработках современной педагогической мысли в области РКИ, эмпирических исследованиях и реальных потребностях учителей и обучающихся, непосредственно вовлеченных в процесс. Предлагается тезис о первичности морфологии при изучении РКИ. При обосновании тезиса рассматриваются некоторые особенности языковой структуры русского языка и их роль в освоении РКИ. В частности, представлены и подвергнуты педагогической интерпретации результаты исследований в области освоения русского словообразования и словоизменения. Особо отмечается необходимость активизации практиков преподавания РКИ в научном дискурсе. Рассматривая достижения точной науки в контексте студенческой аудитории и школьного класса, глава вносит вклад в уравновешивание теоретической и прикладной областей знания организации обучения РКИ.

Bridging the research-practice divide

Researchers research and teachers teach. The two worlds seem convergent, as both are occupations related to education. However, in reality, they are of a fundamentally divergent nature. Researchers create their own inquiries and move forward at their own pace as their desire, agenda, talent, and time warrant – they can pause if they wish, they may or may not aspire to look into a certain aspect of theory or a detail of practice, and they can change the direction of their inquiry (Xiao & Chan, 2020). Teachers, on the other hand, cannot pause or stop instruction, as they focus on the success of their learners and the instructional process as a whole, rather than any one aspect of it (Hattie & Hamilton, 2020). As an unconscious event, language acquisition simultaneously encompasses phonology, morphology, syntax, semantics, discourse, and pragmatics – the entire landscape of grammar (Slabakova et al., 2020). Therefore, regardless of how (in)conclusive and nuanced the research – for example, on feedback – may be (Mackey, 2020) or how well-(un)informed teachers are about its impact, teachers continue to use feedback in instructional settings to the best of their ability. Numerous constituents of the instructional process of teaching and learning – conveniently pinned motionless and prone to manipulation in their finest components under the researcher's magnifying glass – come together in the dynamics of the classroom, intertwine, and interconnect. The classroom is where instruction lives and grows, its parts interdependent, each one vital for student's success, as organs are for a living being. Given the interconnectedness and interdependence of instructional elements (Brown & Green, 2019), a teacher does not have the luxury of concentrating entirely on one particular component of instruction in real time, and even if we could, which one would it be?

Teachers want to be informed and generally value and appreciate educational research (Groothuijsen et al., 2020; Jefferson Education Exchange, 2019); however, their ideas on research required in education do not coincide with the ideas held by researchers (Groothuijsen et al., 2020). From the practitioner's perspective, research is defined in terms of practice, such as how applicable, consistent, and effective an intervention, method, or result is. Furthermore, "'applicability' is described by researchers as the extent of generalizability," while practitioners describe the applicability of research in terms of feasibility and relevance (Groothuijsen et al., 2020, p. 778). As classroom practitioners further expand on the notion of applicability, they speak of the necessity for research, in addition to being purely theoretical, to be relevant in the context of practice to greater benefit learners and educators (Groothuijsen et al., 2020).

Research holds another key to teachers' acceptance and willingness to consider its implementation: the effects of applying a particular strategy or approach should be well worth of and in proportion to the time and effort invested by the instructor in its conceptualization, implementation, and follow-through. Practice-oriented research can be complex to conduct: "The quality concerns based on the two-sided research and practice perspective of teacher-researchers are more complex than the quality concerns based on the research perspective in the educational literature" (Groothuijsen et al., 2020, pp. 784–785).

There is, of course, teacher action research (Mills, 2018), however, the number of teachers actually engaging with it is inconsequential, particularly in K–12 setting, due to the constraints involved (Manfra, 2019). It is, therefore, important that the two environments – practice and research – communicate continuously in order to benefit the field at large, and especially L2 learners. As practitioners' knowledge of L1 and L2 language processes expands, their choice of and approach to creating materials may also change (Leal & Slabakova, 2017). This chapter, therefore, aims to balance research and practice fields of L2 Russian acquisition by contextualizing research findings in the practice of teaching RFL: I cite research results and relate them to the practice of teaching L2 Russian by providing some specific examples of practice shaped by research, allowing teachers a comfortable starting point for their own classroom inquiry and research application. The chapter also encourages self-reflection for both teachers and researchers of L2 Russian.

Effective pedagogical decision-making

While some research offers interpretation relevant for practice, more often, specific applications for language study are not provided or cannot be derived not only due to the preliminary nature of the findings, but also because knowing that a particular language feature is difficult to learn doesn't provide a path for teaching it (Slabakova et al., 2020). Slabakova and colleagues (2020) present an insightful account of the contributions generative second language acquisition (SLA) offers for practitioners (discussed in later sections) and encourage further research on L2 teaching, concluding that generative SLA researchers should consider pedagogical aims.

For the learners' benefit, teachers have to become savvy consumers of educational research in order to be able to extrapolate from it the most impactful instructional strategies. Given sufficient quantity of input, research literature transforms into vectors of action and cognitive approaches that form the teachers' overarching instructional frame of mind which, in turn, guides teachers' instructional decisions. This self-created instructional frame of thought shapes classroom instruction through teachers' willingness to challenge their current pedagogical mindset and implement new practices to benefit the learner. An individual's pedagogical background and intuition become the catalyst and the medium that transform research findings into specific instructional approaches.

However, as suggested by the following overview, translating research into practice can be a daunting task, as it requires time and access to resources that a teacher may not have. Due to small and fluctuating enrollments in courses of less commonly taught languages, including Russian (Looney & Lusin, 2018; Martin, 2020; Rhodes & Pufahl, 2009), language teaching jobs are not always stable, which has a direct impact on the access to quality professional development for teachers of L2 Russian. Coming from various professional backgrounds (e.g., study of literature, film, or journalism in Russian context), the faculty tasked with teaching of L2 Russian are not necessarily grounded in either linguistics or language pedagogy. Furthermore, many teachers of L2 Russian – just like 41 percent of other language teachers in the U.S. – work as a *department of one* and do not always have the institutional support for their professional development (The State of World Language Teaching, 2020). With various degree of professional support, whether in private enterprises or public institutions, K–12 settings, or tertiary education, practitioners of L2 Russian continuously search for better ways to address the needs of their learners, and, along with teachers of L2 Chinese, often spend ten or more hours a week of additional time planning instruction or grading student submissions – more than teachers of any other language (The State of World Language Teaching, 2020).

It is easy to see why, first and foremost, this chapter (and the volume at large) serves to benefit diverse practitioners of L2 Russian, as it describes time-saving approaches to instruction and the research rationale behind them, serving as a blueprint for turning reflection into an empowering professional exploration. Indeed, why is it important for language teachers to follow the latest research developments? And how *does* research on the role of morphology in L2 learning inform classroom instruction of morphologically rich languages? We will first take a closer look at Russian morphology and establish why it warrants an explicit discussion of its own in an L2 Russian context. The importance of following the latest research developments in the area of inflectional morphology and the potential such research holds in influencing classroom instruction of morphologically rich languages is further discussed next in the context of L2 Russian classrooms.

Russian as a morphologically rich language and its instruction as L2

Language differences have often been a source of fascination, offering various areas of exploration to the human mind. Language differences can lead to interesting and unexpected societal twists. Consider, for instance, two poems from two different languages written in the same meter, with both languages employing syllabo-tonic verse systems, such as English and Russian. The two poems still differ rhythmically. This phenomenon is largely responsible for the two "divergent approaches to the description and analysis of meter and rhythm" in the research of metrists stemming from the two traditions (Scherr, 1980, p. 353).

What is it that makes Russian and English so different that they produce "divergent approaches" in the study of poetry within the two language systems, and might the difference play a role in the acquisition of Russian as a foreign language?

Russian and English are classical examples of a synthetic and an analytic language respectively (Shulga, 2017). Greenberg's scale (1963) is used to determine the saturation of text with morphemes, with its index reflecting the number of morphemes per hundred words of text. Morpheme is the minimal unit of meaning in language, a part of a word with lexical (golf-ER) or grammatical (golfer-S) meaning. Vietnamese with an index of 1.06 (index of 1.06 on Greenberg's scale means that Vietnamese has 106 morphemes per 100 words of text) is classified as an analytic (isolating) language: one Vietnamese morpheme almost always represents one word (Greenberg, 1963). English is an analytic language, as its index of 1.68 falls within the range of 1.00–1.99 (Greenberg, 1963), meaning, there are about 168 morphemes per 100 words of English text. On the other end of the spectrum are polysynthetic languages with an index of 3.00. Russian, with an index of 2.39, has, on average, 239 morphemes for every 100 words of text (Greenberg, 1963). Interestingly, classical Sanskrit has an index of 2.59, which means that the synthetic nature of Russian is 92.3 percent that of Sanskrit (Shulga, 2017). In terms of its morphology, English is closer to the analytical Vietnamese than to Russian or Sanskrit: Russian has about 71 more morphemes per every hundred words than English. Below follows an illustration of how this concept manifests itself in the way words are created in Russian. I begin with a short description of Russian morphology as it pertains to the acquisition of L2 Russian.

As Russian has 239 morphemes per 100 words, it can be inferred that Russian words are often comprised of more than one morpheme. The following is an abbreviated comparison of English and Russian verb paradigms.

Possible verb inflections for regular English verbs are represented using the past tense marker *-ed*, the marker of continuous action *-ing*, and the marker of third person singular *-s*: paint-ED, paint-ING, paint-S. Learners of L2 English must also acquire an additional group of irregular verbs, where each verb has three or four possible choices in its paradigm. For the benefit of the reader less familiar with Russian morphology, I simplify both English and Russian verb systems and choose a verb with a rather typical conjugation pattern in both systems. In order to further simplify the system of Russian verbs, particiles and reflexive forms of the verb are withheld. There are 16 main verb classes in Russian (Zaliznyak, 1980, pp. 78–70, 91–135), "some of them high-frequency productive and others low-frequency unproductive and with conjugational patterns varying in the degree of regularity" (Gor & Long, 2009, p. 459). The following is a partial paradigm of the Russian verb *рисовать* (imperfective) or *нарисовать* (perfective) [to paint]:

Table 2.1 A simplified conjugation pattern of Russian verbs *рисовать* and *нарисовать* [to paint]

Form description	Рисовать *(imperfective)* To draw/paint	Нарисовать *(perfective)* To finish drawing/painting
	Present *(imperfective)*	**Future *(perfective)***
1st person singular	Рису-ю	Нарису-ю
2nd person singular	Рису-ешь	Нарису-ешь
3rd person singular	Рису-ет	Нарису-ет
1st person plural	Рису-ем	Нарису-ем
2nd person plural	Рису-ете	Нарису-ете
3rd person plural	Рису-ют	Нарису-ют
	Past *(imperfective)*	**Past *(perfective)***
Singular masculine	Рисова-л	Нарисова-л
Singular feminine	Рисова-ла	Нарисова-ла
Singular neuter	Рисова-ло	Нарисова-ло
Plural	Рисова-ли	Нарисова-ли
	Imperative *(imperfective)*	**Imperative *(perfective)***
Informal/Singular	Рису-й	Нарису-й
Formal/Plural	Рису-йте	Нарису-йте

Imperfective aspect (несовершенный вид, 2a in Zaliznyak's system)/perfective aspect (совершенный вид, 2a) paradigm of *рисовать/нарисовать* [to paint] (Zaliznyak, 1980, p. 93). We omit the explanation of aspect and simply state that this verb can be used either with or without the prefix (на) depending on the context (Zaliznyak, 1980, p. 93). Russian *(на)рисовать* is represented by 24 word forms (Table 2.1):

An illustration of a Russian noun comes from Gilabert and Castellví (2019), who observe that a Russian noun "typically has ten different forms, which usually include stress movement, which in turn entails changes in vowel quality due to vowel reduction" (p. 529). By way of example, Gilabert and Castellví (2019) introduce the Russian noun for *дом* [house], explaining that its citation form is used

> in nominative or accusative case; *дома* dama [damá], in plural nominative or accusative case; *дому* domu [dómu] singular dative; etc. It can also entail the generation of new prosodic and lexical structures of the same word, for example in *о домах* o domakh [adamáx] plural prepositive case, in which the preposition is attached to the noun's prosodic word as if it were a prefix.
> (Gilabert & Castellví, 2019, p. 529)

I add a feminine noun *библиотека* [library], to illustrate the change of inflection based on grammatical gender (Table 2.2):

Table 2.2 Declension patterns of Russian nouns *дом* [house] and *библиотека* [library]

Case	Дом House		Библиотека Library	
	Singular	Plural	Singular	Plural
Nominative case	Дом-	Дом-á	Библиоте́к-а	Библиоте́к-и
Accusative case	Дом-	Дом-á	Библиоте́к-у	Библиоте́к-и
Genitive case	До́м-а	Дом-óв	Библиоте́к-и	Библиоте́к-
Prepositional case	До́м-е	Дом-áх	Библиоте́к-е	Библиоте́к-ах
Dative case	До́м-у	Дом-áм	Библиоте́к-е	Библиоте́к-ам
Instrumental case	До́м-ом	Дом-áми	Библиоте́к-ой	Библиоте́к-ами

Information on the case and number of a noun in Russian is encoded in a single inflection. Paradigm forms are chosen based on parameters that consider gender (three grammatical genders), case (six cases with numerous exceptions), animacy (animate/not animate), and number of a noun, all further refined according to the type of word base, more specifically, its ending; the choice is often opaque, as allomorphy is very common in both Russian derivational and inflectional morphology (Lekant, 1988; Zaliznyak, 1980).

Readers familiar with the role of input in SLA probably wonder if this number of verb forms (at least five times more than that of English verb forms) means that there should be at least five times as much input as for the acquisition of the English paradigm of the same verb and five times that of a noun. Consider also that Russian has features encoded in context without explicit lexico-grammatical markings, such as the expression of definiteness, marked overtly in English (Cho & Slabakova, 2014). Citing additional features of Russian morphology, such as number-noun agreement, Gilabert and Castellví (2019) conclude that, "Without a doubt the particularities of Russian morphology pose a considerable challenge for L2 learners and make teachers approach the teaching of Russian with very different conditions from those under which the teaching of English proceeds" (p. 529).

Research focusing on L2 morphology acquisition: what we have learned in recent years

Roumyana Slabakova's aptly expressed summary (Slabakova, 2019) speaks to the hearts and minds of teachers and learners of L2 Russian as it moves this discussion into the research of L2 morphology acquisition:

> adult L2 acquisition difficulties are essentially due to linguistic factors that stem from the language architecture and principled views of cross-linguistic variation. Frequency, redundancy and salience can explain some of the

variation, but they are far from explaining all of it. The functional morphology is responsible for most of the acquisition challenges. Core syntax and semantics come for free!

(Slabakova, 2019, p. 343)

What is it about Russian morphology that makes Russian difficult to acquire for learners of RFL and how can research advances help teachers and inform the practice of teaching RFL? The research I find relevant as a teacher and present here is derived mostly from the generative strand of applied linguistics. In her *Slavic Psycholinguistics in the 21st Century* (2017), Irina Sekerina defines the aim of formal experimental psycholinguistics as understanding the mental mechanics behind human beings' effortless language production and understanding. She names morphology as one of the most essential areas of recent research in various subfields of psycholinguistics and speaks of its important advances. Sekerina's (2017) classification of methods employed by psycholinguistics and domains they deal with is most useful as an introduction to the more in-depth discussion later.

Based on the **methods** employed, Sekerina (2017) describes research in psycholinguistics as characterized by *behavioral* studies (conducted offline, with questionnaires and judgment studies, and online as studies on reaction time and eye movements), *neuroimaging*, such as fMRI, MEG, and ERPs, and the *modality* they work with, namely, spoken or written language. Studies of spoken language have prevailed in the last two decades, possibly due to the emergence of new technology, such as visual eye-tracking paradigms used in studies on language comprehension phenomena. **Domains** of *production* and *comprehension* are the most important and telling area of analyses, as they deal with the core subject matter of psycho-linguistics, where production concentrates mainly on agreement errors and comprehension covers mental lexicon, processing of morphology, and sentence processing. Sentence processing is the most researched area within the comprehension domain of Slavic psycholinguistics, giving rise to studies on ambiguity, complexity, and prediction (Sekerina, 2017).

Sekerina makes an important distinction, pointing out a common confusion in the literature regarding the term "cognitive," which is caused by the fact that it is "also used in the name of the second theoretical approach, that of cognitive linguistics. The latter is a theoretical linguistic model that emphasizes meaning as opposed to structure and draws on other less formally oriented disciplines" (Sekerina, 2017, p. 478). Both strands are relevant for this chapter's purpose, however, the space available dictates narrowing the scope to mainly generative perspective. Particularly relevant to this chapter, Slavic psycholinguistics have recently developed a trend of researching bilingual learners which is conducted within either formal experimental or cognitive linguistic fields (Sekerina, 2017).

The acquisition of L2 Russian morphology, influenced by the advances in psycholinguistics, became a prominent field of study, gaining more attention in recent years. Many researchers within generative, instructional, and other fields of SLA inquiry offered their rationalizations regarding the tendency of L2 learners of Russian to make errors in the use of inflectional and derivational morphology well into advanced levels of proficiency (ACTFL, 2012). Proposed explanations include the *bottleneck hypothesis* (Slabakova, 2009, 2019), L1 negative transfer (Portin et al., 2007), cognitive weight of online (real-time) processing (McDonald, 2006), representational deficits within the *failed functional features hypothesis* (Hawkins & Chan, 1997), and form-meaning mapping deficits (Kempe & MacWhinney, 1998), *inter alia*, with no agreement reached to date. The practice of Russian L2 morphology acquisition appears to be facing a significant challenge, as *whether Russian morphology can ever be fully acquired by L2 learners* has been poised as a research question:

> Does the absence of morphological case and gender marking on nouns and adjectives in English prevent . . . learners from ever fully acquiring these forms in Russian, or can they eventually be acquired through means such as exposure to sufficient input, explicit instruction, and/or conscious self-monitoring?
>
> (Peirce, 2018, p. 96)

Research on the acquisition of morphologically rich languages can be viewed by strands based on the type of morphological process: inflection, derivation, or compounding (Leminen et al., 2019). New words are formed as a result of derivation and compounding, such as assign-MENT or смел-(ый)/ОСТЬ. In contrast, inflectional morphology attends to grammatical forms of a lexeme, as in assign-S or assign-ED, or смел-ЫЕ. All three types are prominent in the Russian language, with their own sub-sets of characteristics, and all three present challenges for L2 learners of Russian (Gor, 2015; Gor & Long, 2009; Janda et al., 2020; Janda & Tyers, 2018; Kireev et al., 2018, 2019; Leminen et al., 2019; Romanova & Gor, 2016; Slabakova, 2018, 2019).

Terminology: Russian philology's perspective

The three base terms of Russian and English morphology – *inflection, derivation,* and *compounding* – may hold the key to understanding some profound differences with implications for learners. Acknowledging the deeply nuanced nature of the subject (where even the main terms such as *base, inflection, root, stem* are still debated in theoretical and descriptive morphology, e.g., Spencer, 2012), for the sake of space and clarity, I base this discussion on two sources representative of two lines of thought: Leminen and colleagues (2019) for English, and Lekant (1988) for Russian morphology. English morphology has a rich, well-developed history of exploration rooted in issues of inflectional (walk-ED), derivational (dark-NESS), and compound (manPOWER) words (Leminen et al., 2019). The same three morphological operations – inflection, derivation, and compounding – are discussed in Russian philology as well. In Russian, these terms are named to reflect their function; however, the functions are conceived differently by the two respective linguistic traditions. The following contextualizes translation terms for the benefit of readers not familiar with the Russian language or the Russian philological tradition of its study. In Russian linguistics, *inflection* is referred to as *словоизменение* or *word-change*, and its participants are, therefore, *словоформы* [*wordfoms*], not *слова* [*words*] per se. This is in clear opposition to **derivation**, *словообразование* [*word-derivation*] (along with its Russian synonym of *деривация* [*derivation*]) – the process of creation of new words, with **compounding** nested within **derivation** as one of its many integral parts. Following the logic of the terminology of Russian linguistic tradition, all words of the Russian language are treated within a dichotomy: they are either a result of a *word derivation*, making them "words," or a result of a *word change* or *inflection*, making them "forms of words." In a university-level Russian textbook for philologists on the subject of Russian language, *словообразование* [*word-derivation*] includes treatments of both word derivation and word inflection, and is a heading in its own right along with other areas of language study, presented in the following order: Lexicology [Лексика], Phonetics [Фонетика], Graphics/Orthography [Графика/Орфография], Word-derivation and word inflection [Словообразование], Morphology [Морфология], Syntax [Синтаксис] (Lekant, 1988, pp. 413–416; Rozental' et al., 2017, pp. 436–444).

Russian inflectional morphology and its L2 acquisition

Understanding whether Russian words with complex morphology are broken down by learners into individual morphemes, requiring reassembly during production, is particularly useful for L2 Russian teachers. This depends largely on L2 learners' access and retrieval mechanisms of multimorphemic (composed of several morphemes) words, with empirical evidence offering some preliminary answers. Indeed, if morphologically complex words are processed as a whole by learners during phonological form-meaning mapping, explicit conversations about Russian morphology are of little use in an L2 Russian class. If, however, the words are decomposed into morphemes as L2 learners attempt to access lexical meaning, then there is merit in focusing on morphology during instruction.

This question can be viewed through Lardiere's (2008, 2009) feature reassembly hypothesis (FRH) for L2 learning, which states that learners first try to deconstruct morpholexical features of the L1 and then reassemble the required meaning using features of the L2. This two-step process may not always occur in its entirety, with the cognitive work involved requiring various amounts of time and energy and not always leading to exact matches of L1 and L2 features. The FRH for L2 Russian was investigated and supported by Cho and Slabakova (2014). Additional evidence for the FRH has been provided by research on Arabic and Hebrew (Freynik et al., 2017).

In recent years, interest in the processing of L2 morphology has brought significant advances in understanding how complex morphology is accessed and processed by L1 and L2 learners. Coming from the Universal Grammar perspective, Gor's (2015) comprehensive overview concludes that L2 learners accessing multimorphemic words rely on largely the same processes as L1 speakers, but only once they reach a certain level of language proficiency. "L2 learners need time to understand the morphological structure of the L2 and then practice becoming efficient at using L2 morphology in native-like ways. Reliance on the same processing mechanisms and successful processing are not the same thing" (Gor, 2015, p. 198). Romanova and Gor (2016) found differences in gender and number agreement processing by L1 and L2 Russian speakers, noting that L2 learners of Russian employ different processing instruments, which was found to be true even for advanced learners (Romanova & Gor, 2016; for more on differences in Russian L1 and L2 language processing see also Gor, 2017; Gor & Cook, 2018).

Gor and Long (2009) describe two possible mechanisms of production as they draw on the body of previous research regarding the storage and online computation of inflections: (a) as the inflected form is stored in memory, frequency plays a part in its processing; (b) if morphemes comprising the word are added together by the speaker in real time, there is no pronounced frequency effect; and (c) type frequency impacts linguistic processing. Gor and Long (2009) conclude that

> It is type frequency, or the frequency of the rule or pattern, that influences linguistic processing. Research on the processing of Russian verbal morphology shows that this third possibility is, indeed, the case and connects the probabilistic aspects of L2 processing to properties of the input.
> (Gor & Long, 2009, p. 457)

The last statement speaks volumes in terms of instruction of L2 Russian and indicates that work on patterns, building on individual isolated language events or presented to learners as a concept, can yield significant results in terms of acquiring inflections. In L2 processing, learners may not know some lexemes, as vocabulary size and depth directly correlate with proficiency level, however, they can generalize declension and conjugation meaning-bearing patterns as they develop an understanding of the patterns' limits. In simple terms, this would mean that if an L2 learner of Russian encountered, for example, the genitive of класс [*class*] – *у класса*, they can be taught to deduce the genitive of лес [*forest*] – *у леса*, without having to re-calculate the entire process. Recognizing the crucial role of input "or in case of L2 learners . . . intake" and highlighting the implicit nature of knowledge of type frequencies and its effect on L1 and L2 processing, Gor and Long (2009) stress that, "This does not necessarily mean that this processing is not based on abstract symbolic rules" (pp. 466–467). In other words, instructors can facilitate students' observation and explicitly show ways of generalization in order to help develop learners' understanding of how Russian words are built and how meaning forms through the elements and structures of Russian grammar.

Teaching to see patterns in language, in turn, begs the question of how to help learners to not overgeneralize.

As mentioned earlier, L1 speakers can either process (make choices) online (in the act of using) or retrieve an inflected wordform from memory, taking the fastest route while both methods are activated. For L2 learners, however, there are additional factors: token (individual instances) and type frequencies (patterns), conjugational/declensional complexity, and learner characteristics, such as proficiency level, which correlates with the number of inflected forms available from memory (Brezina & Pallotti, 2019). As such, while associative patterning may be helpful for Russian morphology acquisition, it is not readily available to beginner learners with limited vocabulary and must be addressed during instruction. Beginners' online agency is also limited; therefore, instructional goals in beginner classrooms should include both *implicit and explicit pattern-building* in meaningful contexts in order to enable learners to move along the proficiency continuum:

> More advanced L2 learners can potentially take advantage of associative patterning, as well as abstract rules, and in order to do so, adult L2 learners will make use of both implicit and explicit inputs on the way to successful mastery of inflectional morphology.
>
> (Gor & Long, 2009, p. 467)

The following contextualizes research findings in pedagogical setting by considering how teachers can help L2 students of Russian understand the morphological structure of the Russian language and become efficient at using L2 morphology in native-like ways.

Associative patterning, language mining, Russian Constructicon, and root nests

Associative patterning: The fact that an inflected wordform can be acquired, stored, and accessed as a solid unit without parsing by L2 learners underscores the benefits of patterns in input. Work with associative patterning of word formation includes noticing patterns and learning to build similar structures based on the ones just noticed or already acquired. In my teaching experience and collegial observations, university students are not readily doing it on their own, requiring explicit effort to draw students' attention and help them discover, dissect, and learn to build on familiar patterns without overgeneralizing. While we worked with patterns in every text we encountered, most students loved to do this with song lyrics. As poetic language often employs patterns not typically used in regular communication, some phrases had to be given a more common appearance, which in turn presented productive noticing (observations), as well as production by rephrasing:

> Попытайся ладони у мёртвых разжать [try to unclench the dead hand's grip]

И оружье принять из натруженных рук [and accept the weapon from the tiered overworked hands].

(В. Высоцкий; V. Vysotskiy)

This might turn into a more common and less poetic *Попытайся разжать ладони у мёртвых и принять оружье из натруженных рук* [same sentence with a more direct word order]. One way to do this would be to give students cards with individual words and ask them to assemble a meaningful sentence with the use of dictionaries encouraged. After a few minutes of small group discussion or a jigsaw activity (for a description of jigsaw and input flood, see Rahimi et al., 2020), one student from each group switches groups. This gives students a chance to move the new group's work along or realize a mistake. The goal is to *arrive* at an acceptable word order when the placement decisions are *discussed and justified* based on the previously acquired patterns, rather than simply *giving* the correct answer. Building on the detected patterns, the students may later produce sentences and simple phrases such as *попытайся разжать руки/кулаки и успокоиться* [try to unclench hands/fists and calm down]; *попытайся написать статью* [try to write an article], or *попытайся сделать* [try to do]. Working in a small group serves as a form of scaffolding in learning to manipulate language and recognize the morphemes that contribute to pattern creation. Taking a short time to complete, such instructional episodes make comfortable scaffolds in larger-scale meaning-oriented activities.

For beginners, the same work may be done with simpler texts such as

Жил да был черный кот за углом [There lived a black cat around the corner]
И кота ненавидел весь дом [And the cat was hated by the entire house].

(М. Танич; M. Tanich)

Following the same process, the students (a) **simplify** the text by changing the text register from poetic to conversational with more direct word order: *Черный кот жил за углом. Весь дом ненавидел кота* [same text, more direct word order]; (b) use familiar patterns to facilitate and **justify** understanding **and build patterns** with shorter sentences or phrases: *Глупый сосед жил за углом* [Foolish neighbor lived around the corner]. *Он ненавидел слона* [He hated the elefant]. *Весь день,* [All day]; (c) **use** base phrases, as well as newly created phrases by building on the patterns of base phrases to "spice up" (in student terms) their conversation and writings in the larger meaning-oriented activities; and (d) **reflect** on the process. In their reflections, the students expressed feeling satisfaction in being able to use the structures they considered challenging only a short time ago; some felt the activity was difficult, so they had to watch others work before being able to contribute to group effort. Learning to leverage patterns received positive rating from beginner, intermediate, and advanced university students alike. In the open-ended part of their comprehensive end-of-semester course evaluations and in progress-tracking questionnaires (a routine monthly formative assessment in my courses) many spoke of it in terms of empowerment.

Language mining: A similar instructional approach is presented in literature as "language mining," albeit without any work on patterning. *Language mining* is used in the discussion of praxis in task-based language teaching by Feryok (2017): "new language that learners have 'mined' from tasks" (Feryok, 2017, p. 724). The term is also used within the instructional space of Chinese as a FL by Han (2020). According to Han (2020), language mining "involves exploring language input, extracting expressions, and utilizing them in output production . . . language mining, as I intend it, means extracting language constructions from input for meaning expression" (pp. 4–5). Han (2020) draws on additional input reading and feedback findings of Coyle and Roca de Larios (2014) and Kang (2020), refining the *language mining* construct and positing it within the broader scope of input processing, asserting that language mining "contributes to language acquisition, and, in turn, the ability to predict while reading, and ultimately to reading and writing fluency" (p. 5). This is an interesting example of how researchers and practitioners can think alike, taking different routes to arrive at the same approach as they look for ways that allow deeper processing of L2 input and facilitate transfer-appropriate processing.

Russian Constructicon and root nests: Work on patterning is also reflected in recent advances in computational linguistics in grammar construction which have led to the creation of the first Constructicons, with the Russian Constructicon including over 2,200 entries, far exceeding the analogues of any other language to date (Endresen et al., 2020; Endresen & Janda, 2020). The Russian Constructicon is an area well worth practitioners' exploration, as it may be instrumental for L2 learners of Russian. In particular, the Russian Constructicon may be helpful in facilitating learners' ability to recognize morphological transparency. In Gor's (2015) research on morphological transparency, L1 English speakers better process derived words when derivation is more semantically transparent, such as driver-DRIVE. Russian *однокоренные слова* are a group of words stemming from the same root, such as the English drive, driver, driven, overdrive, driveway. Building on the narrative of associative patterning of word formation discussed earlier, we can assume with some confidence that Russian *однокоренные слова* may be easier learned when a root nest, or morphological family (Gor, 2015), is made visible to the learner, for example, through a language mining exercise.

An illustration of a classroom activity based on this finding (beginner through advanced level) is learning to recognize morphological nests through structured input (VanPatten & Sanz, 1995; see also Benati, 2017) and can also be accomplished through input flood (Ellis, 2003; Rashtchi & Etebari, 2018). As students gradually build stamina, they become more confident in distinguishing root nests from false relatives. For instance, *комнатный* [indoor], *командовать* [to order], and *ком* [ball] all begin with *ком-* but belong to three different root nests. The *комнатный* [indoor] morphological nest includes *комната* [room], in contrast to the noun *команда* [team] of the root nest of *командовать* [to order], while neither is connected to *ком* with *комкать* [to crumple] and *скомканный* [crumpled] in its morphological root family. Proper root identification for an L2 learner of Russian, as well as for an L1 Russian speaker, is, in turn, important in accessing derivational formations and inflectional assembly and ultimately contributes to building L2 fluency, as it is clear now that the root words of large morphological families are accessed faster (Baayen et al., 2007). In addition, explicit instruction in growing learner's ability to recognize morphological nests builds L2 Russian reading comprehension skills and is instrumental in learners' use of language references (Comer, 2014).

Derivational and compound morphology of Russian and their acquisition by L2 learners

Derivational morphology is routinely present in L1 English language pedagogy, and there is a substantial body of research addressing its role in the instruction of L1 English (Levesque et al., 2018; McQuillan, 2020). Levesque and colleagues (2018) use the terms *morphological awareness* and *morphological analysis* to distinguish between the ability to manipulate morphemes (awareness) and infer the meaning of new multimorphemic lexemes (analysis). They point to L1 students' increased reading comprehension over time when students are taught to infer the meaning of new complex vocabulary using morphemes. An increased general morpheme awareness appears to support this process. Notably, the authors looked at derivational, not inflectional morphology. For L1 speakers, morphological analysis facilitated reading comprehension, while morphological awareness was instrumental in advancing the skills of morphological analysis, which led to gains in overall reading comprehension (Levesque et al., 2018).

If we assume the line of thought that L2 language acquisition processes are, at least partially, similar to those of L1 (Gor, 2015; Rankin & Whong, 2020; VanPatten et al., 2020), then explicit instruction in L2 Russian derivational morphology, given its prominent place in L1 Russian pedagogical landscape (Kanakina & Goretskiy, 2021; Razumovskaja et al., 2020; Lekant, 1988, *inter alia*), may play a crucial role in advancing the fluency of L2 Russian learners. Interestingly, similar explicit work on deeper awareness and understanding of L1 English morphology for native English-speaking students is routinely advocated by literacy experts in U.S. schools, as they cite manifold literacy gains from explicit derivational morphology instruction and practice compounding over time (Beyersmann et al., 2021; Chan et al., 2020; Kirby & Bowers, 2018; Levesque et al., 2018; McQuillan, 2020).

In her extensive review of the research on the processing of L2 morphology, Kira Gor (2015) concludes that L2 learners, except beginners who are inclined to memorize language chunks, process multimorphemic words using decomposition, similar to L1 speakers. Gor (2015) also points to definitive differences between the two groups, specifically noting that morphological decomposition is a demanding cognitive task and learners are not always successful at it; semantic transparency becomes the agency that facilitates the process of decomposition, similar to L1. Gor (2015) further clarifies that

> Even L2 learners may have whole-word representations for high frequency inflected words, and will use the direct access route. In the case when both decompositional and whole-word access routes are available to the L2 learner, the choice of the route will depend on the task.
>
> (Gor, 2015, p. 196)

Gor (2015) maintains that stem allomorphy (strong-strength; *ухо-уши*, [ear-ears], Lekant, 1988) is tied to L2 proficiency, stating that learner's ability to decompose the words with complex allomorphy grows as L2 proficiency increases. In the pedagogical context, the earlier-cited research invites a series of questions: What instructional practices will help learners of Russian become more successful at processing Russian derivational morphology? How can instruction facilitate its understanding and acquisition by students? What strategies could facilitate practice in order for learners to, in Gor's terms, "become efficient at using L2 morphology in native-like ways"?

Understanding the processes of derivational morphology and an awareness of its features do not come intuitively to L2 learners; moreover, they are explicitly addressed in education of L1 speakers, as discussed earlier. There is documented evidence of L2 Russian teachers using morphological word analyses in instruction, particularly at advanced levels (as stated in Comer, 2012b, p. 213). This practice should also be made accessible to novice learners. The following is an illustration based on practice with beginner high (ACTFL, 2012) L2 Russian students in tertiary setting. Several pop-up grammar explanations and an explicit class discussion on the derivation of Russian compound adjectives with "*много-*" [multi-] were necessary for this group of learners. Following this, the students started using compound adjectives in their output and appeared to enjoy working with them.

It started when my university students in their second semester of studying Russian encountered a compound adjective "*многонациональный*" [multinational]. This was followed by a short grammar pop-up discussion on how the adjective was formed. The students seemed interested and genuinely involved. For the next class, as an extension of learning, I prepared a Quizlet set of flashcards to help students capitalize on their knowledge and branch out deeper into the Russian language. The set was entirely composed of words with *много-* [multi-] and all flashcards followed the same pattern: "*многоводная*" [full river] had to be matched with "*река, в которой много воды*" [full river], or "*многолюдная*" [full of people] with "*улица, на которой много людей*" [street full of people]. The function of "*который*" [which] was to be implicitly learned by the students. In order to minimize the cognitive load and help students concentrate on semantics and morphology, all adjectives were in the nominative case and the nouns they modified were represented by all three genders plus plurals; use of dictionaries was encouraged. In my mind, the connections between the terms and their definitions were easy for students to grasp. In class, the students used the cards I prepared in advance and worked with a partner to match each word with its definition.

This activity turned out to be difficult for learners, with students describing it as "work" and "strenuous learning" rather than "empowerment" in their reflections. What I thought of as a quick and fun elementary school-style matching activity that would super-charge student motivation by way of significantly enlarging their vocabulary base with little effort, turned into "hard work." The activity was still well received by students and some referred to it in their monthly reflections as an eye-opening and beneficial experience, but I was not satisfied: the difficulty that the students experienced was unexpected. In the following year, I minimized the cognitive load and increased scaffolding by reviewing the *который* [which] construction ahead of time, replacing some nouns with more frequently used ones, and ensuring the vocabulary choices in compound adjectives overall were less challenging. The students appeared to enjoy the class more and had less difficulties with matching. We continued to use high-yield activities requiring little time and effort that had a significant impact on student production. The students voluntarily undertook mini-projects with "*мало-*" [little] (i.e., *малопонятный* [hard to understand]) and "*трудно-*" [difficult] (i.e., *труднодоступный* [hard to reach]) as extensions to their compound adjectives learning.

This classroom experience is validated by the research of Leminen et al. (2019) on morphological processes in the brain. Reviewing advances in cognitive neuroscience on neural mechanisms underlying morphological processing, Leminen and colleagues separate the findings into three categories of inflectional, derivational, and compound multimorphemic words, noting that studies on compound morphology were few, with most inconsistencies of all three categories (Leminen et al., 2019). The authors illustrate compound formations with "man-POWER" and "MAIL-man" (Leminen et al., 2019, p. 28). In Russian discourse, Lekant illustrates compound formation with *высокоразвитый* [highly developed], *сногсшибательный* [stunning] (Lekant, 1988, p. 162). A summary of research findings by Leminen et al. (2019) presents divergent and at times contradictory conclusions:

> While some studies clearly support views favoring the access to the constituent morphemes prior to accessing the whole compound word, some other neuroimaging studies posit that compounds are processed at a whole-word level. Moreover, while some studies suggest that the semantic transparency of compound words may determine the manner in which these words are accessed, others claim that transparent and opaque compounds are processed similarly. Furthermore, there are studies suggesting that the extent to which constituents can be accessed highly depends on the prior experience with the whole compound, claiming for differences in the morphological decomposition of novel and existing compounds.
>
> (p. 37)

Carte blanche. If someone ever wondered what *carte blanche* directions for classroom instruction would look like, here they are. It seems practical, therefore, to continue looking for strategies that work for students in the acquisition of rich morphology and to continue practicing those that facilitate both language learning and acquisition (Krashen, 1981). This is especially true since even novice L2 Russian learners benefit from explicit instruction on Russian derivational morphology and show gains in grammatical gender recognition using diminutive suffixes, such as frogg*y* and boot*ie* in English and дом*ик* [house, *dim.*] and свеч*ка* [candle] in Russian (Brooks et al., 2011). As reported by Brooks et al. (2011), the learners successfully transferred patterns to new words and showed a diminutive advantage in vocabulary recall. Learned diminutive derivations may reduce learners' cognitive load by decreasing the overall material to be memorized, thereby enhancing word learning (Brooks et al., 2011), with adult learners employing both pattern-based and memory-based learning processes (Kempe et al., 2010). Gor (2015) encourages teaching effective strategies of employing decomposition explicitly and underscores the two-fold benefits this brings: faster access of lexemes and overall more efficient L2 processing.

The central role of morphology in the acquisition of L2 Russian is supported by research in other languages that share some qualities of Russian's rich morphology: Slabakova's *bottleneck hypothesis* (Slabakova, 2009) tested against the *interface hypothesis* (Sorace, 2011) is recently validated in the context of L2 German (Lecouvet et al., 2021), where inflectional morphology, particularly that of case, proved to be a key in L2 acquisition of other areas of grammar and grammar interface with discourse (for definition and discussion of *interface* see Sorace, 2011), influencing L2 acquisition at the syntax-discourse level (e.g., convergence in discourse-to-syntax mappings).

The efforts to measure morphological complexity resulted in the creation of several techniques over the years, to include the recently developed new construct of the Morphological Complexity Index (MCI) (Brezina & Pallotti, 2019). To date, MCI has been applied to Italian, German, French, and English with investigations in other languages underway. According to the first reports of its application, in morphologically rich languages MCI strongly correlates with proficiency, as well as lexical diversity and sentence length. This is not so for L1 and L2 speakers of English, a morphologically simple language, where MCI remains mostly constant across the proficiency levels. The authors conclude that morphological complexity of produced language depends not only on proficiency of the learner and speaker, but also on the language being acquired (Brezina & Pallotti, 2019). This study provides additional indirect empirical evidence to the concept of primacy of morphology in instructed acquisition of L2 Russian.

The role of teachers in bridging the research-practice divide

In recent years, research on L2 morphology acquisition experienced many essential advances that have important implications for effective instruction of L2 Russian with new investigations underway. However, there is currently no definitive answer regarding the mechanics of L1-like systems of L2 acquisition development by L2 learners as they acquire multimorphemic words. Furthermore, the influence of context on L1 expectancy considering the word's morphosyntactic connections in speech processing remains unclear (Gor, 2015). Teachers, therefore, continue to look for effective instructional strategies to develop learners' ability to form a system of inflection expectancy and morphological fluency. Various methods of and approaches to instruction are available for L2 Russian; from the teaching perspective though, there are only two categories: those that are productive in facilitating language acquisition, and those that are not. It is, therefore, important to reiterate that teachers should rely on their linguistic background and professional teaching experience when interpreting and applying various research, as only some findings can be readily translated into pedagogy. Another area to be aware of is that the conditions of educational and research environments vary significantly, and what seems to deliver desirable results in one setting may not be as productive in another (Han, 2016).

Discussing the connections and interdependency of SLA and linguistic theory, Jing-Schmidt and Peng (2018) draw on a substantial body of research to illustrate the research-practice divide as they attend to challenges associated with assuring a meaningful and productive exchange within the larger SLA community, calling to the respective field to abandon practices of condescension and resistance as not productive. Jing-Schmidt and Peng (2018) argue for bridging existing theory-practice gaps and encourage optimism and open-mindedness:

> Hollow calls for theoretically informed teaching fall short to assist pedagogical decision making. So is a perfunctory paragraph about "pedagogical implications" habitually tagged onto a technical linguistic analysis inadequate to accomplish true mediation. To be helpful mediators, the linguists among us need to translate theoretical tenets to comprehensible pedagogical principles, and transfer these in turn to concrete and executable pedagogical actions. . . . This is easier said than done.
>
> (p. 73)

Their words certainly ring true to the greater space of teaching and learning of L2 Russian. The field would benefit from more robust conversations about its instructional practices and from teachers' reflections on using research findings in their classrooms through deliberate practice accounts. Action-based research (Manfra, 2019), a long-standing tradition of research in L2 Russian pedagogy, is mainly institutionalized in tertiary education (see Comer & deBenedette, 2011) and, thus, mostly limited to that setting.

This chapter bridges research and practice by means of a contextualized review of research findings directed at their application to practice instruction of L2 Russian. It lets research findings shine as they transform classroom instruction and give grounding and substance to the teacher's experience and intuition. Only the combined efforts of the two fields – language acquisition research and practice – have the power to advance the field of teaching RFL. Sato and Loewen (2019) speak of teachers' intuition and experience as beneficial and helpful in adjusting instructional strategies. They also caution that a significant amount of imbalance may ensue when either research or practice assumes a dominant role. It is vital for teachers to be aware of the latest advances in research:

> Teachers fully relying on their intuitions and experience sometimes jeopardize the students' learning. As Paran (2017) cautioned, disassociating L2 teachers from L2 research is dangerous because teaching might "become merely the transmission of self-perpetuating, unsupported beliefs and prejudices, based on experience that is never examined" (p. 506).
> (Sato & Loewen, 2019, p. 19)

It is equally important for researchers to provide instrumental accounts of how their findings can help inform classroom instruction to the benefit of the learners, for,

> At the end of the day, it is the teachers who make the change in the classroom, by putting in extra time and effort to improve their pedagogy. However, we believe that the responsibility is on researchers to make their research useful and accessible, given the limited research access teachers are generally afforded.
> (Sato & Loewen, 2019, p. 19)

It may also prove valuable for research teams to include teachers as equitable author-partners during early stages of study design, potentially making the overall efforts of the study to be more pedagogically sound and purposeful. Such equitable partnership would provide researchers direct access to the pedagogical expertise the team may lack otherwise and prove effective not only in shaping the overall research design frame, but also in translating study results into practice. In this respect, the conversation on praxis in L2 teaching holds promise (Feryok, 2017) and awaits its further development in the context of teaching L2 Russian.

Both researchers and teachers owe it to learners of L2 Russian to find the instructional strategies that would allow learners to genuinely enjoy learning, progress more quickly toward their desired proficiency level, and appreciate the innate beauty and richness of the Russian language in the process. It is within our power to ensure our students see the forest behind the trees as they become aware of and learn to appreciate the grandeur of the Russian language behind the seemingly endless choices of inflections, variety of stem patterns, and changes in stress placements, and are able to meaningfully enjoy it – use it. Productive instructional approaches should stem from and be framed by the necessities of meaningful communication. Based on research, they should add efficiency to a truly student-centered and learner-friendly environment all teachers aspire to foster in their instructional space. Such transformed teaching, empowered by enhanced communication and a more prominent teacher agency within the wider field of applied linguistics, would in turn spark future areas of research, elating new spirals in the cyclic nature of language pedagogy.

I would like to thank the volume's co-editor Wendy Whitehead Martelle for creating the two tables I used in this text to illustrate the rich Russian morphology.

Chapter 3

Cracking the Cyrillic code through tasks
Implications for instruction and foreign language teacher education

Nina Kositsky

Chapter summary

Despite the efficacy of task-based language teaching (TBLT), foreign language educators face many challenges in implementing TBLT, which may lead to it being largely underutilized. This chapter describes a pedagogical framework for introducing task-based language instruction to future teachers of foreign languages. Task-based teaching is demonstrated through a Russian language lesson that introduces the Cyrillic alphabet to beginners. This puts future language teachers in the learner position, allowing them to experience the thrill of language learning in a well-scaffolded task-based classroom.

Краткое содержание главы

Несмотря на эффективность целевого задания, преподаватели иностранных языков (ИЯ) сталкиваются со множеством проблем при его использовании. Это может привести к недостаточно широкому использованию целевого задания на практике. В данной главе описывается педагогическая модель обучения будущих преподавателей ИЯ этой методике с тем, чтобы сделать метод целевого задания более доступным для преподавателей ИЯ. Описываемый подход включает в себя урок русского алфавита для начинающих, который ставит будущих учителей в положение учащихся и позволяет им испытать радость от успешного усвоения языка в рамках хорошо организованного урока, основанного на принципах целевого задания.

Introduction

If there is an instructional approach that can instantly transform a language classroom, it is task-based language teaching (TBLT). The efficacy of this language pedagogy has been most unequivocally demonstrated by U.S. government language programs, where students are able to make progress "at a rather rapid pace" and to effectively apply their new language skills in real-life situations (Leaver &

DOI: 10.4324/9781003146346-3

Kaplan, 2004). There is also empirical evidence from other contexts that suggests that TBLT is "superior to traditional teaching" in promoting language acquisition (Ellis, 2009, p. 226). Ellis lists the following advantages of a task-based approach:

- TBLT offers the opportunity for 'natural' learning inside the classroom.
- It emphasizes meaning over form but can also cater for learning form.
- It affords learners a rich input of target language.
- It is intrinsically motivating.
- It is compatible with a learner-centered educational philosophy but also allows for teacher input and direction.
- It caters to the development of communicative fluency while not neglecting accuracy.
- It can be used alongside a more traditional approach.

(p. 242)

In addition, the literature abounds in examples of teaching practitioners' positive attitudes toward TBLT (see, for instance, Faez et al., 2011 and Edwards & Willis, 2005), who consistently acknowledge increased student engagement and motivation due to intrinsic interest of task-based activities. For example, Poupore (2005) writes, "As I observed my students pursuing their task goals, they looked totally engaged. It really seemed as though they had lost track of time. This led me to continue using tasks in the classroom" (p. 242).

However, data and anecdotal observations alike indicate that TBLT "continues to have a somewhat limited influence on actual second language teaching practices in many contexts" (Ogilvie & Dunn, 2010, p. 161). Partially, this can be attributed to the fact that more conventional approaches to language teaching, such as grammar-based instruction for instance, lend themselves well to accountability since they generate "clear tangible goals, precise syllabuses, and a comfortably itemizable basis for the evaluation of effectiveness" (Skehan, 1998, p. 94).

Other studies reveal real practical problems and difficulties that teachers face when they actually implement TBLT. Among identified obstacles, teachers' "poor understanding of what a task was," reported by Ellis (2009, p. 240) and Erlam (2016), stands out as most concerning. Leaver and Kaplan's (2004) list of challenges reported by TBLT course instructors includes significant investment of time in planning task-based lessons, paucity of materials, and need for faculty development, among others (p. 57). Ogilvie and Dunn (2010) extend this list by pointing out the lack of support for student teachers in language teacher preparation programs. As Ellis (2009) emphasizes, "These practical problems . . . will need to be addressed if TBLT is to be made to work in actual classrooms" (p. 240).

What follows is a description of a pedagogical framework that aims to address the earlier-identified challenges and, potentially, to make TBLT a more practical endeavor for language educators. The framework is grounded in the author's teaching experience in a language teacher preparation program and involves four

Table 3.1 Four-stage TBLT training framework

1. Reading Lee's (1995) article *Using Task-Based Activities to Restructure Class Discussions* (or an alternative comparable reading) to build some background knowledge about TBLT.
2. Participating in the Russian language learning simulation *Code Breakers* (see later), which puts language teachers in the learner position and allows them to experience the thrill of language learning in a well-scaffolded task-based language classroom.
3. Whole-group discussion to reflect on participants' experience learning the Russian alphabet through a task and to establish connections between the theoretical framework outlined in Lee's (or alternative) article and the structure of the Russian lesson *Code Breakers*.
4. In-class mock teaching (during subsequent class sessions): course participants design and teach task-based lessons that incorporate key TBLT principles and insights learned from participating in the Russian language learning simulation *Code Breakers*. Each mock teaching is followed by a feedback session.

---

stages designed to help teacher candidates internalize core principles of TBLT and apply them to their own lesson planning and teaching (Table 3.1).

Understanding what a task is

As the name suggests, a *task* is the pillar that defines TBLT. Therefore, attaining a clear understanding of what *task* is in a language classroom and, moreover, learning "to think in terms of tasks" (Leaver & Kaplan, 2004, p. 57) are two critical competencies that teachers need to develop in order to be able to implement TBLT.

Resorting to the TBLT literature for insights reveals a wide range of perspectives, definitions, and uses of the term *task*. As Shehadeh (2005) points out, "Some researchers have examined tasks from an interaction perspective, others from an output perspective, others from a cognitive perspective, and still others from a socio-cultural perspective" (p. 20). On the one hand, such a variety of views, approaches, and task typologies appears to provide flexibility for teaching practitioners to adapt TBLT to their specific contexts. On the flip side, the sheer ubiquity of often-conflicting views on what constitutes *task* in a language classroom and of corresponding pedagogical implications make it more difficult to build a coherent task-based instructional framework – a process that might feel like attempting to construct a jigsaw puzzle picture using pieces that belong to different sets.

To construct the framework presented in this chapter, we have drawn on existing TBLT research and the author's teaching experience in a language teacher preparation program to extrapolate and to articulate essential design features of task (Table 3.2) that distinguish it from other types of classroom activities. These task attributes make up a sufficiently comprehensive and yet accessible and generalizable instructional framework that can be applied to different teaching contexts, to all foreign languages, and to all language proficiency levels. Furthermore, *if used*

Table 3.2 Design features of task

1. Task is a goal-oriented activity where participants have to work toward a specified outcome (Willis, 2004).

   A task is completed when the specified outcome is achieved.

2. Task creates a genuine reason for communication.

   Communication is an interaction between at least two independent (i.e., not exercising control over one other) participants, one of whom may benefit from the other's skill in making the interaction succeed (Lee, 1995). As they communicate, they engage in the process of "interpretation, expression, and negotiation of meaning" (p. 439).

3. Task induces *negotiative interactions*.

   There is some sort of incompleteness, partiality, problem, or gap that needs to be addressed through negotiations. In addition to negotiation of meaning, there are other types of negotiation that entail genuine communication in a task-based classroom: negotiation of (linguistic) form, task content, task procedure, etc. (Poupore, 2005).

4. Task does not merely *encourage* participation but *requires* it.

   Accomplishing a task entails completing a series of steps of gradually increasing complexity that require learners' active involvement in constructing their own knowledge.

5. Task *enables* participation and communication.

   There are linguistic and conceptual supports built into the task. This scaffolding is fine-tuned to students' proficiency level.

together as a set, identified design features can effectively serve as an operational characterization of task, since coming up with an all-encompassing definition of task has proven problematic (Ellis, 2009; Lee, 1995).

These design features can be applied to the development of different task types conceptualized in the literature, such as:[1]

- *Real-world tasks*: "the hundred and one things people do in everyday life, at work, at play, and in between" (Long, 1985, p. 89), such as making a hotel reservation.
- *Pedagogic tasks*: "tasks that look more like classroom activities" (González-Lloret, 2016), such as information gap activities.
- *Closed tasks*: tasks that have very specific goals, are highly structured, and have only one right answer or solution, such as "spot the difference" activities (Willis, 2004).
- *Open tasks*, where the content and style of the end-product vary between different learners, such as experience-sharing tasks (Willis, 2004).
- *One-way tasks*, where only one participant controls the flow of information and others are listening and doing something, such as listening and arranging a sequence of pictures (Willis, 2004).
- *Two-way tasks*, where two or more learners interact to achieve a specific outcome (Willis, 2004), such as agreeing on a list of movies to watch over a weekend.

- *Focused tasks:* tasks that "aim to induce learners to process, receptively or productively, some particular linguistic features, e.g., a grammatical structure" (Ellis, 2003, p. 16), such as having students give each other advice on how to solve a particular issue, eliciting the present unreal conditional – "If I were you, I would. . . ."
- *Unfocused tasks:* those that encourage students to use freely any language they have at their disposal, without concentrating on specific forms (Willis, 2004), such as having students interview people for a project, where they are not given specific phrases or samples of language to use (Lys, 2005).

It is very common for a language classroom to integrate different types of tasks in order to achieve various language development goals. Therefore, following a unified set of principles to design various tasks can make lesson preparation more efficient.

Learning to think in terms of tasks: Russian to the rescue!

Unless it is one's lived experience, learning to think in terms of tasks might take time. To accelerate this process, the author developed and taught a model TBLT lesson – *Code Breakers* (later) – as part of a language methods course in a university teacher preparation program. It is a Russian language lesson designed for the novice low proficiency level. Course participants are teacher candidates preparing to teach ESL/TESOL or foreign languages (such as Chinese, French, German, Portuguese, or Spanish) who have no Russian language background.

When a group of language learners with zero skills in the target language is told that in about 25 minutes, they will read and write basic words in that language, one can expect a mixture of skepticism and excitement. Indeed, language learning experiences of most people do not include such an immediate return for the effort of learning. However, even a short well-designed task-based lesson can produce substantial, tangible gains in students' language acquisition. And Russian, with its reputation of being "difficult," makes a perfect language for demonstrating the effectiveness of TBLT!

The lesson *Code Breakers* capitalizes on two specific affordances of the Russian language:

- Russian is a largely phonetic language, which means that a word's pronunciation can often be predicted from its spelling, and its spelling – from its pronunciation.
- Russian and English share some cognates – words that have a similar meaning, spelling, and pronunciation: e.g., бар/bar, видео/video, президент/president.

Our lesson uses an inductive method to introduce the Russian alphabet, i.e., "an approach in which learners first see letters in context and are then guided on their own to discover the sound-symbol correspondences" (Bown et al., 2007, p. 90). Inductive instruction lends itself well to TBLT, as it promotes learners' active involvement in constructing their own knowledge while they are solving a particular problem or filling in a (knowledge) gap. In addition, research on learning the Russian alphabet suggests that inductive methods "may lead to quicker and more accurate acquisition of the Cyrillic alphabet" (Bown et al., 2007, p. 90).

Code Breakers consists of a series of interconnected focused pedagogic tasks, which expose students to the same linguistic input in a cyclical manner – a subset of letters in the Russian alphabet (see Table 3.3). Students encounter the same letters in different words in the context of different tasks. Repeated but varied engagement with such finely tuned input[2] ensures internalization of target linguistic structures and concepts – Russian letter formation and sound-letter correspondences, while the task prompts intrinsically engaging negotiative interactions among students and creates reasons for genuine communication. The lesson revolves around negotiations of form (Poupore, 2005), as learners have to puzzle out Russian grapheme-phoneme patterns in order to achieve concrete goals specified for each task.

To enable negotiative interactions among novice Russian language learners and to scaffold their acquisition of letter-sound knowledge, the lesson makes use of students' native language (L1) – in this case, English. This approach is consistent with a socio-cultural view of second language development, where L1 is seen as an important tool in mediating the learning process and in promoting collaborative dialogue. Proficiency level of the students and cognitive demands of the task are key factors that determine the role that L1 can potentially play in a L2 classroom: "if the activity requires complex cognitive processing, then the best (and perhaps, only) way for the learner to engage in the activity is by 'talking it through' in the first (strongest) language" (Swain et al., 2015, p. 43). Drawing on relevant studies, Swain et al. (2015) continue: "L1 use can both support and enhance L2 development, functioning simultaneously as an effective tool for dealing with cognitively demanding content" (Behan et al., 1997 cited in Swain et al., 2015, p. 43).[3]

Table 3.3 Code Breakers

Task title:	Code Breakers
Task goals:	• To introduce the Russian alphabet • To enable learners to make appropriate letter-sound connections in Russian
Setting:	Adult/University/PD workshop
Proficiency level:	Complete beginners
Task type:	Focused; pedagogic
Can-do statements:	• I can infer correspondences between Russian letters and their sounds • I can read some basic words in Russian • I can write some basic words in Russian
Assessments:	Ongoing informal formative assessment, orally and with white boards

Student handout

Task introduction: a mission to accomplish

You are a cryptanalyst who has to break a new code. This time it is the Russian alphabet! Follow the prompts to figure out the algorithm that will allow you to decode and encode a series of incepted Russian words. Remember: whatever you do, do not stop making inferences about letter-sound correspondences!

Task 1

Below is a list of words in Russian and their equivalents in English.

1. As you listen to the instructor read the Russian words out loud, make inferences about letter-sound correspondences.
2. Repeat the words after the instructor, keeping your eyes on the Russian words to confirm or, if necessary, to adjust your inferences about letter-sound correspondences. Try to emulate the target pronunciation.

America	АМЕРИКА
Boston	БОСТОН
Massachusetts	МАССАЧУСЕТС
India	ИНДИЯ
Jack London	ДЖЭК ЛОНДОН
Michael Jackson	МАЙКЛ ДЖЭКСОН
Dostoyevsky	ДОСТОЕВСКИЙ
Physics	ФИЗИКА
Cosmos	КОСМОС

Task 2

1. Individual work: Match each Russian word with its meaning. Try not to look at the table introduced in Task 1 as you complete the activity.

An American writer	АМЕРИКА
The capital of Massachusetts	КОСМОС
The universe, the space	ИНДИЯ
A Russian writer	ФИЗИКА
A continent and a country	МАССАЧУСЕТС
An American pop singer	ДЖЭК ЛОНДОН
A country in Asia	БОСТОН
A scientific discipline	ДОСТОЕВСКИЙ
A state in New England	МАЙКЛ ДЖЭКСОН

2   Form groups of three to compare your answers and to adjust them if necessary.
3   Share out as a whole group – do not look at the English equivalents while reading!

Task 3

1   Choose one Russian word from Task 1 "to study": the goal is to learn to write it in Russian from memory, recreating the shape of the Russian letters.
2   Go to the board and write the word you "studied" from memory.
3   Read your word out loud.

Task 4

1   Make up an interesting yes-or-no question **(in English)** that you would like to ask your fellow cryptanalysts. **Example:** Are you a good chess player?
2   Walk around the room eliciting your colleagues' responses to your question.

   - If the answer is "Yes," your peer will say "**ДА**," and you will write "**ДА**" next to that person's name.
   - If the answer is "No," your peer will say "**НЕТ**," and you will write "**НЕТ**" next to that person's name.

3   Share your "**ДА**" and "**НЕТ**" lists with the whole group.

Instructor manual only

Task 5

1   Students pair up to spell some basic words in Russian as they hear the instructor pronounce them. The words are made up of the letters that the students have already encountered a few times while completing Tasks 1–4. Thus, the expectation is that they will be able to write the words as they hear them by enacting their understandings of the letter-sound correspondences they gained during the previous steps.

> он, сон, нос, сок, май, мой, дом, фото, фокус, Борис, я, Москва

2   Whole group sharing after each introduced a new word: students volunteer to write their version of the word on the board – to compare with other students' spelling and to get the instructor's feedback to ensure accuracy.

Challenges of teaching RFL

Learning the Russian alphabet is both one of the "first orders of business in any beginning Russian class" (Bown et al., 2007, p. 89) and one of the first potential difficulties learners of Russian may experience. As Comer and Murphy-Lee (2004) wittingly put it:

> Some students . . . wonder aloud about how many months it takes to master the [Russian] alphabet; others . . . have the idea that Russian is virtually like English, but coded in strange letters; still others dismiss learning Russian as a daunting task in which an unfamiliar and uninviting alphabet is only the first of many impossible hurdles.
>
> (p. 23)

Some of the well-documented challenges associated with learning the Russian alphabet include mistaking some letters of the Cyrillic alphabet for Latin letters (e.g., "Р" as in "Река" for "P" as in "Plot"); missing/not seeing small visual distinctions between Russian letters (such as "Э" and "З") or between Cyrillic and Latin letters (such as "И" and "N").[4] At the same time, there is evidence that early mastery of letter-sound correspondences predicts success in beginning Russian courses (Comer & Murphy-Lee, 2004). These data underscore the high-stakes nature of teaching the Russian alphabet and highlight the importance of choosing teaching methods that can give novice language learners a quick and meaningful return for the effort of learning.

Lessons learned

The way a task is framed and introduced can impact student engagement. For instance, framing a task as a game facilitates a playful stance and increases student motivation. This is consistent with research that suggests that play and playfulness promote learning and performance (Heimann & Roepstorff, 2018). The researchers maintain that playfulness as "an attitude, mode or mental stance" allows for an exploratory engagement with learning materials and enhances participants' feeling of competence and, consequently, increases their "motivation for the task" (p. 1).

To illustrate, our *Code Breakers* simulation was initially introduced as a "lesson" that "guaranteed" a specific outcome – the ability to read and write basic words in Russian. Even though the lesson design – i.e., a sequence of well-scaffolded, interconnected tasks that gradually build requisite competencies – ensured the attainment of a desired learning outcome, reframing it as a "code-breaking mission" effectively activated students' playful stance towards the lesson activities and changed their perception of the experience from purely academic to game-like. Importantly, asking students to be cryptanalysts also helped to focus their attention on the goals set for them – to break the code of the Russian alphabet by puzzling out Russian phonological and orthographic patterns. Interestingly, task reframing did not require any modifications of the original task design: we kept all the original tasks intact and only changed the wording, i.e., modulated task framing.

This experience taught us that it is possible to design focused pedagogic tasks that pursue specific goals and to tweak task design later in the process in order to introduce a playful stance and, therefore, to increase a task's intrinsic motivation – a trademark of TBLT.

Conclusion

We have described an approach to task-based language teaching that foregrounds design features of tasks as defining characteristics of this instructional framework. Applying design principles to task development in a foreign language classroom involves leading students through a sequence of meticulously scaffolded assignments and activities that enable language learners to *gradually* and *systematically* build requisite skills and understandings. The proposed framework requires that the instructor should consider linguistic competencies and subskills that need to be taught and practiced at each stage of the teaching and learning process before asking language learners to perform more linguistically advanced tasks.

Engaging students in a series of interconnected tasks of increasing complexity, modulating difficulty levels of assignments, thoughtfully calibrating linguistic scaffolding, and engaging students with target linguistic structures in a spiral manner accelerate language acquisition. In addition, strategic integration of L1 as a scaffolding tool into the flow of instruction can facilitate L2 acquisition within the context of meaningful pedagogic tasks, if tailored to the students' level of language proficiency and cognitive demands of specific tasks. Applying outlined considerations to one's lesson planning and teaching allows maximizing *each* student's active engagement by not simply *encouraging* participation but *requiring* and *enabling* it.

While well-designed tasks create reasons for genuine communication in a language classroom, their built-in linguistic supports allow for systematic enforcement of form-meaning connections. Such contextualized attention to form helps to ensure *noticing* – "a requisite for language acquisition to take place" (Ellis, 2009, p. 232; Schmidt, 2001) and minimizes language fossilization.

To facilitate the internalization of core TBLT principles, we recommend engaging course participants in an authentic experience that puts them in the language learner position, such as our *Code Breakers* simulation. For best results, teaching content that participants are not familiar with is preferable. Within the author's context, the Russian alphabet served as an effective tool for introducing TBLT to teacher candidates in a university educator preparation program.

To reach a wider audience of foreign language teachers, the presented four-stage training framework (Table 3.1) can also be used to introduce TBLT in professional development workshops to seasoned language educators in higher education and K–12 settings. Insights from TBLT research and practice show that after initial investment in training, "savings in preparation time have been the typical experience of teachers who move into task-based teaching" (Leaver & Kaplan, 2004, p. 57).

The goal of this pedagogical narration is to present an instructional framework that would clarify the construct of a task and demonstrate what a task may look like in a language classroom. We do so by translating available TBLT research into an actionable, practical pedagogical framework that is applicable to a variety of foreign language teaching contexts. Additionally, we have tackled one of the key challenges associated with learning the Russian language – mastering its letter-sound correspondences. Our lesson *Code Breakers* demonstrates how focused pedagogic tasks can serve as an effective tool for acquiring complex linguistic content in an intrinsically engaging manner. To echo Pylypiuk (2004), "Our success in shaping positive attitudes towards the Slavic languages will be determined by the quality of our tools and our teaching" (p. 7), and TBLT is one such tool in our pedagogical arsenal.

Notes

1 It is beyond the scope of this chapter to provide an exhaustive list of task typologies or to discuss them in any depth. For more information, please consult the referenced works.
2 Finely tuned input is "language which has been very precisely selected to be at exactly the students' level" and which we select for conscious learning and teaching (Harmer, 1991, p. 75).
3 For a comprehensive discussion of the role of L1 in foreign language learning, see for instance Turnbull and Dailey-O'Cain (2009).
4 For a comprehensive list of challenges associated with learning the Russian alphabet, see Comer and Murphy-Lee (2004), among others.

Chapter 4

Learner corpus as a medium for tasks

Aleksey Novikov and Valentina Vinokurova

Chapter summary

This chapter argues for the use of a learner corpus in task-based teaching of Russian. First, the chapter provides the definitions of tasks and discusses texts in task-based teaching. Second, we elaborate on focused tasks in light of the principles of language awareness and introduce Data-Driven Learning (DDL). And finally, we describe the two types of focused tasks, namely structure-trapping tasks and DDL tasks, and explain how a learner corpus can be seen as a medium between the more traditional structure-trapping tasks and innovative DDL tasks.

Краткое содержание главы

В главе предлагается модель использования корпуса изучающих русский язык для преподавания русского как иностранного (РКИ) в рамках метода коммуникативных заданий. В водной части главы даются определения коммуникативных заданий. Затем внимание читателей заостряется на сфокусированных заданиях, нацеленных на конкретные лингвистические формы в рамках теории языкового сознания. Далее в статье излагается метод обучения на основе данных (Data-Driven Learning; DDL), с помощью которого были построены сфокусированные коммуникативные задания, представленные авторами. В статье также описываются примеры коммуникативных заданий и предлагается объяснение того, как корпус изучающих русский язык может быть использован для их разработки.

Introduction

While there are multiple definitions of task and versions of task-based instruction, there is usually an agreement that tasks should be meaning-centered, involve real-world language use, have a communicative purpose, and promote learning by doing (R. Ellis, 2003; Long, 2016; R. Ellis, 2017). According to R. Ellis (2003), tasks can be categorized as unfocused and focused. As such, unfocused tasks "may predispose learners to choose from a range of forms but they are not designed with the use of a specific form in mind" (R. Ellis, 2003, p. 16). The topics of unfocused tasks are derived from real life or the academic curriculum. For example, a task that asks learners to describe their recent trip is an example of an unfocused task. In contrast, focused tasks prompt learners to process, produce, or comprehend a particular linguistic feature, while still satisfying the key criterion of a task, which is using language to achieve some non-linguistic outcome (R. Ellis, 2003).

According to R. Ellis (2003), there are two ways to create a focused task. One way is to design a focused task so that it would elicit target linguistic features; such tasks are also called "structure-trapping tasks" (Long, 2016). For instance, you might ask learners to describe their trip by narrating the places that they went to, and explicitly require them to use certain grammatical constructions (e.g., пошел, пошла, пошли [went]) using sequences (e.g., сначала, потом [first, then]). The second way to design a focused task is to make language the focus of the task, as is the case with consciousness-raising (CR) tasks. An example of a CR task provided by R. Ellis (2003) contains a text passage along with instructions to underline time expressions and to fill out a table by matching time expressions with correct prepositions (*at three o'clock, in March*, etc). In this chapter, we expand on the traditional understanding of CR tasks by including Data-Driven Learning (DDL) tasks, which will be discussed further in detail.

This chapter demonstrates how texts produced as a result of structure-trapping tasks can be used to design DDL focused tasks. In task-based language teaching (TBLT), texts are usually seen as by-products of tasks with one of the methodological principles of TBLT being "using tasks, not text" (Long, 2015, p. 305). Doughty and Long (2003) argue that texts are "static records of someone else's (previous) task accomplishment" (p. 56), and, compared to texts, tasks are "more relevant, comprehensible and memorable" (p. 58). We, on the other hand, side with the multiliteracies approach, which posits that learning happens through the transformational process of engaging with other people's work, where "[o]ne person's Designing becomes a resource in another person's universe of Available Designs" (Cope & Kalantzis, 2009, p. 12). In other words, one person's work can be used as a resource for someone else. For instance, when learning how to write a resume, it is always helpful to look at examples of resumes written by other people, especially in one's field of expertise. Even outside of the learning context, we constantly engage in reading and re-reading other people's documented by-products of tasks. For example, a translator's work is singularly based on the by-product of the task of a writer. Similarly, an admissions officer's task of making an admission decision is based on the by-product of a task performed by a student applicant. For this reason, we propose that texts should be central to task design in TBLT.

In this chapter, the interconnectedness of texts and tasks in the language learning context is demonstrated through examples of DDL-focused tasks. These tasks are designed using texts produced by learners as a result of structure-trapping focused tasks. This is achieved by employing a learner corpus, which is a collection of texts created by learners in their target language. The following sections, in turn, define the concept of language awareness which is central to DDL, elaborate on the DDL approach, and describe the learner corpus entitled MACAWS which was used to design the activities presented in this chapter.

Language awareness and form-focused instruction

Language awareness is a broad framework for L2 teaching that emphasizes focusing learners' attention. Such attentiveness is conducive to the discovery of linguistic patterns and realities of language use through "active engagement between the learner, language data and the learning process" (Bolitho et al., 2003, p. 256). This approach is predominantly inductive, i.e., learners are provided with linguistic evidence and prompted to explore patterns on their own. However, it has been argued that the inductive nature of the task needs to be followed by an explicit collaborative and reflective analysis (Van Lier, 2003; Bolitho et al., 2003) to help learners summarize and/or verbalize what they have observed.

Language awareness is multifaceted in nature. According to Van Lier (2001), it has at least three levels: pedagogical, psycholinguistic, and ideological. In the pedagogical sense, language awareness can lead to positive attitudes to both language and language learning by enhancing learners' motivation. Psycholinguistically, language awareness precedes language acquisition by cultivating learners' readiness which is necessary for acquisition. Ideologically, language awareness promotes sociolinguistic variation by describing and validating language used in a variety of settings and by a variety of users. Because focused attention to linguistic forms and their patterned variation lies at the core of these motivations, language awareness can be seen in opposition to prescriptive instruction that focuses on correctness by deemphasizing "understanding, appreciation and creative expression" (Van Lier, 2001, p. 160).

Understanding, within the language awareness paradigm, is perceived as "a higher level of awareness than 'noticing' . . . and is related to the organization of material in long-term memory, to restructuring, and to system learning" (Schmidt, 1992, p. 213). Still, for understanding to take place, noticing should be the prerequisite. Thus, noticing is at the forefront of various approaches to form-focused instruction, such as focus on form, input enhancement, metalinguistic explanation, input processing, consciousness-raising, and corrective feedback (Schmidt, 1992; Ranta & Lyster, 2018).

Data-Driven Learning (DDL)

A more recent development of form-focused instruction based on noticing, inductive principles of learning, and language awareness is Data-Driven Learning (DDL). DDL is an inductive pedagogical approach for using corpora (plural of corpus) in the classroom (Johns, 1991; Chambers, 2015). A corpus is usually a large body of texts collected and organized in a principled way to reflect a certain linguistic domain of use (Reppen, 2010).

DDL is an innovative approach that uses principles of guided discovery and pattern recognition for language instruction. With this approach, students are provided with selected language data from a corpus of texts and are tasked with playing the role of "language detectives" by identifying language patterns. The language data is usually presented in the form of concordance lines, which are lines of text produced with concordancing tools (i.e., special search engine tools) that help learners see patterns more clearly. These tools are often built into corpus websites (e.g., Russian National Corpus). Although not widely used outside of the field of corpus linguistics, DDL has been shown to be effective (Boulton & Cobb, 2017; Smart, 2014). In their meta-analysis of 64 DDL studies, Boulton and Cobb (2017) found a large effect size (Cohen's d = 1.5) for effectiveness (operationalized as scores on pre- and post-tests with the same participants), and also a large effect size (Cohen's d = 0.95) for efficiency (control vs. experimental groups with the same post-test). More specifically, medium to large effects were found for vocabulary and grammar improvement. These positive effects of DDL are attributed to the inductive nature of this approach (Smart, 2014).

Despite the positive outcomes of DDL, it has been predominantly used for English language teaching (Vyatkina & Boulton, 2017). In Russian, most of the corpus-based pedagogical materials use corpus as a source of authentic examples rather than for DDL (Dobrushina, 2005; Furniss, 2013, 2016; Ponomareva et al., 2016). Most of these materials also use native speaker language, which has been a typical practice in the field of DDL in general (Chambers, 2015). This is partly because there is no consensus as to whether exposing students to negative evidence (other learners' mistakes) is beneficial for learning (Nesselhauf, 2004). One notable study that recommends using a Russian learner corpus in the classroom is by Yatsenko et al. (2012). They argue that a learner corpus of academic writing can be useful for researching areas of difficulty (e.g., for heritage vs. non-heritage learners), creating pedagogical materials, and assessing students' academic writing. While Yatsenko et al. (2012) make a powerful case for using learner corpora in Russian language classrooms, their focus is not on the theoretical grounding of DDL tasks, nor is it on describing how to design such tasks. Thus, we felt it was necessary to build on their work by focusing solely on task design and the theoretical underpinnings of using the DDL approach.

The emphasis in DDL with learner language has been on comparing NNS (or novice users') corpora against NS (or expert users') corpora. Such comparisons are typically made so that students could notice the gap between their production and that of experts, track their development, and correct their peers' mistakes (Chambers, 2015; Lee & Swales, 2006; Belz & Vyatkina, 2008). One such study was published by Cotos (2014), who investigated the effects of combining a native speaker corpus with a local learner corpus. The results demonstrated that using a learner corpus along with a native speaker corpus helped increase learners' motivation and led to greater use of linking adverbials (the focus of the lesson) in a post-test compared to the control group that had access to native speaker corpus only (Cotos, 2014).

While more studies are needed to show the effectiveness of using learner language with DDL to support this pedagogical practice, this chapter seeks to encourage the first step of this process, which is designing and implementing DDL tasks with learner language. The sections that follow provide more information on the corpus that we used and present the tasks themselves.

Multilingual Academic Corpus of Assignments – Writing and Speech (MACAWS)

As the title of this chapter suggests, to mediate between structure-trapping and DDL focused tasks, we used a learner corpus. The corpus we used is called the Multilingual Academic Corpus of Assignments – Writing and Speech (MACAWS) (Staples et al., 2019), and it was built by a group of researchers at the University of Arizona including the authors of this chapter. While the corpus consists of texts in two languages, Portuguese and Russian, in this chapter we will focus on its Russian component. The Russian subcorpus is composed of texts based on tasks that learners naturally perform in their courses, typically as part of their homework assignments (examples of these tasks are provided in the following section). The corpus is available online with authenticated access and is composed of 1,025 texts produced by 100 beginner and intermediate level students of Russian (118,302 words). The corpus includes both written and spoken (transcribed) texts produced in natural academic settings, i.e., essays and video and/or audio assignments submitted by students as part of the L2 Russian curriculum. (In the future, the corpus will also be complemented by a repository of pedagogical materials, such as prompts for the assignments available in the corpus.) The corpus has search functions for individual words and phrases. These searches can also be filtered by course, topic, macrogenre (e.g., narration, description, argument, etc.), draft, mode of assignment (speech vs. writing), and students' L1. The interface also has a feature that allows the embedding of search results (concordance lines) into learning management systems (e.g., D2L or Moodle) or websites (e.g., Google sites).

Examples of structure-trapping and DDL-focused tasks

In this section, we will shift our focus to the tasks themselves. First, we will present two structure-trapping tasks that have been implemented in the existing Russian language curriculum at a large Southwestern university. To remind the reader, by structure-trapping tasks we mean tasks that focus on meaning-making more holistically, but are designed to elicit the use of specific linguistic features.

In structure-trapping task 1 (Tables 4.1, 4.2), first-semester learners of Russian were asked to post a short essay on Padlet, where their classmates could view it. This assignment was titled: "Какие языки вы знаете?" (What languages do you know?). It was framed as a conversation between local students and (imaginary)

Table 4.1 Task introduction: structure-trapping task 1

Title of the task: What languages do you know?
Task goal/s, setting of instruction The meaning-focused objective of this task is to describe someone's language skills. The form-focused goal is to practice the conjugation of communication-related verbs (e.g., говорить, читать, писать, [speak, read, write] etc.), as well as the use of language-related structures (e.g., по-английски vs. английский язык [in English vs. the English language]). The task was designed for first-semester Russian students in a university setting. **Learner needs analysis** The task is used as an increment of instruction; learner needs are determined based on the students' successful completion of the learning goals leading to the use of tasks. **Type of task**: Focused structure-trapping task **Can-do statements** – Students can name languages that they or their acquaintances know – Students can describe their language abilities in 5 short sentences – Students can describe someone else's language abilities in 5 short sentences **Assessment/s used** Students are given a rubric to follow. Their writing performance is assessed based on the rubric (Appendix A).

Table 4.2 Structure-trapping task 1: what languages do you know?

Какие языки вы знаете?
This time, instead of a video, you will write a short essay (post) on our Padlet page to give our imaginary Russian counterparts an idea of what the linguistic landscape is like in our city. Prompt: describe you and your friend/family member's language skills. • Talk about the languages you know, • Where you study and/or studied them, • How well you speak and/or read and/or write and/or understand in these languages, • What language you speak at home. ***Note: using Google translate or any other translator is prohibited and constitutes a violation of the code of Academic Integrity. Please also avoid using your peer's essays as models – this is plagiarism *and* not the best idea because they may have made mistakes in them.

students in Russia, who are interested in the linguistic landscape of the United States. The prompt asked students to write about the languages that they know, their place of study, their level of skills in reading, writing, speaking, and understanding each language, and the language that they speak at home. Prior to their submission of the post, they had access to the grading rubric (Appendix A) that would be used for this task. This rubric specified that learners would be graded on addressing all questions mentioned in the prompt, spelling, length of their post, and on their use of specific linguistic features. In particular, they were warned about the importance of using correct vocabulary, for instance, "английский язык vs. по-английски vs. англичанин" (English language vs. in English vs. Englishman). In addition, learners were asked to pay attention to verb conjugation and the use of the Prepositional case.

In structure-trapping task 2 (Tables 4.3, 4.4), first-semester learners of Russian were asked to post another short essay on the same Padlet page but this time about university life. This assignment was similarly positioned to introduce imaginary Russian students to academic life in the U.S. through personal stories. The specific prompt asked students to include information about their studies including their major, their classes, and the campus. The rubric for this assignment (Appendix B) addressed content, vocabulary use, grammar, and length. Students were not required to use any specific grammatical features but in the vocabulary section, they were prompted to use verbs учиться [study/go to school] and изучать [study/learn], which are the salient features of this task.

Both of these structure-trapping tasks have the main features of a task as defined by R. Ellis (2003). Although the tasks are artificial in terms of situational authenticity, they do have interactional authenticity: the language that results from these tasks is the language of real-world communication (R. Ellis, 2003).

As for the DDL focused tasks in this chapter, they are based on student texts produced as a result of the structure-trapping tasks mentioned earlier. Figure 4.1 shows the process of how structure-trapping tasks were redesigned into focused tasks. The structure-trapping tasks were given to students in class. After they

Table 4.3 Task introduction: structure-trapping task 2

Title of the task: University Life

Task goal/s, setting of instruction

The meaning-focused objective of this task is to describe someone's studies. The form-focused goal is to practice the conjugation of study-related verbs (e.g., учиться, изучать, заниматься [study], etc.), as well as the use of school-related vocabulary (e.g., биология, русский язык, специальность [biology, Russian language, concentration], etc). The task was designed for first-semester Russian students in a university setting.

Learner needs analysis

The task is used as an increment of instruction; learner needs are determined based on the students' successful completion of the learning goals leading to the use of tasks.

Type of task: Focused structure-trapping task

Can-do statements

– Students can describe their university life in 10 short sentences
– Students can describe their apartment/dormitory in 3 short sentences
– Students can explain why they study Russian in 3 short sentences

Assessment/s used

Students are given a rubric to follow. Their writing performance is assessed based on the rubric (Appendix B).

Table 4.4 Structure-trapping task 2: University life

Padlet#4. Университетская жизнь [University life]
Our peers from Russia are ready to get down to business! They are very interested in our university, and they want to know more about the university itself and about the academic aspects of your lives. To help them, you will write a short essay about your school life and post it on our Padlet page.

Prompt: talk about your university life. Below are some questions to guide you. The questions in bold **must** be answered in your essay, and you can pick and choose from or add to the other questions on this list.

- Describe your educational background: where did you go to high school (школа)?
- **Where do you live now and where did you live before?**
- **What is your major?**
- **What year of school are you in?**
- Why do you study at the U of A? (why did you pick this university?)
- **What courses are you taking this semester?**
- Which of these courses do you like? Which of them don't you like?
- **Why do you study Russian?**
- **Where do you usually do your homework?**
- Describe our campus. (libraries, stadiums, etc.)
- What is the dormitory like? What do you have in your room?
- Do you work? Where?

***Note: using Google translate or any other translator is prohibited and constitutes a violation of the code of Academic Integrity. Please also avoid using your peer's essays as models – this is plagiarism *and* not the best idea because they may have made mistakes in them.

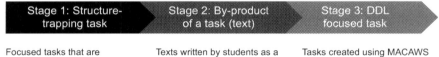

Stage 1: Structure-trapping task	Stage 2: By-product of a task (text)	Stage 3: DDL focused task
Focused tasks that are designed to elicit certain linguistic features resulting in student texts	Texts written by students as a response to structure-trapping focused tasks in Stage 1	Tasks created using MACAWS corpus and data-driven learning (DDL) principles based on student texts from Stage 2

Figure 4.1 Stages of task redesign

completed the tasks, their texts (by-products of tasks) were collected and added to the MACAWS corpus. These texts in the corpus were used to create focused DDL tasks using the MACAWS interface. This design process is cyclical rather than linear in nature because the focused DDL tasks will result in new learner texts (Available Design) that will, in turn, become a resource for someone else's learning (Designing and Redesigning) (The New London Group, 1996).

The focused DDL tasks presented in this chapter are based on some of the most common but also problematic linguistic features from the structure-trapping tasks. The purpose of the focused DDL tasks is to raise learners' awareness of the use of the linguistic features in question.

Focused DDL Task 1 (Tables 4.5, 4.6) includes three parts: noticing patterns, systematizing knowledge, and applying knowledge. In Part I, students are prompted to notice patterns from the concordance lines. The online version of these activities allows for twenty concordance lines in a scrollable format with a sorting function (to the left or to the right of the highlighted word in alphabetical order). The sorting function helps learners to see the patterns more clearly. For example, in Concordance 1 in Focused Task 1, the lines are sorted to the right of the highlighted word allowing us to see the use of the verb говорить before по-русски. In Part II of the task, the students are given an opportunity to compare the patterns that they notice with the rules from the textbook and to complete a controlled fill-in-the-blank activity. Finally, in Part III, students are encouraged to practice the patterns in a free production activity.

Focused DDL task 2 (Tables 4.7, 4.8) is less scaffolded: it is assumed that the students are more familiar with this type of task (from focused DDL task 1). Similarly to focused DDL task 1, this task is made from texts, by-products of structure-trapping task 2, using the MACAWS interface. In addition to noticing, this task includes a focus on free production and a traditional controlled grammar activity. These focused DDL tasks can be their own stand-alone consciousness-raising tasks, or they can be used in tandem with the structure-trapping tasks presented in this chapter. Depending on how comfortable students are with using the features

Table 4.5 Task introduction: Focused DDL task 1

Title of the task: My linguistic background

Task goal/s, setting of instruction

The main goal of this task is for students to notice, verbalize and use patterns associated with the language-related verbs (e.g., говорить, писать vs. знать, изучать [speak, write vs. know, study]) and their complements (e.g., по-русски vs. русский язык [in Russian vs. the Russian language]). The task was designed for first-semester Russian students in a university setting.

Learner needs analysis

The task is used as an increment of instruction; learner needs are determined based on the students' successful completion of the learning goals leading to the use of tasks. This task was implemented in a classroom, followed by feedback from both students and teachers.

Type of task: Data-Driven Learning (DDL) task

Can-do statements

– Students can identify verb patterns in descriptive texts when talking about language skills in Russian
– Students can use these patterns to describe their own experiences with language

Assessment/s used

– Low-stakes self-assessment in the form of fill-in-the-blanks with automatic feedback
– Low-stakes speaking assessment, such as a short question-answer exchange with peer or instructor

Table 4.6 Focused DDL task I: My linguistic background

My Linguistic background

Level: Beginner's Russian

Materials: Textbook *Beginner's Russian* p. 272

Learning Outcomes:
1. Identify verb patterns in descriptive texts about the knowledge of Russian
2. Use these patterns when talking about your own linguistic experiences

Part I. Noticing Patterns

Respond to the following questions:
1. Look at the verbs to the left of the highlighted words, and see if you can notice a difference in verb usage in two concordance boxes that follow. To help you notice the pattern, in your notebook, write down the verbs to the left of the highlighted words from each concordance box. *Hint:* Remember that in Russian, the verb *to be* in the present tense is only implied.
2. These texts come from students of Russian like you! Do all examples follow the standard Russian use? If not, what would be the standard Russian use? Do you think you would make such a non-standard choice?

The lines below are sorted by the word right before the key word in context. Sort by the word after.

т. Моего второго брата зовут . Он очень хорошо говорит по-русски и любит играть в футбол. Ему 22 года. Он учится в Технолог и химию. Я изучаю русский язык потому что мой папа гавapит по-русски. Я занимаюсь в общежитии.
орит по-итальянски. Она любит астрономию. Она хорошо говорит по-русски. Она милая. (She;s nice?)
т-Петербурге, где она изучает историю. плохо говорит по-русски, а она говорит свободно по-немецки. (She;s nice?)
ощадь. Мы ели в ГУМ, мой друг, который не знает как говорить по-русски, они сказали "GYM" и не ГУМ. Я много смеялся. Мы ходили по орю хорошая по-английском и по-французски. Я неплохо говорю по-русски. Я говорю по-английском в доме.
Университете в Аризоне, в Тусоне. Чуть чуть понимаю и говорю по-русски, а неплохо пишу и читаю. Мои дедушка и папа русские, так о-английски, я неплохо говорю по-испански, и я плохо говорю по-русски. Я хорошо понимаю по-английски, я неплохо понимаю по- ис се. Я учусь в Университете Аризоне потому что я хочу говорю по-русски. Я изучаю математику и русский язык. Я люблю оба. Я учусь потому что они любят русский язык, хотят читать литературу по-русски. Я хочу быть переводчик и люблю русский язык. Русски такж я изучаю русский язык в университет, я тоже читаю медленно по-русски, немного понимаю и плохо говорю. Дома моя фамилия говорим язык. Моя подруга была из Москвы. Она заставила меня по-русски культура. Я люблю Америку но Россия красивый. Очень реки и те тоже. Я тоже понимаю по-испански немного. Я читаю и пишу по-русски плохо, а по-испански хорошо. Я говорю и понимаю по-русски по- английски и хорошо говорю по-испански. Я немного пишу по-русски. Я говорю по-английски дома. Моя мама и мой папа свободно

Concordance 1. По-русски [In Russian]

Learner corpus as a medium for tasks   57

The lines below are sorted by the word right before the key word in context. _Sort by the word after._

Я знаю русский язык и учу русский язык в университете. Мой друг знает французский я
Я знаю английский язык и испанский язык. Я изучаю русский язык в университете но изучала испански
ски и свободно читаю французский язык. Я немного знаю русский язык. Я быстро читаю по-русски, но я медленно говорю. Моя мама
te>. Я американка студентка. Моя специальность политология и я учусь в аризонском университете. Я думаю что аризоны
о педагогику в девять часов. Искусства в одиннадцать часов и русский язык. Во вторник и четверг я встаю в семь ча
Я знаю английский язык, испанский язык и русский язык. Моя сестра знает английский язык и китайский язык. Я из
Аризонском университете. Эм моя специальность политология и русский язык. Но сейчас я поступил в Московском государственный универс
ончу университете через 3 году и получу диплом политология и русский язык. Мне нравится слушаю русская музыка и играть в видеоигры.
нас много студентов. Моя специальность физиология. Я изучаю русский язык. физиологию, химию, математику и медицину. Я люблю химию п
- испанский и читаю по-испанский медленно. Сейчас я изучаю русский язык, и тоже читаю медленно по-русски, немного п
уйте! Я хорошо знаю английский. Я читал сербский. Я изучал сербский, испанский и французский языки. Моя ма
ий язык. Раньше я изучал испанский язык, а сейчас я изучаю русский язык. Мой брат и моя сестра изучали французский язык когда он
изучали французский язык в средняя школа. Я сейчас изучаю русский язык. Я свободно говорю, пишу, читаю, и понимаю по-английски.
ом курсе в Томском государственном университете. Э я изучаю русский язык здесь. Томском находится на востоке Сибири. Я окончу униве

Concordance 2. Русский язык [The Russian language]

Part II. Systematizing your knowledge.
Your textbook **Beginner's Russian** provides the following explanations on p. 272.

- Use the adverb по-русски (or по-английски etc.) after verbs that denote the ability **to speak, read, write, or understand a language** (e.g., *Я пишу по-русски. I write in Russian.*)
- Use the adjective-noun combination русский язык after the verbs **знать, изучать and учить**. (e.g., *Они знают русский язык? Do they know Russian?*)

Now using what you have discovered from the concordance lines together with the textbook rules, try this fill-in-the-blank activity. You can check if you answered correctly by clicking on the "Check your answers" button.

Fill in the blanks with the most appropriate answer from the parentheses.

1. Я читаю и пишу по-русски плохо, а (испанский/по-испански) хорошо.
2. Я изучаю (русский/по-русски), потому что мой папа говорит по-русски.
3. Я знаю (английский/по-английски) язык, испанский язык и русский язык.
4. Раньше я изучал (испанский/по-итальянски), а сейчас я изучаю русский язык.
5. Они любят русский язык, хотят читать литературу (по-русски/русская).
6. Я изучаю (русский/испанскую), физиологию, химию, математику и медицину.

Part III. Making it your own.
Now record a video on your phone to record a video of yourself answering the following questions on Flipgrid!

1. What languages do you study/know?
2. What languages do you understand/speak?

Table 4.7 Task introduction: focused DDL task 2

Title of the task: My studies

Task goal/s, setting of instruction

The main goal of this task is for students to notice, verbalize and use patterns associated with the study-related verbs (e.g., учиться vs. изучать [to study]) and their complements (e.g., в университете Аризоны vs. русский язык [at the University of Arizona vs. the Russian language]). The task was designed for first-semester Russian students in a university setting.

Learner needs analysis

The task is used as an increment of instruction; learner needs are determined based on the students' successful completion of the learning goals leading to the use of tasks. This task was implemented in a classroom, followed by feedback from both students and teachers.

Type of task: Data-Driven Learning (DDL) task

Can-do statements

− Students can identify differences in the use of учиться and изучать
− Students can use the patterns they have identified when talking about their studies

Assessment/s used

− Low-stakes discussion questions with a partner
− Low-stakes speaking activity with a partner
− Low-stakes verb-conjugation activity

in the focused DDL tasks, these tasks can come before or after the structure-trapping tasks. Completing focused DDL tasks before structure-trapping prepares students to use problematic linguistic features. The value of planning focused DDL tasks before the structure-trapping tasks is in being proactive, rather than reactive; in Long's (2015) terms: to raise students' awareness of these problematic features before asking them to produce their own meaning.

Challenges of teaching RFL

When developing TB/SLT tasks in the context of teaching Russian as a Foreign Language, it is important to take into account the student population and the language distance between the native and target languages. For example, Russian is arguably more difficult to acquire than French for L1 English speakers. One of the problematic areas in the acquisition of Russian for L1 English speakers is its rich inflectional and derivational morphology. However, challenges in the acquisition of Russian are not always dependent on learners' L1 or unique to the acquisition of Russian. There is one area, in particular, that is often overlooked when it comes to the acquisition of any foreign language, called lexicogrammar. In brief, lexicogrammar explores connections between lexis (vocabulary) and grammar (Biber et al., 1998). However, learners tend to see language in terms of individual words

Learner corpus as a medium for tasks   59

Table 4.8 Focused DDL task 2: My studies

My studies
Russian has several verbs that can translate as "study." If you look closely, you will notice different patterns of its use in English as well. Take a look at these two examples of the word "study" in English:

1. I study Russian.
2. I study at a university.

What differences do you notice in terms of the surrounding words?
So, as you can see, in English the meaning of the word "study" changes depending on what follows the verb in a sentence. In Russian, there are several words that mean "study."

The next concordance box (Concordance 3) has the word "изучаю", while Concordance 4 contains the word "учусь".

The lines below are sorted by the word right before the key word in context. Sort by the word after.

Университете. Моя специальность испанский язык, и	изучаю	испанский, португальский, и русский языкые и лингвистику.
зучали французский язык в средняя школа. Я	изучаю	русский язык. Я свободно говорю, пишу, читаю, и понимаю п
ский потому что английский международный язык.	изучаю	русский язык потому что Русский тоже международный язык, и
он международный язык и его сейчас изучают все. Я	изучаю	Русский язык потому что, Я родилась в России и Я считаю ч
10/29 Я	изучаю	русский язык, потому что люблю России история. Мой друг из
по русски Я	изучаю	русский язык, потому что русский интересен. Мой друг изучал
есный и они думают русский язык очень красивый. Я	изучаю	русский язык потому что я хочу понимать люди в фильмы.
й язык очень красивый и он международный язык. Я	изучаю	русский язык, потому что он близок к болгарскому языку и
ризоны университет – это очень большой кампус. Я	изучаю	международную политику, потому что он нужен в моей будущей
гаю в восемь часов, одеваюсь, и иду на занятия. Я	изучаю	педагогику в девять часов, искусства в одиннадцать часов и
тет. Моя специальность музыкальная композиция. Я	изучаю	её, потому что я люблю писать музыку. Я также изучаю пиано
много студентов. Моя специальность физиология. Я	изучаю	русский язык, физиологию, химию, математику и медицину. Я люб
си, стадион, рестораны и спортзал. Этот семестр я	изучаю	химию, статистику, русский язык и английский язык. Мой люб
испанский и читаю по-испанский медленно. Сейчас я	изучаю	русский язык в университет. я тоже читаю медленно по-русс

Concordance 3. Изучаю [study]

(Continued)

Table 4.8 (Continued)

The lines below are sorted by the word after the keyword in context. Sort by the word before.

17 Сентября 2018 Я учусь в Аризонском Университете в Тусоне. В Аризонском Университет
Привет меня зовут . Мне 19 лет. Я учусь в Аризонском университете в Тусоне. Я на четвертом курсе.
в Тусоне. Это город на юге-востоке Аризоны. Э студентка, я учусь в Аризонском университете на втором курсе. Э моя специальн
и родилась в Финикс в Аризоне. Э мне 20 лет. Я студентка. Я учусь в Аризонском университете. Я живу в Тусоне. Эм я учусь в т
Привет друзья. Я начинаю влог потому что я учусь в России этим летом. Эм о себе. Меня зовут и эм я
Здравствуйте, меня зовут . Мне 20 лет. Я студентка. Я учусь в Санкт-Петербургском государственном университете на трет
джмента организации. Я изучаю на четвертом курсе. В Америке я учусь в университете Аризоны. Учиться буду шесть лет. Мне нрави
ою диплом в университете Аризоны на через два года. Сейчас я учусь за граница в Новосибирске. На Новосибирском государственном
в университет Аризоны. Я на гуманитарном факультете. Сейчас учусь зарубежом в Санкт-Петербургском гуманитарном университете.

Concordance 4. Учусь [study]

Questions

1. Looking at the examples of the word *изучаю* in Concordance 1, what do you notice about its use? Which English examples is it most similar to and why?
   a. I study Russian.
   b. I study at a university.
2. Can you relate to these students' answers from the concordance lines? Do you study similar/different things?
3. Looking at the examples of the word *учусь*, what do you notice about its use? Which English example is it most similar to and why?
   a. I study Russian.
   b. I study at a university.

Additional Questions

1. As you can see, the difference between these two verbs can be a bit tricky for an English speaker, hence you might see some mishaps in how the students used these two words. Do you notice anything that can be rephrased?
2. Now how would you explain the difference between these two words to your friend who wants to learn Russian but doesn't know anything about Russian?
3. Tell your classmate what you study, where you study and which year you're in.
4. As you noticed, all the examples were in the first person singular (я-form). Now conjugate the verb into second person singular (ты-form) and ask your classmate what they study, where they study at, and which year they're in.

and arbitrary grammar structures, thus making lexicogrammar a challenging area for acquisition. One of the goals of this chapter was to present DDL tasks that train learners to pay attention to how words co-occur (e.g., говорить по-русски vs. изучать русский [speak Russian vs. study Russian]).

While designing both types of tasks, the authors met some challenges that are discussed here. With the structure-trapping tasks, the main challenges are related to the language of prompts and the precision of rubrics. While it is recommended to use as much target language as possible, prompts in the target language are limiting in some ways, especially at lower levels. First, instructions in the target language can get overwhelming for the students. Second, when students use language from the prompts, it can make it difficult for the teacher to determine whether the students have acquired specific vocabulary or grammatical structures. Third, it has been shown in previous studies that task complexity results in greater linguistic complexity (Foster & Skehan, 1996; Robinson, 2001a), and that providing instructions in the students' L1 can elicit more complex language. Task complexity is also related to an additional challenge of structure-trapping tasks, namely, how specific the rubrics are. While encouraging students' creativity is crucial, it is also necessary to reinforce what they know/are expected to know, thus requiring students to use certain forms by specifying them in the rubric. If the rubric is not specific enough and there is no explicit requirement to use certain forms, students should not be penalized for not using them.

Similar challenges are related to creating DDL tasks. For example, it is important to write prompts in the students' L1, because the emphasis of these tasks is on language awareness: if the students are at a low level of proficiency, they will not be able to understand the prompts, or talk about the patterns they notice in Russian. It is also important to ask questions that students can understand without substantial linguistic training. In addition, there are challenges that are specific to DDL tasks. The design of such tasks requires one to create (or to locate) a corpus of texts and to select relevant linguistic features. Before choosing what features to focus on with DDL tasks, it is important to take into account both the language areas that are problematic for students (e.g., lexicogrammar, morphology) and the affordances of specific DDL tools. In other words, some of the linguistic features that are challenging for students might not be appropriate or possible to address with DDL. Tasks involving morphology, on the other hand, can be fruitfully explored using the DDL approach.

Conclusion

The purpose of this chapter was twofold. First, we argued for the importance of combining focused structure-trapping and focused DDL tasks in TBLT of L2 Russian. Second, we showed two sets of examples of how to combine these two types of tasks using the MACAWS learner corpus. The structure-trapping tasks presented in this chapter come from the existing Russian language courses at a large Southwestern university, while the focused DDL tasks were created from the texts that the students produced as a result of the structure-trapping tasks. The focused DDL tasks are based on the principles of pattern recognition and language awareness. We demonstrated that a learner corpus is an effective medium between the two types of tasks and can be used to build focused DDL tasks from structure-trapping tasks.

Based on our experience, the approach best enjoyed by students and teachers alike is to combine the two types of tasks in a sequence that goes from more to less focused tasks. As such, our students typically enjoy first working through relevant grammatical features in a focused DDL task and then proceeding to more meaning-focused (structure-trapping or unfocused) tasks. This sequence mitigates anxiety for those students who feel insecure when making mistakes during planned or spontaneous language production. Our experience shows that focused DDL tasks have been effective for our students in preparing for less controlled tasks. While learner and teacher perceptions of corpus-based tasks were not the focus of this chapter, it is important to note that these tasks have been generally well-received by students: such language puzzles are more exciting for them than simple explanations of grammatical rules.

Appendix A

Table 4.A.1 Grading rubric for structure-trapping activity 1

	Отлично! (5 points)	*Хорошо (4 points)*	*Плохо (3 points)*
Content (see prompt)	All content areas mentioned in the prompt are covered	Most content areas mentioned in the prompt are covered	Few content areas mentioned in the prompt are covered
Vocabulary use (especially английский язык vs. по-английски vs. англичанин)	All vocabulary is used appropriately	Most vocabulary is used appropriately	Vocabulary is mostly used inappropriately
Spelling	There are 2 spelling errors or fewer	There are 5 spelling errors or fewer	There are more than 5 spelling errors
Grammar (verb conjugation and Prepositional case)	There are no grammatical errors	There are 3 grammatical errors or fewer	There are more than 3 grammatical errors
Length	The essay is 10 sentences long or longer	The essay is 7 sentences long or longer	The essay is 5 sentences long or longer

Appendix B

Table 4.B.1 Grading rubric for structure-trapping activity 2

	Отлично! (5 points)	*Хорошо* (4 points)	*Плохо* (3 points)
Content (see prompt)	All obligatory (see bold questions in the prompt) questions are answered	At least 5 obligatory questions are answered	Less than 5 obligatory questions are answered
Vocabulary use (especially учиться/изучать/заниматься)	All vocabulary is used appropriately	Most vocabulary is used appropriately	Vocabulary is mostly used inappropriately
Spelling	There are 2 spelling errors or fewer	There are 5 spelling errors or fewer	There are more than 5 spelling errors
Grammar (especially, but not only, case)	There are no grammatical errors	There are 3 grammatical errors or fewer	There are more than 3 grammatical errors
Length	The essay is 10 sentences long or longer	The essay is 7 sentences long or longer	The essay is 5 sentences long or longer

Chapter 5

Task-based vlogs in an elementary Russian classroom

Katie Esser

Chapter summary

This chapter first reviews the theory behind task-based methodology. It then reviews a body of literature on empirical evidence supporting the effectiveness of technology-based assignments in a communicative or TBLT classroom and their potential in improving vocabulary acquisition and decreasing affective variables. Next, two video-based assignments from an elementary Russian classroom are described detailing their task-based goals, themes, and grammatical and lexical targets. Finally, both assignments are analyzed in accordance with previous research to provide suggestions for instructors who wish to adapt the tasks described here for their own classrooms.

Краткое содержание главы

Глава предлагает примеры преподавания РКИ на основе целевых заданий и обобщает существующую литературу эмпирических данных, обосновывающих включение педагогики целевого задания в курсе РКИ. Особо отмечается улучшение словарного запаса обучающихся и положительное влияние метода целевого задания на мотивацию студентов. Описаны два видео-задания для начального курса РКИ, которые представлены в контексте их грамматических и лексических целей и тем. Оба задания анализируются на основе существующей литературы. Представлены рекомендации по адаптации данных целевых заданий при использовании в отличных от описанного контекстах.

Author background

When I began learning Russian as a first-year Linguistics major, I was curious about how evidence-based study could be applied to the development of language curricula. I loved my Russian class, where my professor would get us excited about memorizing all the nuances of the genitive case. But I also wondered if there was a way to introduce creative assignments into the classroom that would get us speaking even at an elementary level. As I continued my studies in Linguistics, I became enamored with

DOI: 10.4324/9781003146346-5

applied linguistics and language teaching methodology. I learned about communicative and task-based language teaching (TBLT) and became excited about how they could be applied to my own studies of Russian. In my senior year, I became a teaching assistant for elementary Russian. Entering the year, my professor and I wanted to move the curriculum in a more communicative and task-supported direction to allow students to use Russian *creatively* even when they lacked a wide range of grammar and vocabulary. This narrative account describes how we used task-supported video assignments in the form of vlogs in an elementary Russian classroom.

Introduction

For the past decade, technology in education has become ever prevalent and essential in engaging students in the learning process. New tools such as Blackboard and Canvas are used at thousands of institutions (Duffy, 2018) to allow instructors to share presentations and assignments and to facilitate discussion through forums, blogs, and/or videos. Feedback from students using technology for at-home assignments has indicated that these blogs, forums, and videos are positively perceived as ways to reduce anxiety related to expression, create a community outside of the classroom (Harrison, 2011), allow work to be done at one's own pace, and engage with supplementary materials (Unal & Unal, 2017).

Utilizing these technologies is beneficial to language education specifically, as development of productive skills is a key step in language acquisition. Doing so in the Russian classroom is particularly important, given that Russian is considered to be a typologically distant language from most American college students' L1 English. Several of its features including lexical stress (Hayes-Harb & Hacking, 2015), verbs of motion (Gagarina, 2009), and case declension (Rubinstein, 1995) present L1 English students with great obstacles in acquisition.

In the university classroom examined in this case study, the online communicative elementary Russian textbook *Mezhdu Nami* (deBenedette et al., 2015), was utilized as the core material for instruction. The body of this textbook consists of story-based dialogues that are written and read by native speakers. Those dialogues are supported by explicit grammar instruction in a separate section of the website. In teaching with *Mezhdu Nami*, homework and classroom activity booklets that referenced events and characters from the story were assigned to students. These short activities target specific forms and functions of Russian language use (e.g., case, gender). To further support the textbook, the author (a Teaching Assistant) and the primary instructor decided to design communicative and task-supported assignments that bootstrapped homework activities and in-class instruction.

Considering the growth in popularity of tech-based assignments among instructors and students, it was decided that video assignments ("vlogs") would be a great medium to allow students to inform and relay opinion through newly targeted forms (e.g., new cases or verbs). In doing so, the aim was to reduce the negative influence of some affective variables (e.g., anxiety) present in day-to-day live instruction and increase motivation to learn and practice the language.

In this case study, a discussion on the pedagogical theory behind the assignment design as well as evidence from previous literature to support the effectiveness of vlogs as a task-based/task-supported strategy will be presented. Next, the assignment structures and how they align with this classroom's pedagogy and existing literature will be described. The results from the vlog implementation will be reviewed and will be followed by a discussion on their connections to results from previous evidence. Finally, the case study will conclude with implications on introducing these assignments into a broader RFL context.

Literature review

In designing and implementing the vlogs, the author and the course's instructor assumed Comer's (2007) synthesized definition of "task." Under this framework, a task entails:

1 Work carried out by learners engaging in receptive and/or productive skills.
2 Focus on meaning to fill an information or opinion gap.
3 An easily identifiable objective.
4 Use of language to achieve a specific outcome.

(p. 183)

This elementary Russian classroom emphasizes key structural concepts such as gender and case declension paradigms in its instructional design. To ensure that students achieve these grammatic milestones in a productive, communicative way, the author and course instructor wanted to assume a definition of "task" that would create space for quantitative communicative (1, 2, 4) and linguistic (4) goals. In the vlogs, students engage in productive skills and fill an information *and* opinion gap to achieve a specific communicative outcome. Through these three actions, they also achieve the objective of using key grammar or vocabulary topics.

Alongside Comer's (2007) definition, integration of existing evidence from literature on video assignments in the second language classroom was equally considered in the assignment design. The scholarship summarized in the following describes the evidence suggesting the ability for video assignments to foster motivation and aid in grammar and vocabulary acquisition.

Gromik (2012) describes an EFL classroom in Japan in which students made weekly 30-second videos of themselves speaking English. Students were told that they could re-film their videos if necessary before turning in their final product to the professor. They also were encouraged to view each other's videos to compare linguistic performances and hear other opinions. After completing the course, students filled out a questionnaire which revealed a strong self-reported improvement in speed, fluency, and confidence in their speech. Students also commented that they appreciated the ability to compare speaking styles and opinions among their peers. There was additionally a quantitative improvement in word production among students. Similar results were found in Wulandari's (2019) study, which concluded that both proficiency (e.g., vocabulary size, language use) and student confidence and motivation improved after deploying vlog assignments in the classroom.

Similarly, Aksel and Gürman-Kahraman (2014) explored how student opinion and motivation play a considerable role in testing the efficacy of vlogs. They administered a questionnaire to students regarding their opinions on the vlogs' ability to improve language skills. Results from the questionnaire indicated that students had a deep appreciation and excitement toward using technology in the foreign language classroom, positive attitudes toward the effect on their foreign language skills (e.g., daily use, fluency, etc.), and the implementation of the assignments. Students also commented that they appreciated how the assignments afforded them the ability to be creative and self-reflect (e.g., opinions, grammaticality). From this data, the authors concluded that students enjoy using technology and vlogs in the foreign language classroom for its impact on the learning process and its potential to encourage self-reflection and creativity.

Speaking from a quantitative perspective, Sildus (2006) presented a case study focused solely on proficiency. The results from the implementation of a topic-centered video project indicated that students who participated in making vlogs retained vocabulary better than those who did not participate in the project. In the following section, the evidence summarized earlier is used to support the claim that task-based vlogs have the potential to increase student motivation and the acquisition of grammar and vocabulary.

The assignments

In the vlogs, students were tasked to describe aspects of their daily life to a fictional Russian friend and express opinions about their hometown (e.g., what sights to see, which restaurant is the best in town, etc.) While the focus of the assignments was on filling an information and opinion gap (Comer, 2007), students were required to attend to form as well. For example, in the hometown assignment, students were asked to use un-prefixed, unidirectional verbs of motion and five newly learned activity verbs. These targeted forms were identified in the instructions and were accompanied by an example as well as a model video demonstrating what merits a satisfactory score. Although examples were provided to students, they were encouraged to get creative in their language use and filming. By synthesizing these communicative and form-based objectives, students were able to achieve important early language milestones in informing and relaying opinion.

The students were asked to record two videos where they describe aspects of their daily life to a fictional Russian friend in two scenarios: (1) in their hometown over spring break and (2) at home during COVID-19 quarantine.

Hometown video assignment ("vlog")

Table 5.1 Hometown vlog task introduction table

Title of the task: Hometown Video Assignment
Task goal/s, setting of instruction: The goal is to create a short video for a Russian friend describing the daily life of an American university student on spring break. This task was assigned to college students in the first semester of elementary Russian over spring break. ***Learner needs analysis:*** These students were low beginners and had challenges distinguishing between location and direction, which caused confusion in the use of accusative and prepositional cases. The aim was to improve students' accuracy in the use of accusative and prepositional cases and to encourage practice of newly learned verbs of motion. ***Type of task:*** Task-Supported Language Teaching (TSLT) – focus on form and communication ***Can-do statements:*** Students can practice their speaking skills through filming a daily vlog. Students can name five activities of their daily routine during spring break. Students can recommend one destination in their hometown. Students can use nouns in accusative and prepositional cases in short sentences. Students can name two places they go to using идти and ехать. ***Assessment/s used:*** Students were formally assessed on their ability to meet the linguistic objectives set in the instructions as well as provide information and opinions about their routines during spring break.

The instructions for this assignment were to "create a short video for a Russian friend describing the daily life of an American university student on spring break." In detailing the requirements for a satisfactory score, students were further tasked to describe their daily routine in their hometown as well as to comment on their favorite local attractions, tourist activities, and what they recommend their Russian friend to do. The following details how the assignment was designed based on Comer's (2007) definition of task:

- Students film themselves and narrate the video in Russian
- Students fill an information gap by providing their friend some details on their routine in their hometown during spring break.
- Students fill an opinion gap by giving recommendations (e.g., favorite restaurant/activity).
- Students meet specific linguistic objectives such as using verbs of motion (see Appendix A for a description of the assignment).
- Students use the language to achieve the outcome of an informative vlog for their Russian friend.

Alongside the linguistic objectives included in the assignment instructions, students were provided with examples of target forms and vocabulary that would need to be present in each video for a satisfactory score. Specific grammatical and vocabulary targets made the assignments easier for students to comprehend and the clear guidelines also made it easier for the instructors to grade submissions.

Task design was informed by the findings of the earlier literature review. The potential to increase vocabulary and improve grammatical accuracy was one of the primary reasons why this assignment was implemented. For example, from homework corrections preceding this assignment, it was observed that students had difficulties with determining when to use the prepositional case (location) versus the accusative case (direction), so this distinction was integrated into the vlog assignment design. Students were also expected to practice newly learned verbs of motion. Although advancing student language proficiency was crucial to the assignment design, affective factors were equally important; namely, increased motivation, confidence, and self-reflection, all of which have been found to be a common thread in research (Gromik, 2012; Young & West, 2018; Wulandari, 2019) on using the target language through vlogs. Both the course instructor and I remember being former beginning Russian students, and how important these affective factors can be. We thus recognized that getting students engaged, excited, and motivated to complete a task and most importantly *communicate* in their new language was crucial at this early stage.

Final video assignment ("vlog")

Table 5.2 Final vlog task introduction table

Title of the task: Final Vlog/At-Home Oral Exam
Task goal/s, setting of instruction: The goal was to create a short video for a Russian friend describing one's daily routine during the COVID-19 quarantine. This task was assigned to college students as a portion of the final exam for the second semester of elementary Russian. The instructions and examples were provided to students via Blackboard and during a synchronous session of the class through Microsoft Teams.
Learner needs analysis: These students were beginners that had not had face-to-face Russian instruction for nearly three months. The aim was to allow students to practice the target language despite the limitations of distance learning while improving accuracy of the newly learned concept of aspect.
Type of task: Task-Supported Language Teaching (TSLT) – focus on form and communication
Can-do statements: Students can practice their speaking skills through filming a short vlog. Students can understand and provide comments on their classmates' vlogs. Students can provide information about their daily routine during quarantine through the use of verbal aspect and various time expressions. Students can express what they like and do not like about quarantine. Students can compare and contrast peers' routines. Students can use nouns in the dative case in short sentences. Students can practice a new grammar topic (aspect) while communicating information and opinions to their Russian friend.
Assessment/s used: Students were formally assessed on their ability to meet the linguistic objectives set in the instructions (see Appendix B). They were also assessed on their ability to provide information and opinions to their Russian friend about their routines during quarantine.

The second vlog was implemented as an alternative to a final oral exam, which would typically be delivered in a face-to-face setting without scripting. However, as the COVID-19 crisis interrupted the semester, there was an opportunity to assign an additional video task in place of the oral exam. Unlike a traditional oral exam, this task allowed students to engage with current events in their target language. As students and instructors became reliant on remote instructional methods, the task was implemented not only as a means to gauge cumulative student performance, but also to allow students to express themselves in such a difficult climate. Furthermore, this assignment allowed for more engagement and interaction during this period of self-isolation, in which students were deprived of typical face-to-face interaction.

Similar to the spring break assignment, students were asked to describe their daily life, this time during quarantine. However, with this task, an element was added that would allow students to interact with the content they submitted (see task description in Appendix B). Students were required to comment on each other's videos to demonstrate their ability to comprehend and express opinions in Russian. This assignment was designed to fit Comer's (2007) definition of task in the following ways:

- Students film themselves and narrate the video in Russian.
- Students fill an information gap by providing their Russian friend with details on their routine during the COVID-19 pandemic.
- Students fill an opinion gap by expressing their likes and dislikes (e.g., "I do not like quarantine") and comparing/contrasting peers' videos (e.g., "I really liked your video! I found out that you do X, and I do Y!").
- Students meet specific linguistic objectives such as using a verb in both aspects (see Appendix B for a description of the assignment).
- Students use the target language to achieve the outcome of an informative vlog showing how current events impact their daily life to their Russian friend.

Similar to the first vlog, examples of target structures and vocabulary were included in the instructions (Appendix B). The author and course instructor considered this to be particularly important during remote learning as students had less exposure to the kinds of interpersonal communication and negotiation for meaning that are afforded during face-to-face interactions. Some of the target language structures were quite challenging for students. In particular, verbal aspect was a common error on quizzes at the time, so it was decided that it would be beneficial to require use of both verbal aspects.

In addition to the instructions and guidelines for completing the assignment, students were provided an optional word-bank of vocabulary that was related to current events: (карантин [quarantine], самоизоляция [self-isolation], маски/носить маски [masks/to wear masks]). While not all of the students utilized this optional vocabulary, many did. Some students chose to expand their efforts beyond the requirements and express what they miss from before the pandemic and what they hope to do after the pandemic using constructions such as: до карантина [before quarantine], после карантина [after quarantine] alongside newly learned structures (e.g., скучать по чему/кому [to miss something/someone], imperfective "I used to do X" versus perfective "I just finished X"). In doing so, students achieved *their* own communicative aims, and I also learned another way to facilitate productive practice of new vocabulary and grammar.

Results and lessons learned

In reviewing both vlogs for grading, my first observation was that it was incredible to see how much students were able to produce at such an elementary level. From the first to second vlog assignment, it was evident that students were able to produce more complex sentences. As mentioned earlier, students utilized vocabulary related to current events to communicate their opinions through targeted structures (e.g., the dative "to miss someone/something" construction in the final vlog). Furthermore, students were also tasked to compare and contrast their daily routines, which required practice of conjunctions (e.g., the commonly confused "а" versus "и"). As a result, students expressed more nuanced thoughts that met content, opinion-based, and linguistic objectives.

As for motivation, it was clear that students enjoyed the creative freedom afforded to them. Several students showcased their pets, family members, roommates, and their musical talents. Some even gave their loved ones lines to say in Russian. The second task seemed to have given the students an extra boost of motivation after several weeks of self-isolation. Students narrated their actions, showing their peers how they entertained themselves during lockdown. Roommates exchanged jokes in Russian from their apartment in their newly deserted college town. The author and the course instructor observed that many students progressed in the language despite the pandemic-related challenges the semester presented. The students expanded their Russian vocabulary, produced longer sentences, and incorporated humor into their videos. Giving these students a chance to get creative, express themselves, and meaningfully use Russian was an ideal assignment for distance learning.

This experience is in line with the research on affective variables (Aksel & Gürman-Kahraman, 2014), documenting that students expressed the most satisfaction with the impact of vlogs on their language learning and how technology was able to facilitate the process. Students also commented that the editing and re-filming processes allowed them to self-reflect before turning in assignments. In this way, vlogs stimulated both motivation and meaningful repetitive practice of target language

As for proficiency, Sildus' (2006) case study suggested that vlogs can improve vocabulary retention. Likewise, Gromik (2012) found that in a classroom in which vlogs were incorporated as a continuous expectation for students, word production increased noticeably over a semester-long period.

Discussion

Implications related to technology in the classroom

Calls for increased adoption of technology in education are not uncommon. González-Lloret and Ortega (2014) argue that engaging in technology has become a task in and of itself. In response to the coronavirus pandemic, video conferencing and remote instruction increasingly became a part of everyone's daily lives. Including task-based assignments into the language learning curriculum allows students to improve not only upon their proficiency goals but also upon their technological literacy.

Like many other disciplines, language education hopes to develop skills beyond those of content. The knowledge and practice put to work through vlogs are widely applicable in our technologically advancing world. When all students have equal access to technology required to complete a vlog (e.g., smartphones, webcams), we should encourage their use to develop both content-specific and professional skills.

Implications related to the broader RFL context

The tasks described in this chapter were implemented alongside existing curricula of *Mezhdu Nami* (deBenedette et al., 2015). By working on task-supported vlogs, students can further map form to meaning as they link images and scenes they film to the language they aim to produce as students' language proficiency improves (Gromik, 2012).

For the acquisition of Russian, frequency of vlogs is important. Many L1 English university students perceive Russian to be a difficult language to learn, particularly due to the time commitment required to master elements of the language (e.g., vocabulary) in comparison to other previously learned languages such as French or Spanish (Kulikova, 2015). Assigning task-based vlogs that allow for creativity and self-expression is just one way of breaking down the walls of inhibition L2 Russian students face. If instructors can make the act of learning Russian more fun and engaging, students can potentially pick up the language at a quicker pace the more they practice.

Unlike learners of EFL, learners of L2 Russian face a unique challenge in communication. In my experience of leading a conversational group of English learners, even at high-beginner or low-intermediate levels, they were able to elaborate and explain when they encountered a lexical gap in a themed conversation. EFL instructors can ask clarifying questions, arrive at a mutual understanding with students, and provide learners with the new word they seek. At that same level in my own Russian studies, it was difficult to overcome communication gaps.

Hacking and Tschirner (2017) have indicated that vocabulary size in L2 Russian is strongly correlated with reading proficiency, an important skill in acquisition. By introducing more assignments that put vocabulary to practice, such as vlogs described here, students may be able to increase their lexicon and improve their proficiency. Additionally, Russian instructors have suggested that assignment repetition incorporating previously studied grammar can be beneficial for students at lower levels of proficiency (Petukhova et al., 2020) and we adopted this approach, by encouraging practice of previously learned cases and newly learned verbs of motion.

The difference between the challenges that Russian learners and English learners face can be influenced by many factors – typological distance between languages, learning environment (foreign language vs. second language), amount of target language use, etc. However, it should also be recognized that teaching methodology is another key factor. A large body of literature in communicative language teaching and TBLT is available in the context of EFL classrooms, with results indicating increased student motivation and proficiency. Russian instructors should follow suit with such innovations. Asking students to engage in tasks, meaningfully use Russian, and express their creativity will grant them the ability to be as productive as EFL learners. Task-based vlogs are just one potential step to creating a more engaging and successful Russian language classroom.

Appendix A

Hometown vlog instructions

(1) Describe and show at least **five** things you do in your daily routine: я чи́щу зу́бы (I brush my teeth), за́втракаю/обе́даю (eat breakfast/eat lunch), принима́ю душ (take a shower) . . . actually, don't show us that part:) Use as many new verbs from the Unit 5 vocabulary list as possible.

(2) Use **two** verbs of motion (идти и ехать/go by foot and go by vehicle) to describe two places you go to.

(3) Show at least **three** different destinations in town to tell where (куда́ / to where) you go – don't forget the preposition "to" (в/на) + the accusative case!

   (3a) Example: Я е́ду в зоопа́рк, Я иду́ на рабо́ту. (I drive to the zoo, I walk to work)

(4) Tell your friend your favorite thing about your city! Be creative about how you introduce it – feel free to use any of the following cases (prepositional, nominative, accusative, or genitive).

   (4a) Example: Я люблю́ есть в э́том рестора́не, Я о́чень люблю́ э́ту це́рковь. (I love to eat in this restaurant, I really love this church)

(5) Finally, include **one sentence** about what tourists like to do in your town and **one sentence** about what you recommend doing!

   (5a) Example: Тури́сты лю́бят фотографи́ровать це́рковь, Я сове́тую идти́ в музе́й. (Tourists love to photograph the church, I recommend [you] to go to the museum)

Appendix B

Final vlog instructions

(1) **Comment on two classmates' videos**. Your comment should include a brief comparison of what you vs. they do/did/will do. You might write something like the following:

   (1a) Хорошее видео! Ты встаёшь рано, а я встаю поздно. (Good video! You wake up early, and I wake up late.)

   (1b) Мне понравилось ваше видео! Я узнал, что ты готовишь ужин каждый день, и я тоже часто готовлю! (I liked your video! I found out that you make dinner every day, and I also often make [dinner]!)

(2) If you want to say you spent **all day** reading (process): Вчера я **читала** эту книгу весь день. (Yesterday I read this book all day.)

(3) But – if you want to say you finally finished the book: Я наконец **прочитала** книгу. (I finally finished reading the book.)

(4) Time expressions

   (4a) Раньше, часто, редко, никогда не, каждый день, каждую пятницу (Earlier, often, rarely, never, every day, every Friday)

(5) Dative case

   (5a) Who do you miss? Я **скучаю по** (**моим друзьям, моей подруге** . . .) (I miss my friends, my girlfriend)

   (5b) Calling/texting: Я часто **звоню** (или **пишу эсэмэски**) **моим друзьям** из университета (I often call/write texts to my friends from university)

   (5c) Нравиться: Мне не **нравится** карантин, конечно, но мне очень **нравится** моё новое расписание, потому что я могу ложиться спать и вставать поздно! (To like: I don't like quarantine, of course, but I really like my new schedule because I can go to bed and wake up late!)

Chapter 6

Russian and Russia through tasks for beginners
Applying task-based language teaching at a low proficiency level

Vita V. Kogan and Maria Bondarenko

Краткое содержание главы

В этой главе мы рассматриваем различные существующие в литературе попытки определить методологию задачного подхода, чтобы выделить концептуальное пространство, благоприятное для теоретической адаптации задачного метода (ЗМ) к начальному уровню. Мы анализируем понятие коммуникации/общения, лежащее в основе определения "задачи", начиная с конца 1980-х годов. Согласно нашей гипотезе, сужение понятия "коммуникации/общения" до устного взаимодействия с присутствующим собеседником и необоснованное уравнивание продвинутых лингвистических навыков с высшими когнитивными и коммуникативными функциями (такими, как анализ и аргументация) сыграли важную роль в формировании негативного отношения к использованию ЗМ на начальном этапе обучения. Мы предлагаем несколько конкретных стратегий построения урока русского языка начального и пред-среднего уровня (ACTFL), основанного на ЗМ, и приводим примеры задач. Имея сложное предметно-тематическое содержание (экономика, жилищные условия и политика современной России), эти задачи стимулируют критическое мышление и в то же время подразумевают доступный для начинающих язык.

Chapter summary

In this chapter, we review several attempts to refine the conceptual space of task-based language teaching (TBLT) and to make TBLT suitable for beginner learners. First, we problematize the notion of communication in tasks tracing the evolution of the task definition since the 1980s. We conclude that limiting the concept of communication by the notion of oral interaction and focusing on higher linguistic and cognitive skills have shaped the negative attitude towards using TBLT at the beginner level. We compile specific design strategies (principles) that can help to make tasks accessible for low-level Russian language learners and provide sample tasks successfully implemented at the Novice Low and Novice Mid (ACTFL) proficiency levels. These tasks have the content that has been traditionally assigned to advanced level language study (Russia's economy and living

DOI: 10.4324/9781003146346-6

conditions) and that enhances the thought value; however, the proposed tasks are still approachable in terms of the language they incorporate.

Introduction

Task-based language teaching (TBLT) that originated from the evolution of communicative teaching (Howatt, 1984; Richards & Rodgers, 2001) constitutes one of the most promising approaches to second language (L2) instruction. Associated with student-centeredness, meaning-based instruction, authentic material use, textbook-less, and theme-based curriculum design, TBLT provides a set of techniques that supports and, for some theoreticians (e.g., Long, 2015; Nunan, 2004), encompasses content-, project-based, and collaborative learning.

Common beliefs that TBLT is not suitable for beginners

Despite a wide range of definitions and interpretations, TBLT has rarely been conceptualized from the perspective of proficiency level. Many earlier publications related to TBLT focused "on highly qualified students at intermediate stages of the second language development" (Duran & Ramaut, 2006, p. 47). Only a limited body of research explores TBLT in application to beginner learners (e.g., Duran & Ramaut, 2006; R. Ellis, 2001, 2009, 2018; Erlam & Ellis, 2018, 2019; Prabhu, 1987; Shintani, 2016; Willis, 1996), and even these studies often limit the tasks suitable for beginners to vocabulary-centered activities (e.g., Erlam & Ellis, 2018, 2019; Willis, 1996).

Such lack of attention to TBLT at the beginner level might be explained by the shared beliefs long established in the field of L2 education. Duran and Ramaut (2006) and Erlam and Ellis (2019) state that many teachers assume that the language input integrated into task-based activities is too complex for absolute beginners who "lack the basic speaking skills needed to exchange information" (Duran & Ramaut, 2006, p. 47). Therefore, practitioners believe that "it is necessary to first teach language directly to build up the linguistic resources that will enable learners to participate effectively in performing tasks" (Erlam & Ellis, 2019, p. 491). This belief is partially justified by the previous research that has shown that novice learners have difficulty attending to form and meaning simultaneously while processing input within meaning-based instruction (R. Ellis, 1997; VanPatten, 1996). Consequently, there has been a lack of attention to TBLT at beginner levels, whereupon a general trend in L2 communicative teaching has been to emphasize explicit form-based teaching in initial stages of learning, in order to "lay the linguistic foundation" for more implicit meaning-based approaches at later stages (N. Ellis, 2005).

TBLT and languages with rich morphological structure

When the target language has a rich morphology and is typologically different from the students' first language (e.g., Russian for English native speakers), the development of fluency and accuracy might present an additional challenge for novice learners due to the necessity for acquiring a large number of morphological patterns. Since most of the reflections on implementing TBLT in L2 teaching comes from the limited repertoire of typologically close languages often belonging to the Romance and Germanic language families, there is little advice on how to design tasks for languages with different structural profiles. With highly inflectional languages at a low proficiency level, it is generally believed that there is the necessity to concentrate on grammatical acquisition as opposed to purposeful communication (Comer, 2012a; Isurin, 2013; Kempe & Brooks, 2008). This position reinforces the belief that TBLT may be inappropriate for Russian L2 beginners.

Lost in translation: the Russian analogy to the term task

The implementation of TBLT in Russian L2 teaching practice may be constrained by the lack of consensus in the understanding of what a task is. Among teachers of Russian as an L2, we can observe a confusion related to the term *task* that can be translated into Russian both as "задача" [a problem to solve] and "задание" [an assignment to execute]. We must also add a large gap between the Russian and English methodological and terminological traditions. The rare Russian publications on TBLT are mostly authored by TESOL (Teaching English as Second Language) professionals and students. They translate TBLT either as "метод коммуникативных/целевых *заданий*" (Насс, 2020; Блик, 2015) or "методика, ориентированная на выполнение *задач*" (Бойкова, 2013) with no comments about their terminological choice. None of the terminological adaptations is widely accepted. We are leaning towards the terminological variations based on "задача" (for example, обучение языку, основанное на выполнении задач, или задачный метод). This translation avoids the ambiguity of the Russian word "задание" applicable to any activity with a specific objective (цель). Also, "задача" allows to shift the semantic focus from "a given assignment" towards "a problem to be solved" and to highlight the active position of the student as essential features of TBLT. And finally, translating "task" as "задача" instead of "коммуникативное задание" helps us to avoid the ambiguity associated with the concept "communication"[1] that we will discuss further.

We argue that the obstacles in implementing TBLT at a low proficiency level can be overcome. It is possible to design and implement relevant tasks of high interest to learners with limited complex linguistic skills, and in order to do this, we need to review our understanding of TBLT from a proficiency point of view as well as our representation of the beginner learner. In this chapter, we review several past attempts to define the task-based approach and identify the conceptual space where we place our understanding of TBLT, which can be suitable for any level of Russian. We problematize the notion of communication that underlies the definition of a task since the 1980s and believe that certain misconceptions of "tasks" have resulted in an adverse attitude towards the usage of TBLT at the beginner level. To demonstrate that TBLT can be implemented with beginners, we explore design principles that can help to create beginner tasks. We also include a sample implementation of such a task in an intensive language Russian program at the Novice Low and Novice Mid (ACTFL) proficiency levels.

Searching for the definition of a task suitable for the beginner level

As many definitions of tasks exist nowadays and "there is no single task-based teaching approach" (R. Ellis, 2009, p. 221), there are several conceptualizations of TBLT, which can be useful for Russian L2 instruction at a low proficiency level.

Initial focus on reasoning in the early definitions of "task"

One of the earliest references to TBLT can be found in the seminal work of Prabhu (1987) who defines a task as "an activity which requires learners to arrive at an outcome from given information through some process of thought" (p. 24). The cornerstones of this definition are a tangible outcome and the engagement of higher cognitive skills. With regard to the latter, Prabhu (1987) distinguishes three types of gaps that can be resolved with the help of higher cognitive skills: information gap, reasoning gap, and opinion gap. In this work, higher cognitive skills were not connected to higher linguistic skills, therefore, this original definition of tasks was applicable to beginner learners. According to Prabhu (1987), the cognitive skill of reasoning (e.g., processing of numeric information/diagrams) is the most important at the beginner level, because of its potential to act as alternative "languages" in which some of the thinking can be done. For that reason, with beginner learners, Prabhu (1987) recommended using information- and reasoning-gap tasks rather than opinion-gap tasks (p. 44).

Student-centeredness

Nunan (1988a, 1988b, 1989, 2006) introduced student-centeredness as another important aspect of TBLT. According to Nunan, tasks should be tailored to students' needs and objectives; students should be allowed to discuss which tasks they find useful and which tasks should be included in the curriculum. This important characteristic stays relevant to many TBLT theoreticians (Long, 2007, 2015; Skehan, 1996, 1998).

Switch to communication as oral interaction between learners

At the same time, Nunan (1988a, 1988b, 1989, 1991) put forward another important element of the task definition – focus on communication. Since the 1980s, the emerging communicative approach to language teaching has received prominent attention from TBLT theoreticians. Initially, communication in TBLT was viewed mostly as a focus on meaning as opposed to a focus on language: "Task involves communicative language use in which the user's attention is focused on meaning rather than linguistic structure" (Nunan, 1989, p. 10). Thereafter, the understanding of communication shifted towards the oral interaction among learners who are following native speakers as an example. Thus, in 1991, as the first feature of TBLT, Nunan (1991) stated: "the emphasis on learning to communicate through interaction in the target language" (p. 279). Simultaneously, higher cognitive skills, so important for Prabhu (1987) in application to beginners, become compulsorily tied to higher (oral) language proficiency, and, therefore, not accessible for beginners. Thus, in Littlewood's (1981) list of skills necessary for successful implementation of the communicative approach, the first requirement is as follows: "The learner must attain as high a degree as possible of linguistic competence. That is, he must develop skills in manipulating the linguistic system, to the point where he can use it spontaneously and flexibly in order to express this intended message" (as cited in Nunan, 1989, p. 13).

Later task definitions shift attention to new aspects, such as personalization, including freely shared personal experiences (Willis, 1996; Willis & Willis, 2007) and authenticity (Skehan, 1996), yet, oral interaction has consistently been an important premise. Some TBLT researchers might argue that a task should inherently include speaking and, therefore, can be implemented only when speaking in L2 is possible (Nunan, 1989; Skehan, 1996; Swan, 2005; Willis, 1996). This focus on oral interaction between learners imitating native speakers makes it difficult to introduce tasks at the beginner level of Russian taught to non-Slavic language speakers. It might take months and years until learners attain the required linguistic competence.

Input-based tasks as best suited for beginners

Recent developments within TBLT, possibly as a reaction to the "ultra communicative" approach, began considering tasks where speaking was not a primary tool and objective (R. Ellis, 2003, 2009, 2018; Erlam & Ellis, 2018, 2019; Shintani, 2012, 2016). R. Ellis (2001) proposed a promising distinction between *reciprocal* vs. *non-reciprocal* tasks that he reconceptualized later in terms of *output-based* vs. *input-based* tasks (R. Ellis, 2009). Reciprocal tasks "require a two-way flow of information between a speaker and a listener; they are speaking tasks," while non-reciprocal tasks "require only a one-way flow of information from a speaker to a listener" (Ellis, 2003, p. 49). Erlam and Ellis (2019) explain the lack of attention to beginners in TBLT with "a hidden assumption that task-based instruction necessarily involves production-based tasks" (Erlam & Ellis, 2019, p. 492) and present their input-based approach to tasks as an innovation that opens new horizons for the application of TBLT at the beginner level. They consider non-reciprocal tasks as best suited to beginner-level learners (Erlam & Ellis, 2019, p. 492) because this type of tasks "enable learners to develop not only the ability to comprehend input but also the grammatical resources they will need to speak and write" (Ellis, 2009, p. 137). The latter aspect gains particular importance in learning and teaching a language with elaborate morphology as Russian.

Teacher-led interpersonal oral interaction

R. Ellis (2001, 2009, 2018) allows for further distinctions in oral interpersonal communication related to TBLT. Oral communication can be autonomous, i.e., between a learner and another learner or between a learner and a native speaker; but it could also be between a learner and a teacher. The latter mode of communication is usually not included in a canonical understanding of authentic communication. However, the ecological perspective on L2 education (van Lier, 2004) acknowledges the teacher's essential role in oral dialogues with beginners and includes interpersonal teacher-student interaction to the authentic communicative environment.

Erlam and Ellis (2018, 2019) and Shintani (2012, 2016) provide examples suggesting that teacher-student oral communication (as opposed to autonomous student-student oral communication) is optimal for the beginner learner. In this case, a teacher provides a linguistic model and corrective feedback in the form of recasting (Lyster, 2001; Nabei & Swain, 2002) at the same time. It is also an opportunity for dialogic repetition that has been shown particularly beneficial for generalizing rich grammatical paradigms (Ullman, 2005). Gatbonton and Segalowitz (2005) also reflect on the benefit of so-called "inherently repetitive tasks" where "repetition is the means by which the activity goal is attained" (p. 332).

Solo-task based on interaction with environment

Long's (2015) recent definition of a task breaks definitively with the dominating tradition of oral interpersonal communication in TBLT by considering both the cognitive aspect of the task-based activity and many kinds of everyday task-based social actions, instead of only interpersonal speaking-oriented ones. By a task Long (2015) means any complex situation that contains "an information gap" that requires decision-making and that constitutes any authentic (real-world-like) interaction between a learner and an environment, which may or might not include other people. Long (2015) observes that not all tasks – real-world mundane activities that people plan and do every day – require language use. Consequently, we cannot ignore that the world is full of solo tasks. With the increased availability of technology, there is a growing number of solo language tasks that learners have to perform in everyday life: e.g., buying lunch from an automated teller at McDonald's, making purchases online, and obtaining information by searching the Internet. Thus, in the past decade, language proficiency guidelines on both sides of the Atlantic have been integrating solo tasks as part of digital literacies. The ACTFL's *21st Century Skills Map: World Languages* (ACTFL, 2011) suggests considering the following tasks related to information, media, and technology skills: creating a social media profile, browsing a familiar website or watching an advertisement in one's target language, searching online and analyzing the food pyramid from a target culture (ACTFL, 2011, pp. 12, 13, 14). CEFR's *Companion Volume with New Descriptors* introduces a new type of competence – *goal-oriented online transaction & collaboration*, which includes, among other things, purchasing products and services online and engaging in transactions (CEFR, 2018, pp. 92, 98). Such tasks might be complex conceptually (requiring multiple steps or critical thinking) but not linguistically because the language they employ is often suitable for beginners.

Cognitive complexity of tasks vs. language complexity

Another factor that contributed to the lack of attention to beginners in TBLT may be a hidden assumption that linguistic limitation is associated with limited cognitive behavior, however, Martel (2016) argues that beginners' cognitive skills should not be confused with their restricted linguistic skills. Additionally, Klimanova and Bondarenko (2018), using data from a multilingual telecollaboration project, demonstrate that the writing capacity of a beginning learner is routinely underestimated. Clifford (2016) and Corin (2020) suggest reviewing the traditional ACTFL guidelines based on the direct association between a gradual increase of linguistic skills and cognitive task complexity. Research has shown that even before the first utterances are made in a foreign language, a learner is capable of sophisticated L2 behaviors, such as comparing or sorting information according to a given principle, evaluating and merging input from various sources, and making decisions in response to linguistic input (Richards, 2015). By propelling topics with simplistic cognitive content that are habitually introduced in the beginner classes we deny our students the intellectual joy of meaningful learning.

Tentative definition

We would like to restructure the definitive space of a task by expanding the communicative component understood as autonomous oral interaction to include: prioritizing the authentic nature and cognitive complexity of tasks, and addressing interaction with the environment (including the teacher). This does not mean that we do not support the communicative approach in second language learning/teaching – quite the opposite. However, we would like to reflect and build on the notion of oral communication as not limited to one specific type of interaction. From this perspective, an effective task for beginners:

- Focuses on *interaction with the environment*, i.e., the learner has to interact with the world around them and the linguistic resources located in it by *using* the language *purposefully;*

- Requires the learner to draw on *their cognitive resources with an emphasis on complex cognition at all levels to solve a problem based on different types of gaps;* the cognitive complexity of a task should not be used as motivation to assign it to a more advanced proficiency level, but rather to provide strong support (scaffolding) and motivation;
- Can be based on oral input provided by the teacher within teacher-student meaningful dialogue which includes corrective feedback;
- Promotes *learner-centeredness* which includes learner's needs and interests, but also *participatory democracy and learner autonomy*;
- Results in *a measurable output* for constructive assessment, preferably linguistic but not necessarily (it may be *an action* or *a decision* based on the interaction with the linguistic material).

This inclusive definition would make it possible to design meaningful tasks at any level of language proficiency with any language of study.

TBLT at a low proficiency level: design principles

In this section, we suggest some design principles that ensure the implementation of the proposed task definition in the beginner Russian classroom. Most of them belong to the *matrioshka/spiral-like design* that has been proposed to complete meaning-oriented L2 teaching by taking into account the cognitive needs of beginner learners to acquire a complex morphological structure (Bondarenko, in press). *Matrioshka/spiral-like design* is grounded in a number of trends from Cognitive L2 Pedagogy. Without elaborating the contribution of each of these trends in our design model, we will mention the most relevant ones, such as general task pedagogy based on cognitive load theory (Paas & van Merriënboer, 2020), Natural L2 Learning Theory (Krashen, 1981) completed by awareness studies, noticing hypothesis (Schmidt, 1995), feedback (Lyster, 2001; Nabei & Swain, 2002), output hypothesis (Swain, 1995, 2000), and focus-on-form approach (Long, 1991, 1998; Shintani, 2016), Open Architecture Curricular Design (OACD) approach (Campbell, 2018; Corin et al., 2021), research on practice distribution and task repetition in L2 learning (Ahmadian, 2012; Ahmadian & Tavakoli, 2011; Bird, 2010; Bygate, 1996, 2001; Bygate & Samuda, 2005; Gass et al., 1999; Fukuta, 2016; Lambert et al., 2017; Suzuki & DeKeyser, 2017), studies from neurolinguistics (Ullman, 2005; Ullman & Lovelett, 2018) emphasizing the importance of retrieval from memory and spaced repetition, and the neurolinguistic approach to L2 learning (Germain, 2017).

We also respect the general framework for task sequence – *pre-task, implementation of the task,* and *post-task* (Prabhu, 1987, Skehan, 1998, Willis, 1996), which we interpreted in the light of *the* c*ircle of literacy* (Germain, 2017). The circle of literacy consists of iterative stages *of oral interaction – collaborative writing – reading* and emphasizes oral teacher-student interaction with immediate corrective feedback (a recasting in the form of a form-negotiation dialogue integrated into a content-based discussion). After the initial teacher-governing oral dialogue, students have an opportunity to collaboratively compose a short text based on previous oral discussion and then to read aloud the same or a more complex text to practice pronunciation.

In line with the focus-on-form approach (Long, 1991, 1998; Shintani, 2016) and consciousness-raising tasks (Willis & Willis, 1996), we employ what we call an *inter-task*, which serves as a deliberate interruption of a task to raise students' awareness of the linguistic tools involved and to take the form of a meaning negotiation conducted in L2: *Do you understand what the word X means? What is the opposite of X? How to say X in English?*

Taking the theoretical principles from this research to inform our task design (e.g., VanPatten, 1996, 2003; Long, 2015; Germain, 2017), we recommend the following design principles for creating task-based activities in Russian L2 language instruction at a low proficiency level:

Principle 1

Conduct needs analysis with an emphasis on learners' interests and objectives.

Principle 2

Based on the results of the needs analysis, co-create tasks together with students as the course progresses. Discuss (with elements of the presentation if needed) with the students the objectives, content, and the strategy to implement a task at the pre-task stage.

Principle 3

Select topics and tasks that are cognitively stimulating (based on information, reasoning, and opinion gaps) and adapt them linguistically with the help of different techniques including the use of cognates, non-verbal language, and visual support.

Principle 4

Prioritize authenticity and functionality over a specific skill (e.g., speaking).

Principle 5

Prioritize oral input before writing and reading; use task activities as tools and scaffolding for developing speaking skills; do not consider a speaking ability as a prerequisite skill to accomplish the task.

Principle 6

Integrate multiple types of input and the reproduction of new patterns into task definition and task implementation process.

Principle 7

> Prioritize task repetition and "inherently repetitive tasks" within a task-based activity.

Principle 8

> Consider inter-task and post-task discussions as an important step to summarize learners' gains both in terms of content and language.

Principle 9

> Prioritize strong but flexible scaffolding.

Principle 10

> Prioritize a series of task-based activities on related topics within a common theme; a coherent transition across themes and subthemes allows for the recycling of language and for spaced pattern repetition which enhances pattern internalization.

Principle 11

> Rely on learners' L1 and digital literacy to facilitate access to authentic L2 resources and to reduce cognitive load by dealing with familiar genres and environments.

TBLT at the low proficiency level: an implementation

This section introduces an example of TBLT for low proficiency learners of Russian that was implemented in the 2019 Summer Intensive Language Program at The Middlebury Institute of International Studies (SILP MIIS) in Monterey, CA. The SILP MIIS constitutes an eight-week L2 course that prioritizes task- and content-based language acquisition in immersive settings. SILP MIIS immersive settings are different from "full immersion" as students do not stay in a shared linguistic space with their instructors throughout the day and are not required to speak the target language after classes. Five hours of daily classroom instruction are supplemented with co-curriculum cultural activities twice a week. Depending on the level and circumstances, there are about ten students in a typical SILP class. Besides teaching, the instructor is also responsible for developing a curriculum and course materials based on OACD (Campbell, 2018; Corin et al., 2021), with the weekly theme-based syllabus.

The program follows ACTFL standards to define proficiency levels and distinguishes between three sub-levels of beginners: Novice Low, Novice Mid, and Novice High. The sequence of tasks described in the following has been

Table 6.1

Title of the task: ЖИЛИЩНЫЙ ВОПРОС В РОССИИ [Housing conditions in Russia]

Task goal/s, setting of instruction: Interpret authentic statistics and data related to Russian housing and write a short summary of the data. Eight-week summer intensive language program with five hours of daily classroom instruction, supplemented with co-curriculum cultural activities twice a week. The sequence of the tasks described in what follows has been implemented at the Novice Low level (after 20–25 contact hours of instruction) that corresponds to the A1.1 level (CEFR).

Learner needs analysis: Needs analysis in the form of an open-ended online survey was conducted at the end of the first week of the course, revealing that the students' interests in Russia revolved around two topics: (1) food and (2) Russian/USSR life and mentality from social, political, and cultural perspectives.

Task type: primarily an input-based task (R. Ellis, 2001, 2009) involving information-, reasoning and opinion-gap investigations (Prabhu, 1987).

Can-do statements
- I can understand a simple text and interpret statistical data that relate to various types of Russian housing.
- I can write a paragraph describing my living conditions and housing in America.
- I can understand and respond to questions related to living conditions in Russia.
- I can describe what different types of housing look like in Russia.

Assessment
In-progress evaluation through formative assessment:
- Questions to individual students and groups of students during the learning process to determine what specific concepts or skills they have learned.
- Targeted feedback that teachers provide on student work, such as collaborative writing samples that are subsequently reviewed and improved by students.
- Online diagnostic tools such as www.socrative.com/ to quickly estimate comprehension.

Other suggested assessments:
- Self-assessment requiring students to think about their learning process.
- Peer assessment that allows students to use one another as a learning resource.

implemented at the Novice Low level (after 25 contact hours of instruction) that corresponds to A1.1 (CEFR).

In this section, we present a sequence of tasks and task-based activities that focus on the acquisition of complex content (Russia's economy), yet, are tailored to beginner learners (our students were Novice Low/A1 students). Students used higher cognitive skills to solve a variety of linguistic and pragmatic problems that reflect real-life scenarios (e.g., interpreting statistical information on a chart) without the expectation of autonomous spontaneous oral communication.

Defining a theme for a task-based activity

The task-based activities under the common name ЖИЛИЩНЫЙ ВОПРОС В РОССИИ [Housing conditions in Russia] were conducted during five days within the second week of a weekly theme-based syllabus. According to design Principle 10 (see the list earlier), the chosen theme was closely related to the themes of the previous and following weeks (e.g., the activities of the first week were organized around the theme МОЙ ДОМ – МОЯ КРЕПОСТЬ [My home is my fortress]). By the end of the first week, students wrote an essay based on previous discussions, reading, and mini-essays (Principle 5) МОЙ ДОМ: ЧТО ЭТО ЗНАЧИТ ДЛЯ МЕНЯ [What does my home mean to me?].

By the end of the first week (25 hours of classroom instruction), the students were familiar with the following grammatical patterns: МЕНЯ ЗОВУТ (all forms), ЕСТЬ-based construction, У МЕНЯ ЕСТЬ (all forms), У МЕНЯ НЕТ + Gen., ОКОЛО + Gen. (noun only), nouns in plural, Adjective + noun agreement in Nom. (singular and plural) and Prep. (singular) (Я ЖИВУ В БОЛЬШОМ ГОРОДЕ, В БОЛЬШОЙ СТРАНЕ). The following imperfective verbs – ЖИТЬ, РАБОТАТЬ, ЛЮБИТЬ, ГОВОРИТЬ, ЗНАТЬ, ДУМАТЬ, ЧИТАТЬ, ПИСАТЬ, ОТВЕЧАТЬ, СМОТРЕТЬ, ВИДЕТЬ, СПРАШИВАТЬ, ЭТО ЗНАЧИТ . . ., КАК СКАЗАТЬ . . . were introduced in the present tense. The following questions were familiar: ГДЕ? ЧТО? КТО? ПОЧЕМУ? КАКАЯ/КАКОЙ/КАКОЕ/КАКИЕ? СКОЛЬКО? The students were expected to demonstrate the ability to use the following language functions: *introducing, greeting, description, supporting simple opinions* on the topics of *family, nationalities, origin, friends, hobbies; country, city, house,* and *room,* and the following text types: *sentences, a string of sentences* and occasionally – *short paragraphs.*

Needs analysis (Principle 1) was conducted at the end of the first week and consisted of an open-ended online survey with five questions regarding students' professional occupation, interests, learning expectations, and goals. The outcome of the survey revealed that the students' interests concerning Russia revolved around two topics: (1) food and (2) Russian/USSR life and mentality from a social, political, and cultural perspective. Based on the needs analysis and considering the students' previous knowledge, we designed task-based activities for the second week around the theme: ЖИЛИЩНЫЙ ВОПРОС В РОССИИ [Housing conditions in Russia]. Concerning Principle 10, this theme, on one hand, continued the conversation of the first week but from a new social and historical perspective (as opposed to a personal one). On the other hand, as the question about poverty and wealth was naturally integrated into the exploration of housing conditions, the suggested theme, provided an opportunity to initiate a thematic umbrella КОМУ НА РУСИ ЖИТЬ ХОРОШО: БЕДНОСТЬ И БОГАТСТВО В РОССИИ [Who is happy in the Rus': Poverty and richness in Russia]. This umbrella theme covered several interrelated themes that were developed in the following weeks. Thus, three weeks after the students had explored housing conditions in Russia, they resumed their investigation on poverty and wealth with a new investigation into Russian peoples' living conditions and the cost of living in Russia.

The set of task-based activities ЖИЛИЩНЫЙ ВОПРОС В РОССИИ comprised the next five units with interrelated topics (Principle 10):

Day 1 (Unit 1): Бедные и богатые в России (Introducing the umbrella theme).
Day 2 (Unit 2): Жилищные феномены: коммуналка, хрущёвка и сталинка.
Day 3 (Unit 3): Жилищные феномены: коммуналка, хрущёвка и сталинка (история, примеры, актуальные проблемы).
Day 4 (Unit 4): Жилищные феномены: где живут олигархи (рублёвка и элитные квартиры).
Day 5 (Unit 5): Обобщение: жилищные условия и менталитет.

Each activity consisted of several blocs/discussions based on a combination of reasoning-, information- and, occasionally, opinion-gap tasks (Principle 3) involving authentic non-verbal online resources and facilitated by cognates (Principles 3, 4, and 11). Each block was structured according to the circle of literacy initiated by a teacher-led oral discussion (Principle 5) and ensured multiple repetitions of patterns (Principles 6 and 7). Inter-tasks were also implemented in order to slow the dialogue and introduce new patterns or draw attention to linguistic difficulties (Principle 8). A more detailed description of an implementation of a discussion from the first unit can be found in the Appendix.

Discussion: towards a Russian TBLT for beginners

In this chapter, we addressed the underlying issue that often prevents teachers of Russian from implementing TBLT at a low proficiency level – the traditional understanding of a task developed over the long history of TBLT. This understanding is based on the idea of mandatory communication as oral interpersonal interaction between students imitating native speakers and it is also related to associating linguistic and cognitive skills involved in completing a task. Our example of successful integration of tasks into a Russian L2 curriculum for beginners provides an argument in favor of using TBLT at a low proficiency level – not only as a single occasional activity but also as an instructional macro-strategy that underlies the entire curriculum.

Following our theoretical reflections supported by practice observations, we suggest reviewing the existing understanding of a task by moving the emphasis from oral student-student communication (which is limited at a low proficiency level) to other components: interaction with the environment including the teacher, meaning and authenticity (real-world settings), learner-centeredness, the need for the learner to draw on their linguistic and (higher) cognitive resources, purposeful interaction with the language, and orientation on the tangible outcome.

Task-based needs analysis accounting for interests of specific groups of learners

It seems that more research is needed to determine what kinds of tasks are effective for beginner learners. Long (2015) emphasizes employing a task-based needs analysis that prioritizes tasks that are relevant for a particular group of learners.

Some groups of learners (e.g., university students or professionals specializing in politics, economics, anthropology, history, international security, etc.) may be interested in conceptually and cognitively complex topics from the onset of language acquisition. These topics can range from economy and politics and business to philosophy (e.g., Philosophy-based Language Teaching; Shahini & Riazi, 2011). As long as the material is accessible linguistically, i.e., tailored and scaffolded to the learner level, the content can be intellectually sophisticated. For example, instead of memorizing a list of clothing vocabulary and practicing standard shopping situations that become increasingly rare (e.g., "У вас есть зеленая шляпа 38-го размера?" [Do you have a green hat of size 38?]), learners can be invited to reflect upon cross-cultural differences in dress codes in Russia and the U.S. A simple sorting activity that requires learners to assign outfits to either Russians or Americans might lead to pragmatic insights and help learners to navigate a follow-up activity, such as online shopping by using an authentic Russian phone application. A rich "essential" question that invites students "to consider subject matter from multiple, often conflicting viewpoints and do not have simple, declarative answers" (Martel, 2016, p. 115) such as *"When in Rome should we do as the Romans do, or is it important to preserve your identity in any cultural context?,"* could be a central theme for a series of thought-provoking and awareness-raising activities that would later be translated into specific linguistic behaviors. On the other hand, older learners who moved to a new country might not need to communicate orally in a target language and often need to acquire a conceptually different set of skills as opposed to undergraduate students who are preparing to study abroad.

To select tasks, Long (2015, 2016) recommends checking task descriptions for professions and roles and observing real-life situations, but most importantly – working closely with learners, which can contribute to an organically developing, fluid, and open-ended curriculum. To understand what a particular group of learners needs to be able to do in the language of study, Long (2015) recommends recording target situations observed in life.

Linguistic patterns selection based on frequency

Since implementing TBLT at a low proficiency level of Russian involves a careful selection of grammatical patterns that would allow accomplishing a task, we need more research related to the functional value of morphosyntactic patterns. Grammatical structures should be selected based on functionality and relevance as opposed to morphosyntactic complexity. First, it is still a matter of debate which grammatical structures are "easier" for beginners to learn. Second, so-called "easier structures" (e.g., the canonical use of the Instrumental case "Я пишу ручкой" [I write with a pen] or the subject-verb-object word order) might not necessarily be the most frequent, the most relevant or helpful for the learner.

The competition for the cognitive resources of the beginner learner is fierce: in this sense, only the fittest grammatical structures survive. Supplying the beginner learner with the necessary functional language early on will spin the motivational wheel, thus enabling the learner to progress to the next level quickly and avoid the motivational plateau – so common after the first few weeks of language instruction (Novice Mid/High or upper A1). From this perspective, it is not "ecological" (in terms of van Lier, 2004) to overload the beginner learner with grammatical structures that are linguistically simple, but peripheral in everyday language. For example, the dative case in the Russian language corpora is overwhelmingly represented by the pronoun paradigm, such as "мне" (663,428 contexts) or "ему" (442,620 contexts) (Russian National Corpus, 2020). Dative case-based expressions such as "мне/ему/ей нравится" (2,964), "мне/ему/ему нужно/надо" (15,281), personal "мне сказал/а" (3,085), and impersonal "мне сказали" (1,820) and "мне дали" (1,032) dominate the conversational discourse in comparison to "мне дал/купил/послал/подарил/написал/а" (together 1,007 contexts) and "мне купили/послали/подарили/написали" (together 269 contexts) (Russian National Corpus, 2020). Nevertheless, when the dative case is presented, the latter expressions are traditionally introduced first (Davidson et al., 1996; Lubensky et al., 1996; Nummikoski, 2011). Considering how much time the beginner learner spends on acquiring the noun declensions, it is better to equip them with the maximum amount of functional language. Therefore, we advocate for integrating language structures based on their frequency (see also Almutairi (2016) or Samburskiy (2014) on corpus-driven grammar instruction) and not on linguistic complexity.

TBLT and Russian: challenges of teaching RFL

For us, the implementation of TBLT with Russian at a higher proficiency level (B1 and higher) does not differ significantly from the implementation of TBLT in other languages. However, due to the morphosyntactic complexity and semantic opaqueness (not many cognates shared with other Indo-European languages) of the Russian language, early focus on speaking is somewhat problematic. This sets Russian apart from the Germanic-Romance languages commonly taught at the university level, and we believe it important to consider language typology in discussions of TBLT. Each language has a set of challenges unique to it that is especially pronounced at the onset of language acquisition. For Russian, it is undoubtedly the complex morphology. Historically, this challenge has been overcome through focusing language instruction primarily on the form within the traditional Presentation-Practice-Production (PPP) syllabus supported by a specific skill acquisition model. Soviet and post-Soviet L2 pedagogy has been traditionally based on the psychological model which is similar to Anderson's (1983) and DeKeyser's (2007) Skill Acquisition Theory. According to this model, the development of linguistic competencies (навыки) happens through a graduate transformation of declarative knowledge (знания) into procedural skills (умения) by the means of automatization (Леонтьев, 1975; Ильин, 1986). Focused on the automatization process, the traditional PPP syllabus reduces the task to an automatization tool in the format of mini-dialogues on basic (usually not connected) conversational topics and shies away from meaning-based, project-, reasoning- or exploration-like activities. For example, such an understanding of a task as an automatization tool has been recently presented by Бердичевский (2020), an influential Russian L2 methodologist.

TBLT is a promising development within second language acquisition theory and practice, and it is helpful in guiding our understanding of the learning process and curriculum design. We believe it is beneficial to propel TBLT across as many languages and as many proficiency levels as possible because it delivers fast and optimal learning outcomes. In order to achieve such outcomes, we should be able to recognize what is essential in a task and what is optional. We propose that implementing authentic customized and interactive tasks that engage learners cognitively is essential and oral communication as optional in a task. We hope to contribute to a fruitful discussion that would make task-based instruction more accessible for a variety of learners at all proficiency levels.

Appendix

The following is a sample task-based activity that occurs first in a series of activities within the theme ЖИЛИЩНЫЙ ВОПРОС В РОССИИ [Housing conditions in Russia].

Note: A fragment marked with an asterisk (*text) constitutes a transcript of a sample of oral discussions between the teacher and the students. A *text in italics* refers to the written production that resulted from collaborative or individual writing based on oral practice. A framed text represents a suggestion for reading. Inter-task activities are interspersed throughout and aim to introduce new patterns or to draw attention to linguistic difficulties.

Unit 1, part 1 (5 hours of face-to-face instruction): introduction of the umbrella theme *Бедные и богатые в России*

ДИСКУССИЯ 1: ЕСТЬ ЛИ В РОССИИ БЕДНЫЕ И БОГАТЫЕ?

Pre-task: an oral dialogue (task description)

*Дома вы писали текст (сочинение) на тему "Мой дом: что это значит для меня". Вы/мы американцы и ваш/наш дом – это Америка. Сегодня у нас новая тема. Это тоже "Дом", но в новой перспективе. Это российская перспектива. Российская федерация – это большая, красивая и интересная страна. Там живут россияне. Россия – это их дом. Как они живут? Хорошо? Плохо? Мой первый вопрос: как вы думаете, в России есть бедность? Вы знаете, что значит слово БЕДНОСТЬ?

> **Inter-task:** Focus on new vocabulary and word structure (explanation through contrasting visual support): БЕДНЫЙ ДОМ – БОГАТЫЙ ДОМ, БЕДНЫЙ ЧЕЛОВЕК – БОГАТЫЙ ЧЕЛОВЕК, БЕДНЫЙ ГОРОД – БОГАТЫЙ ГОРОД, БЕДНАЯ СТРАНА – БОГАТАЯ СТРАНА, БЕДНОСТЬ – БОГАТСТВО; – ОСТЬ – это абстрактный суффикс, – СТВО – это тоже абстрактный суффикс.

*Как вы думаете, в России есть бедность? В России есть бедные люди? В России есть богатые люди? An expected answer: Я думаю, да. Я думаю, что в России есть бедность. Я думаю, что в России есть бедные люди и богатые люди. Я не знаю.

Inter-task: Focus on the ADJECTIVE + NOUN agreement in plural (a recently introduced pattern)

*Вы ХОТИТЕ знать факты? Я ХОЧУ! Я ХОЧУ ЗНАТЬ факты. А вы ХОТИТЕ? An expected answer: Да, я хочу знать факты. Я тоже хочу знать факты.

Inter-task: focus on a new pattern: the verb ХОТЕТЬ in two basic forms ВЫ ХОТИТЕ (ЗНАТЬ)? Я ХОЧУ (ЗНАТЬ)! Throughout the activity, this question can be asked on many occasions: ВЫ ХОТИТЕ СКАЗАТЬ? ВЫ ХОТИТЕ ЧИТАТЬ? ВЫ ХОТИТЕ ПИСАТЬ?

*Отлично! Если мы ХОТИМ знать факты, надо смотреть статистику. Смотрите статистику в Интернете. Смотрите график.

Task implementation

Show a figure of wages across various population segments in Russia (possible source: Опрос ГородРабот.ру: Какую зарплату россияне получают на руки в мае 2020 – Трибуна 24 (tribuna24.ru))

The students work in pairs and analyze an authentic chart (Principle 3, 4, and 11). During this activity, the teacher intervenes to explore the language of the chart reproduced on the screen:

Это старая или новая статистика/информация? (An expected answer: не очень старая, но и не очень новая).

*Что значит слово ЗАРПЛАТА (ЗАРПЛАТА В ДЕНЬ)? Translation (cf. ПЛАТИТЬ). Что значить слово МЕНЬШЕ (ЧЕМ)? Что значит слово БОЛЬШЕ (ЧЕМ)? Translation (cf. cognates БОЛЬШЕВИК – МЕНЬШЕВИК). Что значит ЦВЕТ на графике? Что значит КРАСНЫЙ цвет на графике (An expected answer: Красный цвет на графике значит "богатые люди", у них большая заплата). Что значит СЕРЫЙ цвет (An expected answer: Серый цвет на графике значит "очень бедные люди", у них зарплата очень маленькая, меньше чем три доллара в день)? Что значит РОЗОВЫЙ цвет на графике (An expected answer: Розовый цвет значит "бедные люди", у них маленькая зарплата, меньше чем десять долларов? Какой процент/Сколько процентов "очень бедные"? У них зарплата в день 3,5 (три и пять) доллара и меньше. (An expected answer: шесть). Какой процент/Сколько процентов "бедные"? У них зарплата в день четыре или десять долларов. (An expected answer: тридцать семь). Какой процент/Сколько процентов "бедные, но не очень"?

У них зарплата в день десять или двадцать долларов. (An expected answer: тридцать четыре).

Inter-task: Focus on new or recently introduced vocabulary and patterns: СКОЛЬКО, ЦВЕТ (color), КРАСНЫЙ, ОРАНЖЕВЫЙ, РОЗОВЫЙ, СЕРЫЙ, МЕНЬШЕ (ЧЕМ), БОЛЬШЕ (ЧЕМ), the ADJECTIVE + NOUN agreement. If errors occur, the teacher provides corrective feedback in the form of modeling 'Вы хотите сказать, что. . . .'.

The students answer the questions:
*В России есть бедность? В России есть бедные люди? Что показывает/говорит статистика? An expected answer: Статистика говорит/показывает, что в России есть бедные люди. Какая у них зарплата маленькая или большая? An expected answer: У них маленькая зарплата. Меньше, чем 10 долларов или больше, чем 10 долларов в день? An expected answer: У них зарплата меньше, чем 10 долларов в день. 10 долларов/35 долларов в день – это много или мало, как вы думаете? В Америке это много или мало? Для вас это много или мало? An expected answer: Это не очень много. Это мало.

*А вы знаете рейтинг Форбс? Рейтинг Форбс – это тоже статистика. Как вы думаете, в рейтинге Форбс есть русские люди? Вы ХОТИТЕ знать? Смотрите статистику и отвечайте на вопрос, есть ли русские люди в рейтинге Форбс топ-50 или нет. Если да, кто они, как их зовут.

In pairs the students explore the recently published Forbes data available in Russian on the Internet and select the five first names of Russian billionaires in the top-50. Thereafter, the students share their answers. If errors occur, the teacher provides corrective feedback in the form of modeling 'Вы хотите сказать, что. . . .'

*Сколько русских миллиардеров в рейтинге Форбс топ-50? An expected answer: пять. Это мужчины или женщины? Кто на первом месте? Как его зовут? Кто на втором месте? Как его зовут? Кто на третьем месте? Как его зовут? Кто на четвертом месте? Как его зовут? Кто на пятом месте? Как его зовут?

Post-task: writing

The students write a summary of the previous oral discussion using the mode of collaborative writing. The teacher writes on the board what the students suggest, and they edit the text together to make it coherent and to correct mistakes (an alternative: the students write in pairs and then do peer review).

Статистика говорит, что в России есть бедные люди. У них маленькая или очень маленькая зарплата, меньше чем десять долларов в день. Но статистика также говорит, что в России есть очень богатые люди. Например, в рейтинге Форбс есть русские миллиардеры. У них очень большая зарплата.

Inter-task: Focus on all grammatical and spelling rules, e.g., endings of ADJECTIVE + NOUN in plural, -И (в России).
Focus on new vocabulary: БОГАТЫЙ, БЕДНЫЙ, МЕНЬШЕ ЧЕМ, НАПРИМЕР, ТАКЖЕ.

Post-task: reading

The students read aloud a text based on previous writing and oral discussion.

> Сегодня постсоветская Российская федерация – это страна контрастов. Это значит, что в России есть социальные контрасты и что эти контрасты очень сильные. В Российской федерации есть бедность и богатство. Статистика говорит, что в России есть бедные люди. У них маленькая или очень маленькая зарплата, меньше чем десять долларов в день. Статистика также говорит, что в России есть очень богатые люди. Например, в рейтинге Форбс есть русские миллиардеры (миллиардеры и олигархи). У них очень большая зарплата.

Inter-task: Focus on pronunciation: -ЫЕ (adjectives in plural), and pronunciation rules.
Focus on new vocabulary: ВСЕ, БОГАТЫЙ, БЕДНЫЙ, СИЛЬНЫЙ, ЗАРПЛАТА, ТАКЖЕ. If pronunciation errors occur, the teacher provides corrective feedback in the form of modeling 'Вы хотите сказать, что. . . .'

Subsequent discussions within this unit involve themes related to the most and least wealthy cities and regions in Russia, as well as labor migration in Russia. Task-based activities surrounding these themes led to discussions comparing economic trends in Russia and the United States (or another country).

In the final stage, students make a list of the new vocabulary words and patterns they have observed and used during the unit. At this time, any questions related to the content and the language can be discussed in the L1:
БЕДНЫЙ, БОГАТЫЙ, БЕДНОСТЬ, БОГАТСТВО, СИЛЬНЫЙ, СЛАБЫЙ, САМЫЙ БОЛЬШОЙ, САМЫЙ БЕДНЫЙ, ЗАРПЛАТА, ПЛАТИТЬ. ХОТЕТЬ (Я ХОЧУ, ТЫ ХОЧЕШЬ, ОН ХОЧЕТ, ВЫ ХОТИТЕ, МЫ ХОТИМ, ОНИ ХОТЯТ). ГОРОД-ГОРОДА. ОТКУДА? ИЗ Владивостока, ИЗ Сибири, ИЗ Чечни.

The teacher presents to the students the text they have written together and asks them to suggest a title. The teacher and the students then discuss the assignment to complete at home. For example, they can: (1) read the final version of the text and write an essay; and/or (2) record an oral presentation; or (3) conduct and record an interview with other students based on the classroom discussions: Какие города и регионы в США самые бедные и самые богатые? Почему? Какие города и регионы престижные? В Америке есть социальная (рабочая) миграция?

Note

1 The ambiguity of the concept "communication" in second language learning/teaching has been observed by many authors, e.g., R. Ellis (1982), Gatbonton and Segalowitz (2005), Harmer (1982).

Chapter 7

Teaching Russian in Brazil

Learner-centered task design and TORFL connection

Anna Smirnova Henriques, Nadezhda Dubinina, Yulia Mikheeva, and Volha Yermalayeva Franco

Chapter summary

The issue of teaching Russian in Brazil is barely addressed in scholarly literature. In the present work, we outline the context of teaching and learning Russian in Brazil, describe the application of a task-based approach, and report our experience in implementing the TORFL (Test of Russian as a Foreign Language). The majority of Brazilians study Russian in private language schools or with private instructors. Most teachers are native Russian speakers. In the Brazilian context, they focus on communicative strategies and use a task-based approach. We detail nine tasks commonly applied in three language schools. Finally, we describe our experience in introducing the TORFL in Brazil. The Speaking subtest revealed excellent communication skills of Brazilian test takers, even at beginner levels.

Краткое содержание главы

Вопрос преподавания русского языка в Бразилии недостаточно широко освещен в научно-методической литературе. В данной работе описывается контекст преподавания и изучения русского языка как иностранного (РКИ) в Бразилии, опыт применения метода целевого задания и внедрение в Бразилии теста по русскому языку как иностранному (ТРКИ). Наиболее распространенная форма организации преподавания РКИ в Бразилии – курсы небольших частных языковых школ или индивидуальные уроки. Большинство преподавателей РКИ в этой стране – носители русского языка. При обучении РКИ в Бразилии применяется в основном коммуникативно-деятельностный подход и используется метод целевого задания. В главе приводится девять целевых заданий, которые успешно используются на занятиях в трех бразильских языковых школах. В заключение описывается опыт проведения ТРКИ в Бразилии: выполняя задания субтеста "Говорение", бразильские тестируемые проявили себя как уверенные участники коммуникации.

DOI: 10.4324/9781003146346-7

Introduction

The Russian language and culture were first introduced in Brazil at the end of the 19th century by Russian-speaking immigrants who belonged to ethnic (Russian Germans and Jews) or religious minorities (such as Old Believers) of the Russian Empire (Zabolotsky, 2007). The next waves of the Russophone immigration to Brazil occurred in the 20th century, one after the Bolshevik Revolution and another after World War II (Ruseishvili, 2016). These immigrants founded churches, introduced Russian cuisine, and wrote and translated books. Tatiana Belinky, born in Petrograd in 1919, popularized Russian folk stories in Brazil and translated several Russian authors, such as Nikolai Gogol, Ivan Turgenev, and Mikhail Zoshchenko, into Portuguese (Mellone, 2018). Boris Schnaiderman, born in 1917 in Uman, Ukraine, an undergraduate student of agronomy, was the first teacher of Russian at a Brazilian university: in 1960, he founded an undergraduate course of Russian at Faculdade de Filosofia, Letras e Ciências Humanas (FFLCH) at Universidade de São Paulo (Assis, 2014; Puh, 2020). Boris Schnaiderman translated renowned classic Russian writers, such as Fyodor Dostoevsky, Leo Tolstoy, Anton Chekhov, and many others.

The last wave of Russophone immigration to Brazil began in the 1990s and continues to the present day (Smirnova Henriques & Ruseishvili, 2019). Today Russians are among the top 15 nationalities that receive work permits in Brazil (Quintino & Tonhati, 2017), and they also come to study or for family reasons (Smirnova Henriques & Ruseishvili, 2019; Smirnova Henriques et al., 2020). After arriving, Russophones frequently discover that Brazilians have a great interest in learning Russian. This interest is stimulated by access to translations of Russian literature (20th-century authors such as Mikhail Bulgakov, Varlam Shalamov, Sergey Dovlatov, and the contemporary writer Vladimir Sorokin are also published), by the mysterious image of Russia and the opportunity to travel there without a visa since 2010, and by the Russian cultural landscape that exists in Brazil (Dubinina et al., 2019; Polivanova, 2017).

Brazil's largest city, São Paulo, has four functioning Russian Orthodox churches, three from the Russian Orthodox Church Outside Russia (Vorobieff, 2006) and one from the Moscow Patriarchate (Higa, 2015). In addition to religious ceremonies, they all organize cultural events: concerts, lectures, Russian dinners, and craft fairs. There is a monthly cultural Eastern Europe fair in the district of Vila Zelina, the preferred region of old Russian immigration; there are also Russian singing and dancing groups.

In recent years, several organizations have held festivals of Russian cinema in São Paulo on a regular basis. They mainly feature Soviet films, but several contemporary films have also been shown, such as "Leviathan" and "Loveless" by A. Zvyagintsev, "Dovlatov" by A. German, "Leto" by K. Serebrennikov and "Sobibor" by K. Khabensky. Some international events, such as the 2018 Football World Cup, held in Russia and widely publicized in Brazil, provided an additional motivation for Brazilians to get to know Russia and its language better (Polivanova, 2017).

Even considering the major interest of Brazilians in the Russian language and culture, very little is published about teaching Russian in Brazil. In the following sections, we outline the context of teaching and learning Russian in Brazil, describe the application of a task-based approach, detail nine typical tasks that we have used in our schools, and report our experience in implementing the TORFL (Test of Russian as a Foreign Language). Finally, we conclude with overall reflections and lessons learned.

Background and setting

Courses of Russian language in Brazil

Very few Brazilian universities offer undergraduate courses of Russian: a bachelor's degree in Russian may be obtained at Universidade de São Paulo and Universidade Federal de Rio de Janeiro, both offered since the 1960s (Puh, 2020). Undergraduate students learn Russian language and literature, but do not have special courses of methodology for teaching Russian (Universidade Federal de Rio de Janeiro, 2021; Universidade de São Paulo, 2021a). Universidade Federal do Rio Grande do Sul offers optional courses of Russian (four semesters) and Instrumental Russian (two semesters) for undergraduate students of philology (Castro, 2008).

The graduate program in Russian Literature and Culture that is unique in Brazil, began to be offered at Universidade de São Paulo quite recently: the master's program was approved in 2001, and the PhD program in 2002 (Puh, 2020). In 2019, the program was reorganized, and currently this specialization is part of the graduate program in Foreign Languages and Translation (Universidade de São Paulo, 2021b). The research areas include: (1) semiotics of culture; (2) Soviet Russian prose; (3) Russian literary theory and criticism; (4) theory, aesthetics and criticism of Soviet Russian theater (Universidade de São Paulo, 2008, p. 2). The aims of the program are focused on the preparation of translators of Russian literature, and researchers in the field of Russian literary theory and criticism. Thus, the preparation of teachers of Russian as a Foreign Language and research in the field of methodology of teaching Russian are not mentioned in the priorities.

The most common form of teaching Russian in Brazilian universities is to offer extension courses for the general public (Castro, 2008). These courses accept all interested applicants who pay a fee and matriculate for one semester to attend one class session per week. The programs of these courses are approved at departmental level, and they can be given by graduate students and postdoctoral researchers. Their realization depends on the number of interested people: there is usually a minimum number of students to open a class.

In addition to Universidade de São Paulo with its program *Russo no Campus* and Universidade Federal de Rio de Janeiro, such extension courses are offered by Universidade Estadual de Campinas, Universidade Federal Fluminense, Universidade Federal de Minas Gerais, Universidade Federal de Paraná, Universidade Federal do Rio Grande do Sul, and by some private universities, such as Pontifícia Universidade Católica do Rio Grande do Sul and Pontifícia Universidade Católica de São Paulo. This list is probably incomplete because there is no official centralized list of extension courses in Brazil. Some of them have just one module restricted to teaching the Cyrillic alphabet and are not offered each semester. As far as we know, courses of Russian are not offered in Brazilian general education schools in a regular manner.

In this situation, many Brazilians look for Russian courses in private language schools (Dubinina et al., 2019, 2020), which are the object of the present chapter. São Paulo has four language schools that teach Russian, Rio de Janeiro has two, and Brasilia has three; there are also language schools in Curitiba, Florianópolis, Porto Alegre, and Recife. These offerings are not sufficient, and this brings many private Russian instructors to the field. Both schools and private instructors are not limited to face-to-face teaching and offer online courses; some of them exclusively offer the online option using Skype, Zoom, or Google Meet.

Who are the teachers of Russian in Brazil?

Most teachers of Russian in Brazilian universities are Brazilians who have studied in Russia and specialized in Russian literature. Considering that the majority of Russian learners in Brazil study in private schools or with private instructors, here we focus on the profile of instructors in private education.

Most of the language schools are organized by and solely employ Russian native speakers, while only a few schools are organized by Brazilian descendants of Russophones or by Brazilians who have lived in a Russophone country. Frequently, the teachers do not have formal employment contracts or they are private entrepreneurs, which is possible only for Brazilian citizens or foreigners who have a permanent resident card. Therefore, there are no Brazilian organizations that hire experienced instructors of Russian abroad; many Russophones, especially those who have come to Brazil for family reasons, turn to teaching Russian as a job opportunity. Their professionalization is shaped by experience. Only some of them take courses for teaching Russian as a Foreign Language: these courses are not available in Brazil, and online options offered by Russian universities are expensive, time-consuming, frequently focus on theoretical aspects of teaching and accept only bachelors of philology.

Methodology of teaching Russian in Brazil

The main research focus of Russian programs at Brazilian universities is on Russian literature, semiotics and translation, and so the methodology of teaching Russian to speakers of Brazilian Portuguese remains poorly investigated and described (Castro, 2008; Puh, 2020). An important exception is the study by Castro (2008), who described phonetic interference from Brazilian Portuguese in the spoken Russian of Brazilian students, and devised some exercises to improve pronunciation.

Textbooks of Russian for Brazilians are mainly old and grammar-centered: they include "A língua russa" by Dolenga (1948) and "Breve manual da língua russa" by Potapova (1961). They can still be purchased in online stores. More recent textbooks are scarce, short, and frequently contain errors. The most complete one is the three-volume series "Fale Russo" by Castro (2005, 2006, 2007). However, these textbooks are mainly used by self-taught Russian learners; we do not have any reports of native teachers of Russian, whether they work independently or at language schools, using Brazilian textbooks of Russian. In the survey of 58 Brazilian participants of TORFL examinations (Dubinina et al., 2020), when asked about the material used for preparation, the participants cited 21 different textbooks, mainly published in Russia. The most frequent answer (nine participants) was "didactic materials provided by the school."

An important feature of teaching Russian in Brazilian language schools is the small size of groups: in-person classes frequently have just three to four students. Instructors can adapt the materials and select the themes according to the group profile. Teaching goals are set up based on students' needs: a family that wants to speak Russian with their grandfather, an old immigrant; friends planning to visit Russia; young people curious about the Russian revolution and military parades; polyglots obsessed with Russian grammar; or people interested in Russian literature or the theories of Lev Vygotsky who want to understand the Russian soul.

To sum up, there is no unique and approved system of teaching Russian in Brazil. There is no association of Russian instructors; no annual seminars or conferences focused on Russian teaching; no large choice of Russian textbooks. This opens up a space for creativity: language schools and private instructors produce their own materials and actively use Internet resources and authentic Russian websites to present Russian realia and the Russian language to their Brazilian students. In this situation, instructors are especially motivated to create conversational situations from real life, and stimulate interactions.

Another interesting fact is that more than half of Russophones move to Brazil with no knowledge of Portuguese and learn the language in everyday life activities without formal instruction (Smirnova Henriques et al., 2019). There are very few opportunities to study Brazilian Portuguese in Russia (Arefiev, 2019). The field of teaching Brazilian Portuguese as a Second Language in Brazil is also quite new, and access to language courses and didactic materials is very limited (Miranda & Lopez, 2019). The experience of acquiring a foreign language naturally seems to help Russophones to apply communicative strategies when they become instructors of Russian.

Who are the learners of Russian in Brazil?

In the present chapter, we will focus on adult learners because there is very little data about teaching Russian to children in Brazil. As far as we know, there is one language school in São Paulo and one language school in Rio de Janeiro that teach Russian to the children who live in mixed Russophone-Brazilian families. They have small groups of children and this experience cannot be analyzed in a systematic way.

The profile of adult Russian learners in Brazil is very poorly described. Following our recent report (Dubinina et al., 2020), 38 percent of the 58 Brazilian TORFL participants began to study Russian because of their interest in Russian culture and literature; 36 percent because of a general interest in studying languages; 16 percent were Russian heritage speakers. In examining the raw data, we noted that only two people stated that they wanted to work in Russia, two that they wanted to travel to Russia, and another two stated that they were interested in the history of the Soviet Union. When asked about the way that they had studied Russian, 22 percent of participants mentioned an in-person course in a language school, 22 percent self-study, and 19 percent private online classes. Additionally, 13 percent mentioned an online school and 10 percent in-person private classes; only two participants had studied in Russia and one participant had studied Russian at a Brazilian university. Another interesting piece of information is that 43 percent of the participants had only visited Russia once, and 28 percent had never been there. This analysis describes typical profiles of Brazilian students who intend to take the TORFL exam; the profiles of students who study Russian without the intention of taking the TORFL exam may be different.

There are reports about Brazilians who study Russian because they dream to travel to Russia and take the Trans-Siberian train; others marry Russians and have bilingual children and a mother-in-law not proficient in Portuguese or English; some elderly people believe that studying Russian protects them from Alzheimer's disease: none of them need to take the TORFL to check their level (Polivanova, 2017). Some Brazilians intend to study in Russia; Rossotrudnichestvo (Russian Federal Agency for the Commonwealth of Independent States, Compatriots Living Abroad and International Humanitarian Cooperation) offers fellowships to support the most successful Brazilian candidates (Polivanova, 2017). The Russian city of Kursk has hundreds of Brazilians studying medicine in English: the tuition fee for medicine courses in Russia is much lower than that of a private university in Brazil (Coelho, 2018; Polivanova, 2017). Usually, students who intend to study in Russia take a preparation course in Russian once they have arrived at their destination (Polivanova, 2017).

From our experience as Russian instructors in language schools in different Brazilian cities, we may emphasize that Brazilians have a special interest in conversation and want to communicate from the moment when they learn their first words. This is quite common when even beginner students go to a conversation club, an event, or a lecture in Russian, and interact as best they can. In fact, even for the general education school the Brazilian National Curricular Parameters (*Parâmetros Curriculares Nacionais*, PCN) emphasize the importance of teaching foreign languages through developing communication abilities (Brasil, 1998). The valorization of communication competences prepared the basis for using task-based language teaching (TBLT) in Brazil for teaching English (Lopes, 2014; Emidio, 2017), French (Oliveira, 2015), or even sign language (Lebedeff & Facchinello, 2018). In the next section, we exemplify TBLT strategies for teaching Russian to Brazilians.

Teaching Russian in Brazil through task-based language teaching (TBLT)

In this chapter, we follow the task definition presented by Skehan (1998): the task is an activity in which (1) meaning is primary; (2) there is some type of communication problem to solve; (3) there is some sort of relationship to comparable real-world activities; (4) the assessment of the task is in terms of outcome. Markina (2017) emphasizes that TBLT is mainly used for teaching English where the learner, during the message formulation, can focus on the lexical encoding; the morphological complexity of Russian demands much more attention to the morphosyntactic encoding, and this makes the task design for beginners more challenging. However, even though the speech of beginner learners of Russian is rather basic, they can solve communication problems if these are formulated in an adequate manner (Drozdova et al., 2015; Markina, 2017).

As we discussed earlier, more than half of Russophones move to Brazil with no knowledge of Portuguese (Smirnova Henriques et al., 2019). From our point of view, the experience of immigration and rapidly learning a language on the spot shapes the mind to discover real-world activities useful for language learning. Many Russian teachers also teach Portuguese as a Second Language for other Russophones and are accustomed to dealing with recently arrived immigrants who need to start working or studying immediately, or are about to meet a large Brazilian family not proficient in English or Russian. The immigrants need to organize their everyday life rhythm as soon as possible. In this situation, homework could involve studying a list of pizza ingredients and ordering a pizza; going to a street market and asking how much vegetables cost; going to an exhibition and asking other people what they like; the theme of a class could be a visit to the doctor or Immigration Services. The outcome is assessed by the success of the procedure after the class, in real life. The Russian teachers bring this "foreigner-in-a-new-world" strategy to the Brazilian learners of Russian, even though many of them do not use the term *TBLT*, which is little known in Russia. The few articles about TBLT available in Russian are recent, they focus on the teaching of English and present TBLT as a new approach to language teaching (Blik, 2015; Nuss, 2020; Tsalikova et al., 2016).

In what follows we detail nine tasks commonly applied in three Brazilian language schools. The tasks were developed before the teachers who implemented them discovered the TBLT terminology, and are reconceptualized in the TBLT framework especially for this chapter. We grouped the tasks into three categories: tasks appropriate for beginners, tasks that could be applied to cultural events, and tasks appropriate in online teaching.

Tasks for beginners

For successfully planning tasks in Russian for beginners, it is extremely important to respect the level of students' grammatical knowledge. If the students do not know all the cases, the task should not provoke them to make errors, and should be level-appropriate. At the same time, Brazilians want to communicate and interact in their first classes, which makes TBLT especially useful in this context. Three tasks for beginners are introduced in Table 7.1.

"Счет" [Counting] (Table 7.1, Task 1) could be practiced even before verbs are taught: it focuses on numbers and is used during the first classes. In the pre-task,

Table 7.1 Tasks for beginners

Title of task 1: Счет [Counting]

Task goal/s, setting of instruction: The goal is to practice counting as well as related questions and answers in an interactive manner. The task is appropriate for early beginners.
Learner needs analysis: The students need to know the numbers to take part in future market role-playing, as well as for traveling.
Type of task: focused pedagogical task.
Can-do statements:
- I can count in Russian using the numbers 1–100.
- I can add and subtract using the numbers 1–100.
- I can ask others to add or subtract using the numbers 1–100.

Assessment/s used: The students are assessed informally by their performance during the task.

Title of task 2: "Что ты делал вчера?" ["What did you do yesterday?"]

Task goal/s, setting of instruction: The goal is for students to discover what other students did the day before and answer the instructor's questions about other students (language structure: past tense). The task is appropriate for early beginners.
Learner needs analysis: the context of this exercise is the basis for everyday communication. The students expressed a desire to meaningfully communicate with classmates as soon as possible.
Type of task: focused pedagogic task.
Can-do statements:
- I can ask what my peers did yesterday.
- I can describe in three–five simple sentences what I did yesterday.
- I can understand the stories told by my colleagues about their daily routine.

Assessment/s used: the students are assessed informally in a quick Q/A exchange with the instructor.

Title of task 3: А что я прочитал ... [Look what I have read ...]

Task goal/s, setting of instruction: The goal of this task is for students to discuss the local news of a Russian city. It functions better in a group of 4–5 students. A good option is the online format by a video conference with a shared screen of the news website.
Learner needs analysis: the students' expressed interest in discussing authentic Russian news.
Type of task: unfocused task.
Can-do statements:
- I can restate in three–five simple sentences news about the life of a city from a web-based local newspaper.
- I can explain why I found the news interesting.
- I can ask clarifying questions about the news presented by other students.
- I can express my opinion about the content of the news.

Assessment/s used: The students are assessed informally by their performance during the task and in a quick Q/A exchange with the instructor.

the instructor teaches the numbers up to five, the expression "Сколько будет (a number) плюс/минус (a number)?" [How much is () plus/minus ()?] and the answer "(A number) плюс/минус (a number) это (a number)" [() plus/minus () is ()]. The task is to answer other students' questions, each student asks another and answers questions from others. During the verbal exchange, the students may exclaim phrases in Portuguese such as "Oh my God," "Just a second" or "It's coming!" The instructor writes them down and suggests Russian equivalents as a post-task. At the next class the students perform the task again, and practice using these phrases in Russian. When they are comfortable with the numbers up to five, the instructor suggests extending the scale to minus five (something that could easily happen in real life, for example with a bank account). At the next class, the activity continues, incorporating new numbers. Students taught in this way can not only use Russian numbers, but also express their spontaneous reactions in Russian.

When the students learn their first verbs, focusing the vocabulary on their everyday life opens a space for a conversation task "Что ты делал вчера?" [What did you do yesterday?] (Table 7.1, Task 2). The Russian past tense is very simple morphologically, so a conversation about something that has happened can be managed much more easily than constructing dialogues that require the present tense. Additionally, Brazilians love to share experiences. In the pre-task, the instructor sets the goal to discover what the other students did the day before. The task is performed through the conversation between the students. In the post-task, the instructor asks some of the students what the other students did yesterday. Later "yesterday" is substituted by "this week." Consistently engaged in such conversations at the beginning of each class, students expect them and search for new experiences and words, so they can report something unusual. This type of task requires students to use verbs of motion, but at this stage the suggestion to use the verbs "ходить" [to go by foot] and "ездить" [to go by transport] is sufficient: in the past tense they are regular and the context always would be "go somewhere and back" with no need of unidirectional verbs. Later, when other verbs of motion are introduced, the students already know the bidirectional verbs well and do not confuse them. This task could be modified to ask the students about what they did on each day of the week.

Another modification of this task, after introducing the construction "У меня есть/у меня было" [I have/I had], is "Что у тебя было на обед/ужин?" [What did you have for lunch/dinner?]. The students like to discover, use, and share the names of foods. When they are confident in using the names of basic dishes and ingredients, the task could be upgraded for compiling a Russian menu using websites of Russian restaurant chains such as "Теремок" [Teremok] and "Му-му" [Mu-Mu], which show many options of dishes illustrated with pictures and organized in easily identifiable categories. The students can describe their menu, show pictures when necessary, and ask other students about their options. The post-task is a conversation with students about the most popular and most exotic options.

The use of Russian Internet sites is useful for TBLT at all levels of proficiency, both for in-person and online groups. The tasks following the model "to search for some information; ask other students; share the experience" greatly stimulate communication competence. The strategy includes a pre-task instruction by the teacher and post-task discussion necessary to check how well the students understood each other and to provide feedback from the teacher. These tasks can be performed in many forms and situations. For example, to stimulate discussion, the students can use the Russian railways website to search prices and itineraries or search for souvenirs in online shops. A little more advanced students can select some news from Internet sites and present them to the group in an informal way as "А что я прочитал . . ." [Look what I have read . . .] (Table 7.1, Task 3). In the pre-task, the instructor suggests a website where students can choose and read some news at home. During the task, the students talk about what they read and ask other students questions for a better understanding of news reported by others. In the post-task, the instructor guides the conversation to find out how well the students understood each other and to provide feedback.

To avoid political and economic topics that require an extensive vocabulary, we recommend beginning with local websites of small cities, such as tv2.today from Tomsk. When students select and prepare their news, they are able to use correct constructions before they understand all the grammar behind them and can collect contextualized language structures for future use. We routinely apply this news task in an online group of certified A1 students, and each class brings surprising discoveries. In a class at the end of May, one of the students presented a news story about hot water being turned off for one month. The group could not understand the reason for this procedure, so the next tasks were to search for answers on a special webpage of the city administration, to test some addresses to discover how much time they would live without hot water if they were local residents, and suggest strategies to solve the problem. The students suggested developing a large network of friends in different districts of the city, visiting public baths, heating water in a pot, and installing a boiler or electric shower, – all of which is, in fact, done in Russia in real life.

Teaching Russian in Brazil through TBLT using Russian cultural events

Events connected with Russia and the Russian language and culture create special opportunities for using TBLT. The 2018 World Cup motivated many Brazilians to learn basic Russian for traveling, and Russian instructors developed special courses for travel preparation. In big cities in Brazil, students can go to Russian craft fairs, concerts, films, or expositions, and experience cultural immersion. The formulation of a task during the pre-task, discussion of the experience in the group, and feedback from the teacher turn "just having fun" into a learning strategy. Additionally, if the city does not have Russian cultural events, the students can simulate them using materials available on the Internet. Three tasks that can be implemented in the context of cultural events are introduced in Table 7.2.

Table 7.2 Tasks for application in the context of cultural events

Title of task 4: Пойти на ярмарку [Going to a fair]

Task goal/s, setting of instruction: The goal is to explore and practice vocabulary used at a fair (buying/selling souvenirs, bargaining, asking questions about souvenirs). This task is suitable for beginners. When the fair is simulated, it is desirable to provide some materials such as souvenirs, printed pictures of souvenirs, postcards and printed "rubles."

Learner needs analysis: students' expressed objective of tourism assumes knowing how to shop as one of the needs. This activity prepares students for traveling.

Type of task: pedagogical task in role-playing; target task at a real fair; unfocused task.

Can-do statements:
- I can ask how much something costs.
- I can say how much something costs.
- I can understand numbers greater than 100 when I hear them.
- I can understand details of the description of a souvenir: the material it is made of, where it was made, etc.
- I can give a two–three sentence description of a souvenir.

Assessment/s used: The students are assessed informally in a quick Q/A exchange with the instructor and when sharing experience with other students in the post-task.

Title of task 5: Урок-вечеринка [Party-class]

Task goal/s, setting of instruction: The goal is to share recipes using food-related vocabulary. This task is suitable for beginners. It is a real party where the students should discover how all the dishes were prepared and which ingredients they contain.

Learner needs analysis: students' expressed objectives of visiting Russia as tourists. Therefore, eating out and talking about food are their needs. This activity prepares students for traveling.

Type of task: unfocused task.

Can-do statements:
- I can list 10–12 main food ingredients used in Russian cuisine.
- I can describe in three–five simple sentences how a dish is prepared.
- I can state my personal preferences and dislikes when talking about food.
- I can propose a toast in Russian.
- I can ask if the dish is a part of an everyday meal or if it is prepared for special occasions.

Assessment/s used: The students are assessed informally in a quick Q/A exchange with the instructor and when sharing experience with other students in the post-task.

Title of task 6: Урок-капустник [A class concert]

Task goal/s, setting of instruction: The goal is to conduct a small concert in Russian. It could be applied at any level. Each student brings necessary items for his/her presentation. The instructor can print lyrics of songs that the students will sing together and have some short poems ready for anybody who is not prepared.

Learner needs analysis: Brazilian students like parties and are often very artistic. They frequently request informal activities outside the classroom and are curious about Russian music and poetry.

Type of task: Unfocused task.

Can-do statements:
- I can choose and perform a song or a poem for an informal concert.
- I can perform my piece in public from memory, without consulting notes.
- I can express encouragement to my peers.
- I can ask how my colleagues chose the theme of their presentation and tell someone about it.

Assessment/s used: The students are assessed informally by their performance during the task and in a quick Q/A exchange with the instructor at the next class.

The first task that we present in this category is "Пойти на ярмарку" [Going to a fair] (Table 7.2, Task 4). In the pre-task, students are informed of an upcoming role-play (or a real) fair and asked to conduct online research on popular Russian souvenirs, to look for regular prices of these items and to read about the history of certain souvenirs such as the matryoshka doll. They may share pictures and bring souvenirs to class if they already have some at home; the teacher provides instructions about how to bargain in Russian and formulates the task to obtain better prices. The teacher presents the Russian currency, "rubles." The task itself is a role-play that could be conducted in the classroom if a real fair is not taking place. Some students perform as salespeople and the others as customers, practicing related vocabulary. The teacher prints some "rubles" and distributes them among "the buyers"; if available, the teacher could provide actual souvenirs, along with some pictures, postcards, and Russian books. The whole classroom could be reorganized in order to represent a fair. The post-task is carried out in the form of an experience exchange. The students discuss how they felt completing the task, what they "bought," and share the expressions they used in order to get discounts.

One of the authors of this task had a chance to take her students to the real Fair of Embassies in the city of Brasília. The students walked around, visited the Russian stand, took pictures in national costumes, bargained in Russian, and discovered new food and drinks. This was a special event, and a chance to get out of the class into a real-life situation where they could practice real-life language.

Another interesting experience that we propose is the task "Урок-вечеринка" [Party-class] (Table 7.2, Task 5). In the pre-task, the students discuss the party plan as they negotiate for the music they are going to listen to, the date, the time, the location, and the food. The teacher helps by providing some basic cooking vocabulary and recommends some recipes. The task itself is performed during the party: the students should discover how all the dishes were prepared and which ingredients they contain. The people who made the food answer questions and give detailed information about the recipes. In the post-task, the first session after the party in class, the students discuss all the meals they tried and how to make them; they also compare Russian food with cuisines of other cultures. It would be useful to have some visual material, such as pictures of ingredients, and a word bank, such as a list of adjectives to describe food.

One more idea of a class in the form of a cultural event is "Урок-капустник" [A class concert] (Table 7.2, Task 6). In the pre-task, the teacher proposes to organize a small concert in Russian, which may be connected to a holiday celebrated in Russia or a memorable date. Each student prepares a performance, with the teacher's assistance when necessary. In our experience, many students choose their repertoire without assistance. During the task, they take part in a real concert that happens in the classroom. The task includes speaking with other students after the concert to encourage them and ask how they chose the theme of the presentation. In the post-task at the next class, each student speaks about his/her experience, shares the information received from other students about their presentations, and receives positive feedback and encouragement.

One such concert was conducted as a New Year event. The students were very creative: they recited poems by Vladimir Mayakovsky, Alexander Blok, and even Nika Turbina, reported travel experiences, sang, and even danced to Brazilian music about Cossacks. The school provided Russian food and invited a Ded Moroz who spoke Russian in the style of an "утренник" (morning New Year concert for children), and gave a small souvenir to each student after the presentation. To carry out this task, the instructor should be sure that the students feel comfortable performing. The instructor should prepare some simple poems that are easy to recite as an alternative for students who cannot prepare something on their own.

All the tasks related to the participation in cultural events aim primarily to improve communication competence and to minimize anxiety when trying to construct a correct phrase. They also encourage students to get to know Russian culture better. When the students are exposed to cooking or reciting poetry, the assessment should be very tactful and positive, to stimulate further interest in new Russian "insider" experiences: the focus should be on the communication achievement and not on the quality of the food or the artistic presentation.

Teaching Russian in Brazil through TBLT online

Brazilian students actively use WhatsApp and Instagram, and most teachers create WhatsApp groups with their students to motivate them through online communication. The social networks allow students and instructors to stay in touch, send tips, cultural information, news, photos, memes, podcasts, videos, and other "sparks" to provoke a conversation. In the groups, students can also clear up their doubts, and they often start conversations with classmates or teachers about the weather, holidays in Brazil and Russia, and other topics. To stimulate the conversation, the students may be asked to provide recipes (they can send the recipe, cook, and post the photo described in Russian); to give recommendations on films to watch over the weekend; to record their own podcasts; to share Russian songs they like. These tasks create an atmosphere of having a Russian friend and stimulate the students to take part in the activities and get feedback without the unpleasant feeling of being evaluated.

Some Brazilians live in cities where Russian cultural events are very rare or non-existent, and there is no opportunity for face-to-face interaction with Russophones. These students only have contact with the Russian language in classes, sometimes private, where interaction is limited to the student-teacher pair. In these cases, developing strategies to simulate a real-life situation is especially important. In Table 7.3, we show in what follows some examples of tasks that can be implemented online.

Table 7.3 Tasks for online application

Title of task 7: Заказываем еду в интернете! [Ordering food online]

Task goal/s, setting of instruction: The goal of the task is to create a list for an iFood order from the website of a Russian restaurant. The task is appropriate at beginner to intermediate levels. The teacher shows a website of a Russian restaurant, and the students write down a list of choices from the site.

Learner needs analysis: Students repeatedly expressed interest in typical Russian food. This activity also prepares them for traveling.

Type of task: Focused task

Can-do statements:
- I can read the menu and make a list of what I want to order.
- I can compare my classmates' lists with mine.
- I can talk about food I like and dislike.
- I can talk about my experience with Russian food.
- I can discuss the prices of food.

Assessment/s used: the students are assessed informally with a chat in a quick Q/A exchange with the instructor.

Title of task 8: Приходите в гости! [Come visit me!]

Task goal/s, setting of instruction: The goals of the task are 1. to explain to a classmate how to get to your home from the bus/metro station by sending an audio WhatsApp message and 2. to understand a classmate's message. The task is oriented to the intermediate level.

Learner needs analysis: After learning verbs of motion, students often feel a lack of practice of these verbs in real situations, so we create this situation in this task.

Type of task: Unfocused target task.

Can-do statements:
- I can say how far my home is from the bus/metro station and how long it takes to get there.
- I can give directions using the verbs идти, прийти, перейти, обойти, дойти, пройти etc. and prepositions в, на, к, у, от, из, с, вокруг, за, через etc.
- I can describe the places someone can see on the way to my house.
- I can trace the route on the map according to or following my classmates' directions.
- I can read the map, signs, and distances and say if a location is near or far.

Assessment/s used: the students are assessed informally with a chat in a quick Q/A exchange with the instructor.

(Continued)

112 Smirnova Henriques et al.

Table 7.3 (Continued)

Title of task 9: Почему вы опоздали? [Why are you late?]

Task goalls, setting of instruction: The main purpose of the task is to practice the common situation of being late to class, and how to talk about situations that worry the students. The task is oriented from beginner to intermediate level.

Learner needs analysis: Students are sometimes late or have to miss a class, so they need some constructions to explain the reasons to the teacher in Russian.

Type of task: unfocused pedagogical task.

Can-do statements:
- I can write one or two short sentences stating why I am late.
- I can ask my classmate to communicate a message to the instructor.
- I can discuss the most common reasons for being late.
- I can help my classmates brainstorm solutions to the problem of being late.

Assessment/s used: the students are assessed informally with a chat in a quick Q/A exchange with the instructor.

One of the tasks is "Заказываем еду в интернете!" [Ordering food online] (Table 7.3, Task 7). In the pre-task, a teacher can show some traditional Russian food, talk about the food he/she misses in Brazil and ask students about their food preferences. Then the teacher shows a website of a Russian restaurant, with a well-presented menu displaying pictures and prices. One possible discussion topic is to find special menus, such as vegetarian, gluten-free, and special cuisine and to discuss if it is easy to find these options in Russia. In a group, everybody writes down a list of what they want to order, choosing from the site. In the task, the students send their lists on messenger to the teacher and say what their classmates have ordered and how much it would cost. An optional additional topic would be the price and time of delivery. In another modification of this task, the students send their lists to the group chat. After this, the teacher says that the orders were mixed up and that student A has received the order of student B. Then the students have to say if they agree to accept this wrong order or not, say why they can't accept it, and what they did and didn't order. In the post-task, the strategies and constructions used in the task are discussed.

Another task is "Приходите в гости!" [Come visit me!] (Table 7.3, Task 8). In the pre-task, the students use a Google Maps service to listen to the directions: how to go from the station to our school building. Then students work in pairs performing the task: one explains the route to his/her home and the other makes notes on the map online and asks further questions. Then the second student shows the map and explains where he/she came from using those directions. In the post-task, the class discusses whether the destinations were reached and if not, what should be explained differently. There may also be a competition for who is the fastest to get to the same place.

The last task is "Почему вы опоздали?" [Why are you late?] (Table 7.3, Task 9). In the pre-task, the students listen to an audio clip where a person explains a reason for being late. The task is to discover if other students are frequently late to classes and why. The students write their messages and send them to the group chat or to each other. In the post-task, they read their classmate's messages to the teacher and the group. The group discusses the results, the reactions, and the seriousness of the reasons. The teacher can ask the students if they experience many traffic jams and how they organize their routine in the morning. The students can propose and discuss ways of solving the problem of being late to their colleagues. Another important point is to discuss with the students the level of acceptability of the excuses in Russia and in Brazil; for instance, Russian speakers would not give reasons such as "I overslept" or "I had diarrhea," while Brazilians may not see a problem with these excuses. On the other hand, Brazilians may not easily accept a non-specific excuse such as "I had a health problem" or "I was busy."

The TORFL in Brazil

The Test of Russian as a Foreign Language (TORFL) is called *Тест по русскому языку как иностранному* in Russian, with the acronym *ТРКИ*; the transliteration of the Russian abbreviation TRKI is also commonly used in English. The TORFL is a language proficiency test developed in the 1990s in accordance with the standards of the Ministry of Science and Higher Education of the Russian Federation (Glazunova et al., 2017). It is based on the Common European Framework of Reference (CEFR) principles, and the certificate is recognized worldwide (Council of Europe, 2018). A TORFL certificate (according to the requirements for the level) is required for foreign citizens intending to enroll in a Russian university, to work there, or to hold positions in companies cooperating with Russian partners. An opportunity to take an official Russian language exam motivates students even at beginner levels, and encourages them to learn more about Russian language and culture.

Current coursebooks developed in Russia and abroad are mainly CEFR- and TORFL-oriented. TORFL exams are held in more than 30 countries of Europe (Denmark, Germany, Great Britain, Greece, Italy, Norway, Netherlands, Poland, Serbia, and others) and Asia (China, Japan, South Korea, Turkey); however, little is known where and how often these exams are held in the countries of North and South America (Dubinina, 2020). The first large TORFL session in Brazil was conducted in 2018 by the Language Testing Centre of Saint Petersburg State University (SPBU) and three Brazilian language schools (Dubinina, 2019).

At present, the SPBU Language Testing Centre has a partnership with six Brazilian language schools in São Paulo, Rio de Janeiro, and Brasília (Dubinina, 2020). By the end of 2019, three TORFL exam sessions with a total number of 112 exam participations were conducted in three cities of Brazil. Information about the dates and places of the exams was posted on social networks in advance, and it did not matter whether the test taker was attending a course at a language school or not. Everybody who wanted to take the examination could do so after the registration procedure and were offered to take a placement test. In the majority of 112 exams that were given (89 percent), the test takers succeeded and obtained their certificates.

When asked about the motivation to take the TORFL, 59 percent of 58 Brazilian test-takers who filled out the questionnaire reported a wish simply to check their level of Russian. Considering other common answers, 14 percent of the test-takers followed the recommendation of their teachers, 14 percent believed it would be helpful to advance their career, and 5 percent intended to study in Russia (Dubinina, 2020). The wish to check their level is most common because in Brazil many Russian learners only have the opportunity to speak Russian with their teachers; in addition, all the language schools and private teachers use different materials, often individually adapted to the students' requirements. For language schools and private teachers, this is a great opportunity to provide an official document that confirms the learners' achievements. Each school can issue a document such as a diploma or certificate on their own letterhead confirming that a student has passed a course; however, a third-party assessment, especially from the country of the target language, gives special weight to the certification.

TORFL includes 6 levels from A1 to C2: Elementary Level Test (ELT) /A1, Basic Level Test (BLT)/A2, TORFL-1/B1, TORFL-2/B2, TORFL-3/C1, and TORFL-4/C2 (Appendix A). Each level test consists of 5 subtests: Speaking, Writing, Listening, Reading, and Grammar and Vocabulary. In this chapter, we focus on the Speaking subtest: it is based on an action-oriented approach and is aimed to assess communicative competence in various domains of language use and communicative situations, depending on the proficiency level. We would like to discuss ELT/A1 and BLT/A2 levels, as they are the lowest in the system in which most students struggle with speaking. In Brazil, students most frequently apply for the level ELT/A1 (Dubinina et al., 2020). This level could be characterized as "survival Russian." The learners mostly take this level exam to evaluate their progress before preparing for the higher levels. The BLT/A2 certificate certifies that its holder can communicate in basic everyday situations. The level is sufficient for obtaining citizenship of the Russian Federation, a work or residence permit. The ELT/A1 and BLT/A2 communication topics concern the speaker him-/herself, his/her home, family, friends, and job or studies. The most typical communication situations within the exam are supposed to occur during shopping, traveling, using public transportation, eating out, travelling around the city, going to the doctor, or visiting a pharmacy. The communicative tasks include: introducing oneself, greeting people and saying goodbye, saying thank you, apologizing, asking questions and giving information concerning people, developments and events, expressing a wish, inviting somebody, making a suggestion, agreeing or disagreeing (Appendix B, Tables 7.B1 and 7.B2).

The ELT/A1 and BLT/A2 Speaking subtests consist of two parts covering production and interaction activities (Antonova et al., 2018, 2019). The first part consists of two blocks. In the first block, the candidate takes part in a dialogue and answers the examiner's questions. The questions mostly concern personal topics (such as "Сколько времени вы изучаете русский язык?" [How long have you been studying Russian?]), and the situations are chosen according to typical everyday contexts (such as "Вы в ресторане. Закажите обед" [You are in a restaurant. Order a meal]). In the second block, the candidate initiates a dialogue according to situations offered by the examiner, such as "У вас есть новый коллега – он недавно в вашем городе и ничего здесь не знает. Расскажите ему о магазинах" [You have a new colleague who is new to your city. Tell him/her about shopping in the city]. In the last part of the subtest, the candidate prepares a monologue according to a communicative task. The topics for the monologues generally concern personal topics, such as "Что и где я люблю покупать" [What do I like to buy, and where?].

The assessment criteria for the ELT/A1 and BLT/A2 Speaking subtests, as described by Lazareva (2013), include interaction skills and production skills. The assessment is focused primarily on the communicative achievement criterion. For example, the task based on situations gives 5 or 6 points for each situation; a communicatively irrelevant error (e.g., errors in verbal conjugation or declination of nouns that don't affect communication) costs 0.5 points. The detailed description of the TORFL assessment scheme is of importance only for specialists dealing with the language assessment; however, an awareness of the proportion between these two parameters would be important for language teachers to avoid paying too much attention to grammatical errors while the group is working on communicative tasks.

The TORFL Speaking subtest at the ELT/A1 and BLT/A2 levels sometimes becomes the most challenging part of the exam for the test-takers. The reason is the lack of practice when the language is learned outside the target language country. Nevertheless, Brazilian test-takers appeared to be rather proficient speakers for the beginners' levels and could cope with tasks involving spontaneous speech. We may assume that one of the important factors of good performance in the Speaking subtest is primarily focusing on communication and not on possible grammar or vocabulary errors. Along with the third testing session held in Brazil at the end of 2019, we conducted seminars for Russian learners interested in knowing more about TORFL in São Paulo and Brasília. Even the ELT/A1 and BLT/A2 level learners took part in public discussions according to their level, interacted with other students quite easily and used only Russian, without support in Portuguese. We consider our intention to develop students' speaking skills in Russian worth reporting and believe that student success is linked to applying the communicative approach, including TBLT.

Conclusions and lessons learned

In this chapter, we describe the situation of teaching Russian in Brazil, which is very different from the U.S. and European models, and offer material for reflection about the place and strategy of TBLT in language schools and private teaching. Many Russian instructors in Brazil use TBLT intuitively and do not have access to structured information about the strategy. Here we share some types of tasks that function well for beginners. The students role-play both everyday situations (for example, talking about how their day was, asking directions, apologizing for being late, making an iFood order) and situations especially rich in cultural context, connected with the commemoration of memorable dates, cooking Russian food, buying Russian souvenirs, or discussing local news from Russian cities.

TBLT is widely used in Brazil, and the good results of Brazilian students in the TORFL Speaking subtest (especially considering that they do not have many contacts with Russia) show that this strategy is efficient for the development of communicative abilities. Careful planning makes TBLT in teaching Russian as efficient as for other languages with less morphological complexity: the challenge is to not to scare the students with grammar, and to find simple but real forms to communicate in an efficient way. Here, the use of focused tasks is of great help. We consider that focusing on the communicative task and not on grammatical accuracy helps learners to develop fluency. The assessment in the TORFL speaking subtest is focused on the communicative achievement criterion, and we find TBLT to be quite effective preparation for students taking the TORFL examination. In addition, some recent data collected on Russian learners from Universidad de Barcelona, mainly native speakers of Catalan and Spanish, show that the TBLT was effective in improving the grammar score on the use of verbs of motion both in oral and written performance (Markina, 2018). This was observed both at the immediate post-test and delayed post-test. In these experiments, the accuracy of oral production was also improved for one of two presented tasks, a map task which had the aim to give directions. When higher lexical complexity and developing oral fluency are expected of the learners, data on improving the grammar scores and accuracy open a space for further investigation of the applicability of TBLT.

Brazilian learners of Russian who study at language schools prefer the communicative approach: they are frequently motivated by the idea to travel to Russia and are excited about speaking Russian in situations that imitate real-life activities. However, there are some challenges the teacher should address.

The first challenge is the implementation of tasks in mixed groups of students with different proficiency levels. This may happen, for example, at conversation clubs, which are common in Brazilian language schools, and open for all levels. When some students are much more proficient in speaking than others, they may speak very rapidly and use an extensive vocabulary that other students do not know. This has the potential to demotivate the beginners: they may not understand the discussion and think that they will never be able to speak Russian. The teacher must control the situation and guarantee a space for beginner students without demotivating advanced students. This could be achieved by recasting the speech of the advanced student and asking the beginners what they think about the issue. Another situation is when a new student arrives who has studied Russian in a different way and is not used to speaking. These students need some time and help from the teacher to feel confident.

The second challenge is situations when students would become so excited about the discussion topic that they switch to Portuguese and stop using the target language, overwhelmed with emotions. In this case, our suggestion is to write some target vocabulary on the board and to repeat what they are saying in Russian. However, this problem is especially difficult to control in groups of elderly people that learn Russian as a way to keep social contacts and to improve their memory. The situation becomes even more difficult when some of them have hearing impairments. The strategy of teaching elderly people should be carefully planned according to their goals.

It is important to keep in mind that TBLT should be learner-centered. On many occasions, we have had productive classes that completely deviate from what was planned. The students themselves can propose excellent tasks spontaneously and naturally, and the teacher should simply pay attention to learners' needs and proposals.

Acknowledgments

Dr. Smirnova Henriques is supported by Brazilian postdoctoral fellowship PNPD/CAPES (*Programa Nacional de Pós-Doutorado da Coordenação de Aperfeiçoamento de Pessoal de Nível Superior*) for her project of studying Russian-Brazilian Portuguese bilinguals. We are grateful to Dmitry Ptyushkin, Director of Language Testing Center of Saint Petersburg State University, for his assistance in our work on this paper and for support of Russian language testing in Brazil. We thank Dr. Nataliya Karageorgos, Assistant Professor of the Practice in

Russian, East European, and Eurasian Studies at Wesleyan University, and Dr. Sandra Madureira, Professor of the graduate program in Applied Linguistics and Language Studies at Pontifícia Universidade Católica de São Paulo/PUC-SP, for helpful discussions. We also thank Simon Patterson for the careful revision of the manuscript.

Appendix A

Table 7.A.1 Correspondences between CEFR, TORFL, and ACTFL levels

CEFR, Common European Framework of Reference for Languages	TORFL, Test of Russian as a Foreign Language	ACTFL, American Council on the Teaching of Foreign Languages
A1	Elementary Level (Elementary Level Test – ELT)	Novice Low Novice Mid Novice High
A2	Basic Level (Basic Level Test – BLT)	Intermediate Low Intermediate Mid
B1	First Level (Test of Russian as a Foreign Language First Level – TORFL-I)	Intermediate Mid Intermediate High
B2	Second Level (Test of Russian as a Foreign Language Second Level – TORFL-II)	Intermediate High Advanced Low
C1	Third Level (Test of Russian as a Foreign Language Third Level – TORFL-I)	Advanced Mid Advanced High
C2	Fourth Level (Test of Russian as a Foreign Language Third Level – TORFL-I)	Advanced High Superior Distinguished

Source: Adapted from ACTFL, 2016; Council of Europe, 2018; Glazunova et al., 2017

Appendix B

Table 7.B.1 Conversation topics for TORFL elementary level test /A1 and basic level test /A2

Elementary Level Test /A1	Basic Level Test /A2
"My Family and I"	"My Working Day"
"Shopping"	"My Studies or my Work"
"Cafe and Restaurant"	"My Day Off and my Holiday"
"At the University"	"Famous People of Russia and my Country"
"At the office"	"Russian Traditions"
"Leisure Time"	"My Lifestyle and my Hobby"
"Personal and National holidays"	"Health and Medicine"
"Travel"	"Countries and Cities"
	"Human Nature"

Source: Adapted from Glazunova et al., 2017

Table 7.B.2 Communication tasks for TORFL ELT/A1 and BLT/A2

Elementary Level Test /A1	Basic Level Test /A2
Production: A learner can speak about his or her biographical facts, family, usual leisure activities, holidays, studies or work etc. **Interaction:** A learner can introduce him- or herself, take part in a short and simple telephone conversation and take part in a short and simple conversation in public places; talk to waiters, shop assistants etc.; express opinion on situations, facts, people; greet or thank someone, say goodbye; initiate and keep a conversation.	**Production:** A learner can speak about his or her schedule, holidays, his or her home country, famous people of his or her country and Russia. **Interaction:** A learner can express request, wish, permission or prohibition, advise and suggestion; ask for advice, thank someone, apologize and respond to someone's appreciation or apologize etc.; introduce him or herself and others both in formal and informal situation; take part in formal and informal conversations on telephone or Skype; discuss leisure time plans; talk to employees of various institutions and people in public places; discuss health problems with a doctor.

Source: Adapted from Glazunova et al., 2017

Chapter 8

Task-based learning in the "grand simulation" context

Six principles for success from isolated immersion programs

Sara Nimis, Natalia V. Krylova, and Iuliia Fedoseeva

Chapter summary

This chapter draws on the pedagogy of teaching Russian as a foreign language developed at Concordia Language Villages (CLV; MN, U.S.). The communicative, task-based approach to foreign language teaching and learning has been practiced at CLV long before the emergence of the respective method and theory, and over the course of several decades, has been effectively implemented in various students' groups, as well as linguistic and cultural contexts. The retrospective analysis of Concordia's unique method of instruction is organized in this paper around the six major principles and core concepts of the *CLV Way*, namely, giving learners courage, learner investment, linguistic and cultural authenticity, creating a need to communicate, and experiencing language learning within the context of extended projects. These principles are enacted through a series of task-based assignments, as well as the unique learning environment of *Concordia's* Russian Village. This chapter illustrates the diverse ways in which the six principles of the CLV grand-simulation model are fostering task- and project-based learning with an in-depth discussion of the intelligence gathering simulation and the immigration simulation project.

Краткое содержание главы

Данная статья содержит анализ многолетнего опыта преподавания русского языка как иностранного, который был накоплен в образовательном учреждении "Языковые деревни Конкордии" (США, штат Миннесота) начиная с 1960-х гг. Практика коммуникативного преподавания иностранных языков с опорой на целевые задания сложилась в Конкордии задолго до теоретического оформления этого метода и была апробирована в различных языковых контекстах и студенческих аудиториях. Ретроспективный анализ этого опыта предлагается в данной статье в свете шести ключевых принципов, составляющих основу уникального метода Конкордии, а именно: воспитание языкового бесстрашия; активное вовлечение в процесс; языковая и культурная аутентичность; создание коммуникативных ситуаций; живой опыт использования языка; преподавание через развернутые учебные проекты. Реализация этих принципов иллюстрируется на примерах целевых

DOI: 10.4324/9781003146346-8

заданий программы "Русской языковой деревни", разработанной для детской и взрослой аудитории, в частности, симуляции сбора разведывательных данных и симуляции иммиграционного процесса.

Introduction

The goal of task-based learning in world language instruction is to allow students to practice applying language structures to realistic scenarios. Task-based curricula are built around processes and communication, with student understanding of vocabulary and grammatical concepts developing as a result of their efforts to accomplish often non-linguistic goals (Lai & Li, 2011). Richards (2006) outlines a few key characteristics of language-learning activities in a task-based curriculum: learners depend upon their existing language resources; the outcome is something besides learning about the language; tasks are built around meaning; and learners must use communication strategies and skills to accomplish the task (p. 31). This definition leaves significant space for different approaches in the design and implementation of tasks that teach languages, with some approaches yielding better results in terms of student motivation and engagement and measured proficiency gains.

While the concept of task-based learning has been around for some time (Prabhu, 1987), it has been in practice at the Concordia Language Villages (CLV) since its inception in 1960, long before the very term "task-based learning" and the respective theory about it were developed. Concordia Language Villages programming takes place on eight isolated, culturally authentic teaching sites, called "Villages" nestled on 800 acres of woodland in Northern Minnesota. It offers an isolated environment for immersion programs in fifteen languages, designed for different age groups and levels of language proficiency. The same model was applied to customized training for military linguists at the Language Training Center (LTC), which was established in 2016 with funding from The Defense Language and National Security Education Office (DLNSEO). This unique learning environment satisfies the requirements for task-based learning and serves as a catalyst of resources needed for meeting real-life cultural and linguistic challenges.

A review of the literature on task-based learning (Lai & Li, 2011) found common threads in challenges that researchers report while observing the implementation of task-based curricula. Teachers often struggle to design tasks that feel authentic to students, to create the sense of a genuine need to communicate, when students and teachers are aware that they are in a language classroom. Students in a classroom often expect to take on the more passive role of receiving instruction provided by the teacher. Teachers encounter the opposite problem when students find tasks exciting, but the language is not adequately integrated into design to prevent students from resorting to their first language to accomplish their goals. In other cases, younger students have been observed to get so excited by the invitation to creatively engage that they lose focus or even present discipline problems. Finally, task-centered language learning is most effective when designed to be challenging but not frustrating for groups of mixed proficiency levels (Lai & Li, 2011).

Teaching principles at Concordia that make tasks powerful learning experiences

These common challenges are alleviated in an isolated immersion environment in which learners, cut off from the English-speaking world, must use the target language to meet even their most basic needs. The so-called "grand simulation" of an in-country experience may sound like it would overwhelm novice learners, however, there is an instructional scaffolding system in place to prevent that. Through extended observation of programs at CLV, Hamilton et al. (2005) identified six guiding principles that make it possible for all learners to engage and succeed at the Language Villages. These principles can also be brought into the classroom to mitigate some of the challenges that teachers face when attempting to implement a task-based world language curriculum. The following sections describe the way that task-based learning has been implemented for K–12 youth in Russian programs at CLV and for adult professional linguists at the Concordia LTC.

Linguistic and cultural authenticity

Ellis (2003, 2009) distinguishes "situational authenticity," meaning "real world" tasks such as applying for a visa, purchasing transportation tickets or ordering food in a restaurant, and "interactional authenticity," which can include classroom tasks that require interactional skills that are necessary in the "real world." For example, a genuine information gap forces a student to practice asking for information. The physical site of Concordia's Russian program sets the stage for a variety of situationally authentic tasks. The site evokes "the look, feel, sounds and tastes of communities where the target language is spoken."[1] The first thing that students see when arriving on site is a great brown, red and blue building designed to reflect a traditional wooden architectural style typical of Northern Russia. Because it houses the dining hall and teaching spaces, it is easy for students to forget that they are in the woodlands of Northern Minnesota. Another authentic teaching space is the sauna (called *banya* in Russian). Students soak in the heat, play games and drink tea or *kvas* with counselors who share personal experiences with banyas in Russia, as well as the history and practices surrounding this quintessentially Russian cultural tradition. The function of woolen hats and birch twigs are explained and demonstrated with historical context. During the introductory orientation, instructors expose students to the abundance of cultural implications the banya has in traditional and modern Russian life-styles, literature, cinema, music, social media, to mention but few. Thus, students who later attend the banya during their free time learn vocabulary and vital cultural information without even realizing that they were engaged in task-based learning.

One of the most extensive tasks in the Russian curriculum at *Lesnoe Ozero* [Forest Lake] Village is a simulated immigration to Russia. It was developed as a productional phase in a sequence of modules on Russian geography, ethnic and cultural diversity, as well as the post-Soviet political divides and migration patterns. A table of this task follows.

Table 8.1

Title of the task: Russian immigration process simulation	

Task goal/s, setting of instruction

The task is developed for the professional level (2/2+/3 – ILR) linguists with a range of field experience (0 to 30 years)

Main task goals:

- Summarize information about geopolitical, cultural, and religious diversity of the post-Soviet world;
- Familiarize students with the common roots of immigration to Russia, as well as of major migration patterns;
- Expose the participants to the challenges of the immigration procedures in Russian Federation;
- Test the students' knowledge of the past and current relationship between Russia and neighboring countries;
- Implement their linguistic knowledge for navigating complex formal situations and solving disorienting social dilemmas.

Learner needs analysis

- Students expressed a goal to better comprehend the challenges of illegal migration Russia is facing nowadays;
- Learners expressed the need to strengthen their awareness of cultural diversity in the Russian-speaking population, as well as of the official attitude towards and the societal perception of immigrants in modern-day Russia.

Type of task

Unfocused task, based on the meaning-focused use of language.

Can-do statements

- Students can navigate a variety of real-life situations related to immigration and/or obtaining a work permit, handle common social interactions and implement their language skills to obtain information and express their needs.
- Students can understand the main ideas expressed by native Russian speakers of diverse social backgrounds.
- Students can demonstrate and reflect on intercultural sensitivity in carrying out both formal and informal communication.
- Students can reflect on what went well and what was challenging during the learning experience.

Assessment/s used

This project results in low-stakes summative and formative assessments, including:

- A work permit certification, which students obtain upon successful passing through several mandatory naturalization procedures (border crossing, issuance of temporary residence permit, currency exchange, Russian language and history test, et cetera);
- Students' self-assessment in the form of reflection on their experience;
- Group discussion of the most challenging elements of the simulation process;
- The instructors' feedback referencing the achievements, addressing the gaps in learning, and guiding learners toward their further improvement (feedforward).

During the pre-task stage, each student is assigned a particular role of an immigrant and provided with a short *legend* outlining their identity: their country of origin, age, gender, professional background, marital status, and the purpose of their moving to Russia. In order to enable students to adapt to their new roles, they are provided with authentic ethnic clothing items and accessories, which Concordia possesses in great abundance. At this stage of the project and alongside the preparatory research of information, students are drawn into a transformative process of a virtual identity production. According to Kramsch (2002) and Norton (2000), identity and language are very closely interrelated. Recent developments in social sciences and socially informed language acquisition research have revealed how language development, social practices, evolving systems of values interconnect, and how this complex process may boost the motivation/investment levels and affect the overall personal growth of a language learner. In order to successfully complete this multi-level task, students need to do a great deal of preparatory research, which requires that they review the content previously covered in class and practice acquiring the proper accent and mannerisms of the character they have to impersonate.

The task phase of this activity includes a series of sub-tasks: crossing the border, arriving at the migration center, exchanging their currency into rubles at the bank, figuring out the best route through the bureaucratic maze, taking a formal test in Russian language and culture, as well as a medical exam, and finally, obtaining a work permit. For the duration of this activity, the entire office building at *Lesnoe Ozero* is converted into a large, multifunctional immigration center with an entry point set up as a customs checkpoint. Along with the formal and rather anticipated challenges, a "migrant," as a socially vulnerable individual, may be confronted with various unexpected and disordering social, financial, and cultural dilemmas. These may include: a shady illegal currency trader; a flirtatious language test proctor, a contentious doctor who is unwilling to recognize foreign medical records, or an excessively suspicious customs' officer (all of these roles are played by instructors at the Russian Village). In the process of overcoming these improvised and at times stressful micro-tasks, students are expected to maintain the proper demeanor that the identity of their assigned fictional character dictates, whether that is a 31-year-old Ukrainian taxi driver from the Donetsk region seeking a security guard position in Chelyabinsk; a 25-year-old graduate of an Armenian technical college aspiring to work as a chef in Moscow, or the pregnant wife of an Uzbek construction worker with very limited proficiency in Russian. In order to successfully navigate all the narrow passages of the simulated immigration and naturalization process, the students should not only properly represent the cultural traits of their impersonated characters, but also demonstrate awareness of the official Russian perceptions of the respective regions. For example, because Russia supports the quasi-separatist movement in Eastern Ukraine (Donetsk region), Russian immigration officials in the simulation show favoritism to migrants who list this "republic" on their forms, assuming they are their political allies. The primary "product" and outcome of this activity is the successful completion of the naturalization process when an "immigrant" receives a work permit as the main award.

In the post-task debriefing stage, students and instructors gather together to discuss their experience and share observations and insights. Based on our collected feedback, the elements of this task scenario that present the biggest challenge to the students are mostly rooted in the cultural incompatibilities, such as the difference in perception and representation of masculinity and femininity, behavioral implications of power distance, or recognition of and informed response to certain implicit cultural biases. Reflecting on similar challenges in the outcomes-based language learning environment, Corin (2021) has noted:

> Resolution of such "perspective clashes" required the engagement of critical and higher-order thinking, which is a key academic desideratum, and promoted growth toward the cross-cultural awareness and competences required for professional-level . . . foreign language proficiency.
>
> (p. 52)

Students and teachers report that the experience of taking on the identity of a socially vulnerable individual, and facing even a simulated version of the frustrations that they face is a transformative learning experience, as observed by Corin (2021). Students emerge from this experience more empathetic toward the challenges faced by socially vulnerable people navigating immigration procedures in Russia and elsewhere.

Besides providing tasks that are authentic because they have real-world relevance and complexity, staffing practices in Concordia aim for authenticity from multiple perspectives and resources (Pais Marden & Herrington, 2020, pp. 637–638). Recruitment and hiring of robust teaching teams provide participants (called "villagers") a sense of the linguistic and cultural diversity of Russian speakers. Teaching teams for youth programs hire an average of thirty staff members, while the smaller Language Training Center teams number six or seven, all of whom are first-language speakers of Russian. Instructors are selected to represent multiple Russian dialects, cultural and ethnic subgroups, as well as professional and regional backgrounds. Together, they recreate the atmosphere of the dynamic, though at times conflicting, Russian cultural "melting pot," which a proficient speaker of Russian needs to learn to understand and effectively navigate.

Inspiring courage in learners

Counselors at the Village do not use English unless an emergency arises; thus, the villagers are surrounded by Russian at all times. Navigating this environment can be confusing or frustrating, and students of all ages may be inclined to request more support in their first language (Carson & Kashihara, 2012). For this reason, challenging and complex tasks are scaffolded, with support from friendly and encouraging staff built into every stage (Hamilton et al., 2005). One participant in the LTC Russian program metaphorized his immersion experience as learning to swim in the water versus on the shore: as challenging and stressful as it was, the overall experience turned out to be both rewarding and enjoyable, while instructors served as supportive and skillful lifeguards.

This consistent encouragement is accomplished in part through a repertoire of verbal Village "traditions," which are set phrases (something as simple as "what is there to eat?") that everyone speaks together in a particular context. Village "traditions" rapidly become familiar even to novice learners, allowing them to complete the many tasks that make up daily life at camp without needing support in their first language. For example, villagers need to complete a series of small tasks in Russian before they can serve themselves at mealtimes. The Village tradition of the whole camp asking what there is to eat at once means everyone can participate, but no one is put on the spot when they are hungry. Counselors or more advanced villagers organize meal presentations that include a call and repeat introduction to the foods being served, so that everyone has a chance to practice the names of foods before they need to ask for them at the table. Villagers quickly acquire the necessary vocabulary to get delicious Russian food during the Village's family-style dinner. At the end of the meal, counselors or advanced villagers teach everyone a song that is sung together to thank the cooks. Similarly, in the LTC, daily key practices – "routines" – include reciting tongue twisters, meal presentations, a proverb, joke or word of the day. Participants have rotating responsibility for presenting these elements to the group.

Creating a need to communicate

Students coming from a teacher-centered, predominantly direct instruction learning background may hold back from fully engaging in task-based learning. By contrast, Hamilton et al. observed that the need to communicate emerges organically in the isolated immersion setting (2005). From their arrival in the Village, students are gently directed to a series of tasks that they must complete using the target language in order to get settled into the summer camp environment. As they are continually offered opportunities to engage, villagers get used to having to focus and learn in order to make friends, participate in activities, and make sure their needs are met. For example, when villagers arrive at *Lesnoe Ozero*, they are expected to complete their first task, which is to "cross the border." They have to choose a new identity (by selecting a Russian name), check in their luggage, and exchange a small amount of currency. Students who are complete beginners have to rely predominantly on gestures and cognates, which makes an otherwise stressful experience quite fun.

Even during free time, Village staff create if not a need, then many enticements to communicate. The Village store offers candy and souvenirs, but in order to buy something, villagers must first withdraw Russian rubles from the Village bank. Beginning Villagers have ample opportunities to review the essential phrases needed to complete this simple task. If they did not learn it when it was presented during the tour of the Village on the first day, they will hear villagers ahead of them in line speak the phrase while they wait their turn. Russian heritage speakers generally account for 75 percent of elementary and middle school learners at the Village and about 25 percent of high schoolers. These participants often help the less proficient villagers smoothly navigate their way through daily tasks in the first days. If beginners still need help when it is their turn at the bank, counselors will help them repeat the necessary phrase. The same is true at the Village store, where they can only buy Russian specialties such as traditional candy, drinks, and souvenirs if they have produced the magic Russian words. By the end of two weeks, every villager is able to reliably produce language needed to make a purchase.

Learner autonomy and investment

Research exploring learner autonomy (Holec, 1981; Benson, 2007, 2011; Cotterall, 2008) has suggested that learners who see themselves as having ownership in the process of meaning-making take a more active role in their own learning, resulting in better outcomes. In the immersion programs at Concordia we also observe that the learners are invested in their learning. Norton Peirce (1995) coined the term "investment" in second language learning, as an alternative to "motivation" in an attempt "to capture the relationship of the language learner to the changing social world" that "conceives of the language learner as having a complex social identity and multiple desires," in which an "investment in the target language is also an investment in a learner's own social identity" (pp. 17–18). In the past decades, Norton has further developed the idea of investment as a dynamic and complex concept in which identity, ideology, and capital are entangled (Norton, 2010; Darvin & Norton, 2016), which has become a critical concept in language education:

> Norton's notion of *investment*, a strong dynamic term with economic connotations . . . accentuates the role of human agency and identity in engaging with the task at hand. . . . In the North American context, *investment* in SLA has become synonymous with "language learning commitment" and is based on a learner's intentional choice and desire.
>
> (Kramsch, 2013, p. 195)

Our use of the term *investment* is similar to what Kramsch identifies in this quote, as a "commitment" based on learners' intentions, which can then lead to increased learner autonomy. What this means for task-based learning is that students perform better when they are put in charge of their own learning, when their background knowledge and skills are welcomed and their creativity is rewarded.

Concordia offers four-week programs for high school credit during the summer sessions. Tasks for these sessions are designed to be learner-centered and invite creativity in different ways depending on language proficiency. Novice learners conduct daily interviews with their counselors. Each day students practice talking about a different everyday topic with their teacher: where they live, their family members, and their favorite activities. Then they are sent to use their new language and have conversations with their counselors. Because they are using real language to learn about real people in these interviews, many of whom are first-language speakers of Russian, students gain a significant amount of confidence during this activity.

The task assigned to the intermediate group of learners is to create a short video with a detailed description of how to make a *buterbrod* (an open-faced sandwich), which is a traditional breakfast food in Russia. The task involves multiple phases. First, learners review food vocabulary provided by the teacher, as well as verbs of cooking, sequencing adverbs, imperatives for giving orders, and the genitive case to talk about quantities of items. Students get to choose where they will take the activity from there. They select the ingredients, come up with the best recipe, work together to make a script, and shoot a video for their peers to watch.

The advanced learners are expected to take on more challenging assignments in the form of self-directed projects. These vary from more formal tasks, such as writing a letter to the dean of the Village, to more creative activities, such as producing a TV series. These tasks include multiple steps and require students to collaborate in order to come up with a high-quality final product. Regardless of the language level, students have commented that they felt how time flew by because they learned so much without realizing that they were actually learning. One student put it this way, "I'd have never imagined learning Russian could be so much fun!"[2]

Experiencing the language

Engaging in task-based approaches within an immersion setting can create the conditions for students to develop their interactive and cooperative skills (Pinto, 2018). In the Villages, students "live the language," which means that learning is embedded in memorable experiences that enable learners to retain vocabulary and information. Villagers contrast the intrinsic motivation they feel to engage in hands-on learning with the pressure to perform on a written test (Hamilton et al., 2005). Vivid experiences like jumping in the lake after warming up in the Russian *banya* (this is encouraged, but not required) just as Russians do in the winter, participating in a Red Cross-type triage and first-aid training, or attending a live press-conference with a Chernobyl "liquidator" over Skype facilitate rapid acquisition of vocabulary and structures, but also provide context for the language learned.

One experiential task offered in the Language Training Center is a hands-on "pelmeni"[3] – making cooking class, or, as an alternative option, – preparing *Olivie* salad and a crunchy Tatar dessert "*chak-chak*."[4] Instructors begin by speaking in Russian about the importance of these foods in Russian culture and their own memories and experiences preparing and eating them. Teachers then introduce the individual ingredients and demonstrate the preparation process. Because the process of making *pelmini* is time-consuming and repetitive, staff and students have plenty of time to informally converse about their personal experiences preparing and consuming foods that are important in their culture or that of their family or region of origin. Vocabulary and structures learned during this hands-on task are thus embedded in associations with people, places, and flavors. Such meaningful mental attachments enable students to more accurately interpret and deploy similar language in other contexts.

Experiences of particular value to professional military linguists have been developed for the Language Training Center in collaboration with Military Language Instructors from the 300th MIB of the Utah National Guard, such as an intelligence-gathering simulation designed to allow students to practice drawing conclusions from a variety of authentic cultural products, as outlined in what follows.

Table 8.2

Title of the task:
Intelligence Gathering Simulation

Task goals, setting of instruction

Setting of instruction: isolated immersion or virtual immersion language training
- Proficiency: professional level (2/2+/3 – ILR) linguists with a range of field experience (0 to 30 years)
- Develop/demonstrate familiarity with cultural products associated with different social, ethnic, religious, regional groups in the target-speaking region
- Interpret/analyze cultural products and symbols and draw actionable conclusions

Learner needs analysis
- As a result of conversations with military partners, learners' needs were established to include being able to rapidly analyze various artifacts in the field to draw accurate conclusions about individuals they encounter

Type of task:

Focused task

Can-do statements
- Can draw accurate conclusions from the use of informal elements in personal communications including colloquialisms, informal greetings, and nicknames
- Can identify symbols and cultural products associated with different ethnic and religious groups across target-language speaking communities, as well as non-government organizations in the target language-speaking region
- Can read handwritten script
- Can interpret abbreviations typical of items such as receipts, tickets and coupons

Assessment/s used

Low-stakes assessment in the form of an ungraded answer sheet

TBLT in the "grand simulation" context 131

Figure 8.1 Sample personal items

Teachers set up three investigation stations, each of which included a bag of personal items, comprising wallets with credit cards and identification (passports, driver's licenses, student IDs), clothing and accessories, reading material, personal letters, invitations, airline tickets, currency, metro cards, religious materials, and personal photographs (sample items can be seen in Figure 8.1).

Students were allowed only ten minutes to examine these items in order to answer a set of questions about this person, including: name, religion, personal and professional affiliations, level of education, habits, travel history and plans for the future. Since not every item was needed to answer the questions, students had to analyze and interpret each item quickly.

The activity was followed by a debriefing conversation in which students explained to each other which items led them to draw the particular conclusions that they made. During the debriefing, students were able to reflect on certain assumptions they had made about individuals based on iconography and religion, and they explained which specific weaknesses in their language skills arose when dealing with authentic materials. Some recognized the need for more practice interpreting handwritten texts, uneven print, and formulaic expressions. This activity highlights and raises awareness of the cultural, social, ethnic, and political diversity of Russian-speaking communities. During the task and debriefing, students learned about some of the many overlapping identities of Russian speakers, on the one hand, and grew in their familiarity of cultural products and symbols associated with those identities, on the other.

Learning within extended projects

Well-designed extended projects allow students to engage in multiple, sequenced tasks to develop both their language and critical thinking skills at the same time (Laverick, 2019, p. 8). Teachers provide interesting questions, relevant authentic materials, and a general framework for the project. Students are then given a choice of how they will organize and focus their work, allowing for the needs of students of different proficiency levels to be met. Teaching through extended projects is particularly important within Language Training Center programs because of the high-stakes nature of the real-life tasks that military linguists may be called upon to perform in the field. All LTC programs have introduced extended projects to meet the high level of motivation that adult students bring to their training experiences, resulting in a wide scope of projects, tasks, modules, and cultural and operational activities.

The summative project of every iso-immersion session is a simulated Russian presidential campaign. Successful completion of an elaborate simulation of this kind requires not only a high degree of linguistic competence from the students, but also a significant level of socio-political and cultural awareness. This is exactly what propels our students' personal and professional growth and contributes to the creation of new generations of courageous and linguistically competent global citizens.

Learner outcomes

The outcomes reported by teachers reflect rapid gains in interpersonal, interpretive, and presentational skills. It is in the area of interpersonal communication where task-based learning in an isolated immersion setting delivers surprising results. Leadership at Lesnoe Ozero reports[5] that after a two-week session, a typical villager who attends Lesnoe Ozero with no prior knowledge of Russian will leave being able to exchange greetings and introductions, ask and answer polite questions about how they are feeling and the weather, and recognize whether Russian speakers are making a statement or asking a question, even around unfamiliar topics. By the end of the two weeks of building relationships and navigating the challenges of village life, villagers are able to talk about their family members, where they live, express preferences about hobbies and other activities, and recognize a time or date when plans for an event are discussed. Even villagers who are new to the language rapidly master mealtime language and behaviors. After two weeks, a villager can understand directions for setting the table, ask for food or drink and express preferences for certain Russian dishes over others. More experienced villagers are also able to order food at a simulated cafe or restaurant.

Teacher evaluations highlighted several communicative benchmarks for villagers who spent four weeks in the high school credit program, having arrived with no previous knowledge of the language.[6] Beyond the items already listed, novice credit villagers were able to engage with authentic written and listening

TBLT in the "grand simulation" context   133

materials about food and dwellings in Russia and the U.S., use this information to conduct surveys of village staff, and present findings in the target language. Furthermore, novice learners developed the ability to autonomously notice connections between new and learned vocabulary, and develop their ability to guess meaning from context and to use a limited vocabulary and circumlocution to use zero English to stay in the target language.

Teachers report[7] that villagers arriving with an intermediate proficiency and completing the four weeks for high school credit leave able to understand and engage with authentic written and listening texts on abstract topics, such as organizational environmental impact, and develop and implement a project based on those themes and issues. Intermediate students surveyed the environmental impact of the Village and drafted a letter to the dean on the topic. Intermediate students were also able to teach peers the names of Russian foods by presenting them to the Village before each meal, as well as reciting memorized pieces of poetry, and singing contemporary music Karaoke-style. Teachers report significant progress in students' ability to take part in spontaneous conversation, asking and answering questions on familiar and unfamiliar everyday and sometimes abstract topics. Students arriving with an advanced proficiency in Russian leave after four weeks being able to comfortably express their own perspective on abstract topics with supporting evidence from authentic materials they have read and listened to during in their more formal learning time (on topics including social media, discoveries in science, globalization and career choices and across genres – including reporting, debating, narrating, persuading, and esthetic discussion), both spontaneously and in the form of polished essays, oral presentation, posters and skits. They are able to ask about and respond to opposing viewpoints in language that would be understood by first language speakers of Russian, even those unaccustomed to the accent of first language speakers of English.

Language Training Center programs employing these principles resulted in measurable improvements on a computerized Oral Proficiency Interview (OPI), with nearly half of all participants from the 2019–2020 academic year (21 out of 44) improving by at least one sublevel after only two or three weeks of training. Beyond their gains in interpersonal communication, surveys of participants in the Russian Language training Center suggest that they appreciated task-based program elements for a variety of reasons. Students expressed appreciation for the opportunity to use language in a way that is "relevant to our life," with 32 participants out of 37 who responded to a course evaluation (86 percent) rating the program as "excellent" in terms of its "responsiveness to interests and training requirements." As one participant put it, "I did not feel the stress of just drilling on vocabulary, I was not so much worried about 'getting homework done' but I focused on what I was learning and using it." Students also reported that they were surprised at how much they learned from engaging in tasks in the Village setting: "I can learn just as much, if not more, in different ways." Indeed, 28 out of 37 participants (76 percent) rated the team as "Excellent" in terms of "Ability to support students' individual needs," with the rest rating it as "good." Finally, participants became so comfortable living in the target language that one reported that they "had to actually switch to speaking and thinking in English" after leaving the site.

The outcomes of task-based learning in an isolated immersion setting can be reached just as successfully in other teaching contexts. Since residential programming has been put on hold in the interest of protecting public safety, immersion programs at Concordia have moved to an online/remote format. This has forced instructors to develop linguistically and culturally authentic tasks and extended projects that create a need to communicate without the help of the isolated and authentic physical site. We are observing that online programs that prioritize experiencing the language, learner investment, and giving learners courage produce similar learning outcomes in terms of proficiency gains and student satisfaction.

Notes

1 *The CLV Way*. Access date: 01/21/2021. URL: www.concordialanguagevillages.org/youth-languages/our-teaching-methods/clvway.
2 More task-based teaching materials developed, tested, and refined at CLV are available at the following link: Ravitch, Lara and Marruffo, Sara. *Russian Homestay Simulation*. Access date: 01/21/2021. URL: www.concordialanguagevillages.org/adult-programs/educator-programs/teacher-resources/startalk-curriculum-modules/russian.
3 Pelmeni are Russian meat dumplings.
4 Chak-chak is a fried honey cake, a ritual dessert that was traditionally cooked in Tatarstan for major celebrations and weddings.
5 Summer Common Learning Outcomes (internal document) https://docs.google.com/spreadsheets/d/1GSYnZvPuN2dLp0ZXTkKlQxGs4DGcE7jC6hlzuJugeXw/edit?usp=sharing.
6 Final Evaluations – High School Credit Program, RB64 2019 (internal document) https://drive.google.com/file/d/1eIwAN0ddLLp301PV4HUWcPBF-gXV9ajy/view?usp=sharing.
7 See note 6.

Chapter 9

Использование целевого задания в краткосрочных курсах РКИ для иностранных студентов-нефилологов

Ekaterina Burvikova and Yevgeniya Stremova

Краткое содержание главы

В статье определяется подход к преподаванию русского языка на краткосрочных курсах для контингента студентов, не связанных с русским языком ни профессионально, ни в долгосрочной перспективе. Статья знакомит с опытом организации краткосрочных курсов и определением их содержания с акцентом на практических нуждах студентов, ранее не говоривших по-русски. В статье дается модель обучения с фокусом на практическом применении языка для выживания в языковой среде в виде целевых (коммуникативных) заданий. Студентам краткосрочных курсов требуется качественно иной отбор материала, его предъявление и работа над ним. Преподавание языка, основанное на целевых заданиях, позволяет сделать акцент на обучении общению через взаимодействие и введение аутентичных материалов в учебную ситуацию. Таким образом, у студентов появляется возможность не только погрузиться в русский язык, разобравшись в практической значимости отработки определенной ситуации, которая отвечает их потребностям, но и получить опыт использования языка в реальных ситуациях, что является одним из ведущих компонентов краткосрочного обучения в языковой среде.

Chapter summary

This chapter proposes a task-based approach to teaching Russian in a short-term study abroad course for a cohort of students who do not have professional or long-term connections with the Russian language. The chapter introduces the organization and content of short-term courses with an emphasis on the practical needs of students who have never spoken Russian before. The authors provide a learning model focusing on the practical use of survival language in a study abroad environment. Short-term students require a different selection and presentation of materials and activities. Task-based language teaching (TBLT) emphasizes the learning of communication through interaction and the introduction of authentic materials into the learning situations. TBLT affords students an opportunity to work through their needs in a linguistic environment through real situations and to immerse themselves in the Russian language.

Цели и задачи краткосрочных курсов

Подход TBLT, используемый в рамках программ обучения за рубежом, с одной стороны, требует от студентов максимальной концентрации внимания, с другой стороны, студенты мотивированы своим выживанием в незнакомой лингвистической среде. В зависимости от подхода к обучению, выбранного преподавателем, цели и метод обучения могут варьироваться. В коммуникативном подходе студент учится использовать грамматику и лексику (в западной методике это объединяется методическим термином form) для того, чтобы выразить смысл (в западной методике – meaning), через коммуникативное задание. Несмотря на главенство значения над формой в практике преподавания иностранных языков, в силу морфолого-синтаксических особенностей русского языка, чистота грамматики остается в приоритете: это помогает избежать коммуникативно значимых ошибок в речи, что облегчит формирование рецептивных и продуктивных навыков. Для студентов, которые изучают русский язык на долгосрочную перспективу, грамматический аспект представляет весомую важность.

В краткосрочных курсах фокус, как представляется нам, смещается. Рассмотрим приоритеты краткосрочного обучения. Практика студенческих программ за рубежом – распространенное явление. Краткосрочные программы за границей, посвященные знакомству со страной и культурой, имеют минимальную языковую составляющую, которая часто описывается как микро-курс по обучению языку для выживания. Участвующие в подобных программах обычно не заинтересованы в языке на долгосрочную перспективу, но видят необходимость изучить некоторые аспекты (например, алфавит), чтобы функционировать в обществе в минимальном объеме. Тематическое содержание курса обуславливается практической ценностью, планами студента на поездку и самыми необходимыми для адаптации в языковой среде темами, лексикой, грамматикой и устойчивыми выражениями или клише. Как показывает практика, студенты обычно заинтересованы в следующих темах: знакомство, заказ еды в ресторане, покупка товаров и билетов, поиск адреса и т.п.

В ходе краткосрочного курса студенты обычно знакомятся с азами русской грамматики в клишированном виде, так как не предполагают продолжать изучать русский язык после окончания курса. Вопрос об автоматизации и разнообразии грамматических навыков в осознанной речи не стоит. Конечно, им важно говорить правильно, чтобы быть правильно понятыми, однако навык самоконтроля у них разовьется на минимальном уровне и будет ограничен только теми сферами, в которых приложимы их языковые усилия. Представляется, что суть их "общения" сводится к узнаванию клише и их воспроизведению, запоминанию и воспроизводству материала в реальной коммуникации.

Говоря об особенностях краткосрочных языковых курсов, мы должны также учитывать следующее: и преподаватель, и студенты ограничены во времени. У студента есть минимум времени на усвоение определенного набора слов и синтаксических конструкций, у преподавателя есть минимальное количество часов на вывод и закрепление изучаемого материала в речь.

Кроме этого, необходимо с пониманием отнестись к типу студента, выбравшему краткосрочные курсы, при разработке траектории обучения русскому языку особо тщательно подойти к вопросу мотивации студента, созданию стимулов и условий в заданных коммуникативных обстоятельствах для максимально возможного использования русского языка.

В западной педагогике одним из популярных в настоящее время педагогических форм работы стал концепт открытой архитектуры (Leaver et al., 2021), который опирается на гибкость и адаптируемость процесса обучения и наполнения содержания обучения. Данный концепт применим, когда у преподавателя нет определенного учебника и траектория обучения выстраивается в зависимости от нужд и предложений студентов. Это позволяет иметь определенный набор тем в модульном варианте, которые можно менять, дополнять, изменять их очередность с учетом реальных потребностей нескольких потоков студентов. Как правило, к понятию открытой архитектуры прибегают на высоких уровнях владения языком, считая, что низкие уровни должны следовать учебникам, которые дают студентам солидную логичную языковую и коммуникативную базу, а также позволяют развить различные стратегии изучения языка. Использование принципа открытой архитектуры позволяет покрывать более широкие области языка и учитывать особенности студентов в его усвоении (Krasner, 2018). Во внимание принимается более осознанное развитие прагматической и социокультурной компетенций, анализа дискурса. Нам представляется возможным использовать концепт открытой архитектуры при обучении русскому языку с нуля в рамках краткосрочных курсов. Приведем пример: студенты, приехавшие в Россию и живущие в российских семьях, столкнутся с похожими темами в языковой среде, что и студенты, приехавшие в Россию, но проживающие в общежитии или хостеле. Тема "Дом" и "Общение с принимающей стороной" могут разительно отличаться. В таком случае, модуль "Дом" мы можем расширить за счет отработки коммуникативных ситуаций "Как объяснить принимающей семье, когда я вернусь домой", "Семья рассказывает, как использовать ключи от домофона" для проживающих в семьях, а для проживающих в общежитии или хостеле мы используем коммуникативные ситуации "Разговор с дежурным по этажу для решения разных вопросов". Как будет неоднократно представлено ниже, студенты являются соавторами курса и вносят вклад в развитие материалов благодаря тому, что обсуждают новые коммуникативные ситуации и обстоятельства, возникающие перед ними по мере вхождения в языковую среду. Безусловно, степень "соавторства" студентов-нулевиков немного преувеличена, но благодаря их погружению и уникальному опыту нахождения в среде в различных (иногда непредсказуемых) ситуациях, мы не можем игнорировать их участие в создании курса.

Кроме того, принцип открытой архитектуры открывает большие возможности в выборе метода преподавания, так как преподаватель не зависит от конкретного пособия и диктуемого им метода. Преподаватель варьирует способы подачи, закрепления и контроля материала в зависимости от целей студентов. Рассмотрим пример использования метода целевого задания в рамках концепта открытой архитектуры.

Метод целевого задания

В связи с вышеперечисленными особенностями краткосрочных курсов нам представляется целесообразным обучение РКИ на основе целевого задания. Термин "целевое задание" является переводным, в западной методике понятие "целевое задание" трактуется по-разному, например: как целевая деятельность в рамках курса; как внеязыковая задача, которую студенты должны выполнить; как серия заданий, направленных на решение проблем и принятие решение и пр.

Понятие целевого задания применяется в западном методическом подходе, который получил название Task Based Language Teaching (TBLT). Термин эквивалентен принятому в методике обучения русскому языку как иностранному понятию "коммуникативное задание". Под целевым заданием мы понимаем коммуникативное задание, определяемое в "Новом словаре методических терминов" как "вид задания, являющийся стимулом к выполнению речевого действия, способствующий <. . .> формированию и совершенствованию речевых умений" (Щукин & Азимов, 2010).

О месте коммуникативных заданий в контексте коммуникативного подхода в преподавании РКИ написано очень много работ, но массовых разработок по TBLT в РКИ на сегодняшний момент нет. Всего несколько работ западных методистов описывают использование TBLT в РКИ: Б.Л. Ливер и М.А. Каплан (Leaver & Kaplan, 2004) исследовали опыт Военного института США в рамках преподавания TBLT; В. Комер (Comer, 2007) рассмотрел использование TBLT-подхода для преподавания темы "Еда" на начальном уровне в американской аудитории; Е. Маркина (Markina, 2017) описала опыт создания целевых заданий в испано-каталанской аудитории на начальном уровне; С. Насс (Nuss, 2020) описала возможные причины и пути развития методики и материалов.

Оба термина "целевое задание" и "коммуникативное задание" противопоставляются термину "языковое задание", которое занимает *предшествующее* положение в формировании языковых навыков и речевых умений в рамках традиционного коммуникативного подхода. Стоит отметить, что в рамках TBLT языковое задание является структурным элементом *финальной* части урока. Как отмечают последователи этого метода. Р. Эллис и Д. Нунан, такой перевертыш помогает мотивировать студентов окунуться в нужную им коммуникацию сразу и не заостряет внимание на возможных и закономерных ошибках (Ellis, 2003; Nunan, 2004). Отработка полученных ошибок, связанных с воспроизведением репертуара устойчивых выражений, необходимых для выживания в среде, происходит в конце занятия. Как нам видится, отработка ошибок должна иметь место, так как, по наблюдениям самих студентов, их не всегда понимали носители языка, и поэтому сами студенты требовали определенной работы над ошибками. Ошибки, над которыми велась работа, включали в себя работу над ударением (Можно вОду? У вас есть водА?), работу над минимальной грамматикой (например, разница между "дойти" и "доехать"). Подробное рассмотрение всех ошибок было бы излишним, так как у студентов краткосрочных курсов не было цели дальнейшего изучения языка.

Резюмируя вышесказанное, отметим, что по стандартной схеме процесс формирования умения идет следующим образом: введение материала – отработка языкового знания – отработка речевого навыка – коммуникативное задание. По нашему мнению, в методике TBLT формирование умения выглядит следующим образом: введение материала – отработка речевого навыка – коммуникативное задание в группе/ в парах/индивидуально – презентация коммуникативного задания в классе – работа над языковым знанием на основе ошибок и контроля.

Опытным путем последователи модели TBLT доказывают, что данная технология обучения позволяет с первых занятий создать условия для спонтанного речевого взаимодействия, провоцирует интерес и предоставляет студентам возможность действовать на русском языке, проживать ситуации, с которыми студент столкнется во время своего пребывания в России или русскоговорящей стране.

Благодаря особенностям планирования урока на основе модели целевого задания студент усваивает необходимую для выживания лексику и грамматику, а также учится использовать в речи клише, выражающие такие коммуникативные интенции как, например, согласие/несогласие, прерывание, уточнение, предположение, изменение темы и т.д., что делает речь студента более естественной и позволяет преодолеть определенные коммуникативные препятствия.

Ключевая роль в процесс обучения на основе целевого задания отводится именно студентам: они не пассивные участники, а инициаторы общения, обмена информацией, мнением, впечатлением, выяснения причин. Преподаватель выполняет роль фасилитатора, предоставляющего студенту актуальный и необходимый для выполнения задания материала, наблюдающего за студентами во время выполнения задания, корректирующего их на финальном этапе. По словам Дж. Уиллис (Willis, 1996), у каждого из нас есть "свой репертуар" историй на родном языке, которые мы воспроизводим в подходящий момент (рассказываем, жалуемся, сравниваем, оцениваем, говорим о фильмах, книгах и т.п.). Если мы будем опираться на этот материал при составлении программы и отборе языкового материала, мотивация студента значительно возрастет, адаптация к новым коммуникативным условиям повысится, так как предлагаемое студенту содержание четко отражает его потребности в выражении себя на русском языке.

Методисты TBLT (Ellis, 2003; Nunan, 2004; Willis, 1996) особо подчеркивают, что в ходе занятия особое внимание стоит уделять большому количество устных и письменных примеров на изучаемую языковую единицу или речевое клише.

Успешность краткосрочных курсов определяется четкостью взаимосвязи между предлагаемыми целевыми заданиями на протяжении всего курса. Блоки краткосрочного обучения должны быть взаимосвязаны так, чтобы у студента была возможность повторить уже выученный и отработанный им материал в новых ситуациях.

Особенности отбора ситуаций, лексики, грамматики, коммуникативных интенций

Так как краткосрочная программа по русскому языку обычно "заказывается" университетом, посылающим студентов в страну, создатели курса учитывают следующие факторы: В каких типичных ситуациях окажутся участники курсов? Например, студенты, которые будут проживать в русских семьях, обычно сталкиваются с проблемой объяснения принимающей стороной, как использовать связку ключей или как объяснить, что ты уже наелся и не хочешь добавки. Студенты, проживающие не в семьях, а, например, в хостелах или общежитиях, могут столкнуться с ситуацией, что нужно воспользоваться стиральной машиной или узнать, есть ли спортзал на кампусе и как в него записаться. Современная жизнь предлагает новые обстоятельства использования языка. Так, все студенты сталкиваются с ситуацией, когда им надо узнать пароль от Wi-Fi.

Релевантность ситуаций и их повторяемость можно предугадать, если маршрут путешествия уже известен или хорошо отработан. Многие ситуации будут универсальными, например, заказ еды; некоторые будут специфичными для определенного города или региона, например, покупка жетона на метро в Санкт-Петербурге или покупка билета на одну поездку в Москве, или описание туристской активности в Казани и Москве. Каждое место будет требовать специфической лексики для описания местных реалий, соответственно словник каждого урока или каждой ситуации может отличаться. Как описывалось раньше, метод целевых заданий предполагает активную роль студента в создании материалов к уроку. Как нам представляется, особенно эффективно это будет наблюдаться в процессе отбора лексики. Студент, исходя из своих реальных нужд, уже находясь в стране, безусловно, постарается узнать нужные ему слова для своего уникального опыта.

Что касается грамматики, преподаватель на основе рекомендаций спектра ситуаций, в которых окажется студент, выстраивает типичные конструкции, которые универсальны и могут быть применимы в сходных ситуациях. Как мы отметили ранее, грамматическая правильность, безусловно, важна в контексте программы для того, чтобы студента лучше поняли, но в силу кратковременности своего применения может не быть идеальной. Количество грамматических форм, которые студенты должны будут пропустить через себя, остается довольно большим – это часть падежей существительных и времена глагола, в первую очередь. Лингвистическая компетенция не является целью таких курсов и дает только общее представление о языке.

Опыт краткосрочных курсов с англоговорящими студентами

Мы будем опираться на опыт проведения краткосрочных курсов с британскими и американскими студентами – 5 человек в 2011-ом году, 8 человек в 2016 году, 14 человек в 2017 г., 10 человек в 2019 г – в рамках летних и зимних краткосрочных программ, где на освоение языка для выживания выделялось 15 астрономических часов. С учетом репертуара речевых ситуаций, в которые неизбежно попадает студент, впервые приехавший в Россию, а также принимая во внимание желания и предпочтения студентов относительно содержания курса, предлагается следующий план работы, состоящий из 7 модулей. Наполнение учебного плана краткосрочной программы отличается ориентацией на функциональность (интенции, коммуникативные обстоятельства, роли и т.п.). Согласно исследованиям Х. Кубиллоса и Т. Инвенто, такой тип учебного плана эффективнее отражается на результатах обучения в сравнении с учебным планом, описывающим только лингвистическую компетенцию студентов (Cubillos & Invento, 2019). Обучение алфавиту мы намеренно исключили из описания, чтобы сфокусироваться на основном содержании обучения.

Так как языковой компонент университетской поездки в страну в своем роде типичен и имеет своей целью обеспечить определенную коммуникативную безопасность участникам, набор ситуаций стандартен. В основе использования таких ситуаций лежит их типичность и повторяемость. Практическое усвоение коммуникативных правил действий в таких ситуациях в краткосрочных временных рамках обеспечивается интенсивными дриллами. При наличии большего числа аудиторных часов преподаватель может применить более креативный подход, но, как показала практика, в нашем случае часовой минимум диктовал другие условия выполнения программы.

Ниже приводится таблица этапов работы над каждым модулем, в которой указаны тема, целевое задание, предварительное задание, вариант задания в языковой среде, а также перечислены умения и навыки, которые усваиваются студентом в ходе выполнения задания (подобный список может быть предъявлен студенту для рефлексии и самоконтроля в конце занятия).

1. ТЕМА: Знакомство "А вот и я!"

ЦЕЛЕВОЕ ЗАДАНИЕ: Берём интервью и составляем профайл партнёра.

ПРЕДВАРИТЕЛЬНОЕ ЗАДАНИЕ: Чтение текста о знаменитом россиянине.

Текст задания Вы будете интервьюировать партнера и составлять профайл.

Студенты опираются на список, в котором указаны имя, адрес, семья, профессия, хобби, спорт, еда, план). Какие вопросы вы планируете задать? Попрактикуйте чтение. Уточните у преподавателя, если вам нужна помощь. Работайте в парах.

ЗАДАНИЕ В ЯЗЫКОВОЙ СРЕДЕ	ЧТО УСВАИВАЕТ СТУДЕНТ В ХОДЕ ЗАНЯТИЯ
Во время мероприятия с русскими студентами познакомьтесь с двумя из них. Представьтесь, узнайте их имена, расскажите о себе.	Я умею представиться и узнать, как зовут другого человека.
	Я умею немного рассказать о себе (национальность, чем занимаюсь, из какого я города, что люблю делать).
	Я использую *меня зовут, очень приятно, приятно познакомиться* и т.д.
	Я знаю разницу между местоимениями "ты (тебя)" и "вы (вас)".
	Я знаю некоторые русские персоналии.

2. ТЕМА: "Всё, что необходимо"

ЦЕЛЕВОЕ ЗАДАНИЕ: Составляем список вещей в путешествие по транссибирской дороге на поезде.

ПРЕДВАРИТЕЛЬНОЕ ЗАДАНИЕ: чтение (текст о Транссибе, сколько дней группа будет ехать, что нужно в поезде, что уже есть)

Текст задания: вы собираете вещи для путешествия, вы можете взять только 12 вещей из своего багажа. Что это будет?

Лучше можно заготовить фото для визуализации. Работаем индивидуально, потом в группе. Объясняем, что берем и почему, выбираем лучший список.

ЗАДАНИЕ В ЯЗЫКОВОЙ СРЕДЕ	ЧТО УСВАИВАЕТ СТУДЕНТ В ХОДЕ ЗАНЯТИЯ
У вас есть возможность поговорить со студентами (прошлого года)/ с русскоязычными студентами, которые уже путешествовали по Транссибу. Узнайте, как прошла эта поездка, что было необходимо для этой поездки, попросите дать рекомендации, что обязательно нужно взять с собой и почему. В группе обсудите ваш багаж.	Я умею узнавать, есть ли необходимая мне вещь в наличии (у вас есть/здесь есть . . .?).
	Я умею узнавать, сколько она стоит.
	Я умею попросить продать или показать мне эту вещь.
	Я знаю конструкции "у вас есть", "сколько стоит", "покажите, пожалуйста"
	Я понимаю нормы вежливости в русском языке.
	Я знаю названия типичной русской еды и названия тех предметов, которые нужны в моем обиходе.

3. ТЕМА: "Давай пойдем в ресторан"

ЦЕЛЕВОЕ ЗАДАНИЕ: Выбираем подходящий ресторан.

ПРЕДВАРИТЕЛЬНОЕ ЗАДАНИЕ: Аудирование. Послушайте четырех человек, которые говорят о своих предпочтениях в ресторанах.

Текст задания: посмотрите меню 6–8 ресторанов, предложите каждому человеку из предварительного задания 2–3 места. Объясните, почему вы выбрали эти места.му нужно пойти . . . потому что там есть . . . /там можно). Сравните ответы друг друга. Объясните, согласны ли вы.

ЗАДАНИЕ В ЯЗЫКОВОЙ СРЕДЕ	ЧТО УСВАИВАЕТ СТУДЕНТ В ХОДЕ ЗАНЯТИЯ
Во время мероприятия с русскими студентами пригласить ваших новых друзей в ресторан. Узнайте, хотят ли они пойти туда вместе с вами. Объясните, в какое время вы хотите пойти в ресторан. Пригласите русских студентов пойти в ресторан вместе.	Я умею говорить о времени и месте мероприятия. Я знаю конструкции "давай/давайте", глагол "хотеть", будущее время глаголов, а также выражения времени. (глаголы движения "пойти", поехать" + винительный падеж"). Я понимаю ассортимент русской кухни.

4. ТЕМА: "Где находится. . . . ?"

ЦЕЛЕВОЕ ЗАДАНИЕ: Составляем план города.

ПРЕДВАРИТЕЛЬНОЕ ЗАДАНИЕ: Чтение. Викторина "Хорошо ли вы знаете город?" (5 вопросов с вариантами ответа)

Текст задания: Парная работа: студент А смотрит карту города А, студент Б смотрит на вариант карты города А, где присутствует другая информация.

На картах у студентов есть только часть информации, другую им надо узнать от партнера. Например, на одной карте написано рядом с м. Театральная – Большой театр, а на другой карте не хватает информации или названия станции или названия достопримечательности. Студенты используют вопросы: Где находится? Как дойти/ доехать до?

ЗАДАНИЕ В ЯЗЫКОВОЙ СРЕДЕ	ЧТО УСВАИВАЕТ СТУДЕНТ В ХОДЕ ЗАНЯТИЯ
На встрече с русскоязычными студентами уточните, где рядом со школой/ университетом можно перекусить, купить продукты и лекарство, посетить достопримечательности, как туда добраться.	Я умею узнавать, где что находится. Я умею спросить, как добраться до места. Я знаю глаголы "дойти" и "доехать", коллокации с предлогом "до" (например, до спортзала, до магазина, до ресторана, до библиотеки, до галереи (родительный падеж), наречия места (налево, направо, прямо, туда/сюда). Я знаю, как выглядит типичный русский город.

5. ТЕМА: "Можно билет на одну поездку?"

ЦЕЛЕВОЕ ЗАДАНИЕ: Планируем сайт для города

ПРЕДВАРИТЕЛЬНОЕ ЗАДАНИЕ: Чтение. Текст о Москве (страница сайта), разделённый на следующие части: Что стоит увидеть/посмотреть: где остановиться, где есть, где покупки, ночная жизнь, погода, транспорт.

Текст задания: Вы собираете информацию о городе N. Индивидуально или в парах составьте список мест для каждого раздела. Подумайте и запишите, что и почему можно делать там. Разыграйте диалог между туристом и работником турагентства (в тексте задания будут предложены вопросы для ролевой игры).

ЗАДАНИЕ В ЯЗЫКОВОЙ СРЕДЕ	ЧТО УСВАИВАЕТ СТУДЕНТ В ХОДЕ ЗАНЯТИЯ
Узнайте, сколько стоит билет на месяц. Купите билет.	Я могу узнать стоимость билета и попросить продать мне билет.
	Я могу объяснить, куда я хочу пойти/поехать.
	Я умею использовать выражения просьбы, винительный падеж с глаголами движения.
	Я понимаю разницу и могу правильно использовать глаголы пойти и поехать.
	Я имею представление о некоторых русских городах и их истории.

6. ТЕМА: "Извините, у меня проблема"

ЦЕЛЕВОЕ ЗАДАНИЕ: Мой неудачный день

ПРЕДВАРИТЕЛЬНОЕ ЗАДАНИЕ: Аудирование. Макс и Мария рассказывают о своём неудачном дне в чужом городе

Текст задания: Расскажите о дне, когда вам не повезло, потому что вы столкнулись с 3 проблемами

ЗАДАНИЕ В ЯЗЫКОВОЙ СРЕДЕ	ЧТО УСВАИВАЕТ СТУДЕНТ В ХОДЕ ЗАНЯТИЯ
1. Объясните дежурному на этаже в общежитии или хозяйке квартиры, что у вас не работает холодильник или вы потеряли ключи.	Я могу объяснить свою проблему (потерялся в городе, нет мелочи/билета, телефон не работает).
	Я умею использовать категорию отрицания (с глаголами и с существительными).
	Я понимаю русское слово-концепцию "удача" и его отличие от "успеха".

7. ТЕМА: "Мне очень понравилась Москва"

ЦЕЛЕВОЕ ЗАДАНИЕ: Мои впечатления от поездки (выбор лучшего).

ПРЕДВАРИТЕЛЬНОЕ ЗАДАНИЕ: Работа в паре над опросом о российских городах.

Текст задания: Первый этап: работаем в парах. Проводим опрос. Студент А по своему опросу А опрашивает студента Б. Студент Б по своему опросу Б опрашивает студента А. Используем конструкции: Как по-твоему? Как тебе кажется?

Второй этап: работаем в группах 3–4 человека. Студенты А в одной группе, студенты Б в другой группе обсуждают результаты проведенных опросов и готовятся делиться результатами с группой. Используйте слова согласен, уверен.

ЗАДАНИЕ В ЯЗЫКОВОЙ СРЕДЕ	ЧТО УСВАИВАЕТ СТУДЕНТ В ХОДЕ ЗАНЯТИЯ
Вы побывали в Москве. Сделайте презентацию на заключительном вечере.	1. Я могу рассказать о своих положительных и отрицательных впечатлениях.
Расскажите о себе. Расскажите, куда вы ходили, что вы видели, что вам понравилось или не понравилось. Расскажите о ваших новых друзьях в России. Опишите, где вы жили.	2. Я могу рассказать о своих предпочтениях 3. Я умею использовать глаголы понравиться и любить в прошедшем времени. 4. Я имею представление о современной России, ее культуре, экономике и политике.
Составьте свой рейтинг мест/ впечатлений, обсудите его с одногруппниками.	

Последовательность работы на занятии

Каждый модуль включает в себя подготовительное задание (в терминологии TBLT – pre-task), в котором студент знакомится с темой, прослушивая или читая текст, отражающий реальную ситуацию или соответствующий заданию, которое впоследствии должны выполнить студенты. Так как именно на этом этапе происходит актуализация необходимого лексико-грамматического материала, особенно важно уделить внимание подбору текстов, которые могут включать в себя аутентичную информацию, например, указатели, билет, объявления, экскурсионные буклеты с деталями экскурсий, туристические расписания. На данной стадии можно дать в том числе и модели возможного речевого поведения в обрабатываемой ситуации. Например, для модуля "Давай пойдём в ресторан" можно показать студентам флаер из кофейни с указанием названия напитка и цены, а также следует продемонстрировать и разобрать такие клише как "У вас есть капучино?", "Сколько стоит капучино?", "Можно мне капучино?" и т.п.

Вторая, основная часть урока – собственно этап работы над целевым заданием, в котором выделяют несколько уровней: работа над заданием, планирование, подготовка к выступлению перед классом и презентация, после чего следует работа над языком (анализ использованных средств и тренировка). В качестве домашнего задания студенты получают коммуникативное задание, которое они должны выполнить в среде, вне аудитории, на основе материала, отработанного во время занятий.

В начале разработки краткосрочных курсов закономерно возник вопрос об использовании родного языка учащихся: от объяснения материала, описания инструкций заданий до коррекции с объяснением возможных ошибок. Считаем вполне правомерным использование родного языка в ходе курсов для облегчения понимания и сокращения аудиторного времени на объяснения. Безусловно, в идеале было бы полностью переключиться на русский язык по крайней мере в конце курса, но, имея небольшое число учебных часов, зная специфику студентов и принимая во внимание объем покрываемого материала, думаем, что вкрапления английского языка не повредят.

Остановимся более детально на первой теме курсов "А вот и я!", разобрав ее с точки зрения принципов TBLT и методических рекомендаций по выстраиванию содержания блока целевых заданий по данной теме. Методические принципы, закладываемые в метод TBLT, описываются лингвистами по-разному. Принципы М. Лонга (Long, 2015), по словам автора, более универсальны и могут быть применимы на стандартных, не TBLT, занятиях. Принципы, о которых говорит К. Ван ден Бранден (K. Van den Branden, 2009), учитывают общую организацию курса и касаются вопросов целей обучения, выстраивания хода и подачи материала, а также оценки. На наш взгляд, принципы Нунана (Nunan, 2004) более детальны, на их примере легко выявить суть TBLT. Он останавливает свой выбор на шести концептах: 1. скаффолдинг; 2. взаимосвязь целевых заданий; 3. переработка одного и того же материала; 4. активное изучение; 5. интеграция; 6. переход от репродуцирования к созданию собственного дискурса; 7. рефлексия. Рассмотрим, как эти 7 принципов выражаются в ходе первого занятия "А вот и я!" в рамках нашего краткосрочного курса.

Первое занятие на основе целевого задания предполагает обучение студентов взаимодействию на русском языке в целях знакомства с одногруппниками/носителями языка и получения необходимой информации о новых знакомых (в группе и/или в русскоязычной среде). Для того чтобы эффективно участвовать в диалоге-знакомстве, необходимо усвоить следующие речевые формулы:

Меня зовут У меня есть Я (профессия) Я живу (адрес)
Мне нравится (существительное/инфинитив) Меня интересует (существительное)
Я хотел бы побывать (адрес) Я хотел бы увидеть (существительное)

А также варианты этих словосочетаний с формами Вы/ты (как наиболее вероятные формы для осуществления взаимодействия и решения задачи – познакомиться с носителями языка в русскоязычной стране). Так как мы работаем со студентами, начинающими изучение русского языка, предполагается, что занятие будет включать себя серию учебных задач (в методике TBLT – pedagogical task), которые будут предшествовать целевому заданию. Они будут постепенно приближать студентов к выполнению основного задания, а также будут способствовать запоминанию, усвоению необходимых слов и словосочетаний.

Во время первого блока студенты получают рабочие листы с подписанными фотографиями известных (узнаваемых) людей России или мира. Группе даётся первая учебная задача: используя конструкцию "Извини(те), у тебя/вас есть" при обращении к партнёрам, найти знаменитость, которая есть на всех рабочих листах. Студенты сразу оказываются вынужденными взаимодействовать на русском языке – трудности не вызывает тот факт, что на рабочих листах узнаваемые люди и их имена обозначены, нужно использовать только одну конструкцию для вопроса "У тебя/вас есть"). На всех листах общей будет фотография Юрия Гагарина. Последующая работа будет связана с его биографией.

Следующая учебная задача, которая будет готовить к целевому заданию, будет состоять из двух частей. В первой части преподаватель расскажет о себе (Для особого внимания выделяя голосом: "Меня зовут; У меня есть; Мне нравится; Я живу; Я хотел(а) бы побывать; Меня интересует; Я хотел(а) бы увидеть"), демонстрируя студентам опорный лист с этими конструкциями и опорными сигналами. Например, рядом с "Мне нравится" помещается фотография с изображением баскетбольного мяча или спортивной площадки. Все опорное визуальное наполнение использует интернациональные слова и узнаваемые личности. Во второй части задания студенты получают свою роль (их узнаваемая личность, с опорным визуальным материалом и конструкциями). На следующем этапе индивидуальной работы они должны подготовить монолог о себе по схеме. После подготовительной части им предлагается задание найти свою пару (муж+жена, сын+дочь и т.п.). Таким образом студенты не просто озвучивают свой текст, варьируя формы (я, меня, мне), но и решают задачу найти своего партнёра ("Это мой партнёр! У меня есть муж Брэд Пит. Это Брэд Пит").

Третий шаг – это собственно подготовительный этап (pre-task в методике TBLT), в ходе которого студенты читают текст о Гагарине. Как вариант преподаватель читает текст, чтобы облегчить студентам восприятие богатого формами и ключевыми словосочетаниями текста. Студенты следят за чтением преподавателя. После прочтения необходимо заполнить опорный лист ключевым визуальным рядом (т.е. на листе будут только фразы: Мне нравится; У меня есть и т.д.). Студентам нужно перенести из текста либо слова, либо рисунки. Для этого можно выполнять задание индивидуально или работать в парах. Далее преподаватель читает начало предложения, а студенты повторяют окончание предложения.

Работа в парах: студентам предъявляются вопросы интервьюера. Работая с партнером, они должны соотнести вопросы с ответами в тексте (вопросы преднамеренно стоят в форме "Вы" (так как, выполняя целевое задание, студенты должны будут задавать эти же вопросы своим одногруппникам). После выполнения задания преподаватель прослушивает каждую пару "интервьюер – Гагарин" или просит поменяться партнерами из другой пары и потом повторить чтение вопросов и ответов.

Так как в нашем случае студенты начинают изучать язык с нуля, **принцип скаффолдинга** (или поддержки со стороны преподавателя, выражаемая в представлении нужного для общения лексического, грамматического, коммуникативного материала и направлении деятельности студента) играет огромную роль в процессе организации курса, составлении заданий и оценки коммуникативной деятельности учащихся. Например, при стандартном подходе к обучению языку, представляемый языковой материал не всегда дается в той же последовательности и, возможно, может быть соотнесен с разными уровнями сложности и представления учебного материала на стандартных занятиях (ср. предложения типа "Это" и "Он работает в/на"). В методе TBLT внимание на значении позволяет нам включает разноуровневые элементы в один блок, целью которого является знакомство и отработка определенной коммуникативной установки. Поэтому скаффолдинг становится основополагающим принципом выстраивания траектории обучения.

Преподаватель выстраивает ход урока таким образом, чтобы вся деятельность определялась **целевым заданием**. Предварительный этап помогает студенту разобрать структурные элементы, которые он будет отрабатывать и использовать в процессе коммуникации.

Принцип переработки одного и того же материала позволяет преподавателю организовать работу тематически и последовательно, где каждое последующее целевое задание зависит от успешности выполнения предыдущего. Таким образом, у студентов выстраивается общая картина ясности элементов, ведущих к осуществлению коммуникативных установки и цели.

Принцип *активного изучения* является следствием студентоориентированного подхода. Задания требуют полной вовлеченности студентов, продуцируемые ими коммуникативные клише и ситуации предполагают определенный уровень осознанности и автономии учащихся.

Принцип *интеграции* подразумевает слияние формы и значения. Студенты работают над определенным набором клише/структур, которые при незначительной модификации помогают им выразить себя в определенных коммуникативных обстоятельствах.

Собственно целевое задание

Студенты работают в парах (преподаватель может объединить студентов в новые пары на свое усмотрение), студенты получают списки, подобные уже использованным ими в начале занятия. Студенты знакомятся со своими партнёрами (дополнительно можно ввести конструкцию "У нас много/мало общего"). Целью этого задания будет дать студентам вербальный инструмент сравнения.

После того как интервью с партнером окончено, студенты приступают к планированию своего ответа, в котором выступят с рассказом о партнёре. Для рассказа преподаватель выдает каждому список форм (он/его/ему или она/ей/ ей). Во время планирования студентами монолога о партнёре при необходимости преподаватель помогает с употреблением новых форм. Заключительный этап целевого задания – презентация монологов. Партнеры-одногруппники слушают рассказы о себе и должны услышать историю человека, с которым у них больше всего общего. Они могут дать оценку услышанному, используя ранее представленную им фразу "У нас много/мало общего". Преподаватель комментирует услышанное.

Принцип *от репродуцирования к созданию текста* представляет мастерство студента использовать язык независимо. Насмотревшись, наслушавшись, начитавшись определенных образцов, используя их в репродуктивной речи, учащиеся выходят на новый уровень, обнаруживающий их умение создавать свой собственный текст в заданных коммуникативных обстоятельствах. Безусловно, на начальном уровне создание своего текста не может быть абсолютно автономным, произведенный текст скорее будет напоминать комбинацию клише и заученных фраз.

Принцип *рефлексии* замыкает цепочку принципов TBLT и органически воплощается в обдумывании своего коммуникативного опыта, работой с обратной связью от преподавателя. Несмотря на то, что TBLT часто обвиняют в отсутствии работы с формой (то есть грамматикой), у студента всегда есть возможность вернуться к "прожитому" материалу, рассмотреть его в свете своих грамматических/лексических ошибок и коммуникативных неудач.

Таким образом, студенты за урок проходят ряд учебных задач (pedagogical tasks) и выполняют основное целевое задание (target task), в которых они постоянно находятся в ситуации знакомства, узнавания нового о человеке, вынуждены взаимодействовать с партнером и группой, а также усваивают конструкции, необходимые для передачи информации о себе или для знакомства в русскоязычной среде. Роль и функция преподавателя большую часть занятия сводится к активному вовлечению и сопровождению студентов: преподаватель озвучивает новый материал, раздаёт опорные материалы, контролирует произносительные нормы, инструктирует перед заданиями и при необходимости разъясняет инструкции. Следует отметить, что на первом занятии допустимо использование словарей и родного языка. В таком случае преподаватель помогает с переводом так, чтобы у студента получилось вместить свою мысль в те конструкции, которые у нас уже имеются. Помимо этого, преподаватель учитывает мнение и опыт студента в формировании содержания курса.

В заключение приведем несколько цитат из отзывов студентов на курс: "Инструктор предоставил нам место для разговора и создал непринужденную атмосферу, которая побудила нас активно использовать язык. Он давал нам множество заданий как во время уроков, так и для домашних заданий, которые, как мне кажется, очень помогли в развитии языка. Я считаю, что для летнего курса ее метод обучения был очень хорош". "Мы могли и нам настоятельно советовали много говорить по-русски, что позволило нам улучшить те области, которые мы разработали в автономном режиме. Большое разнообразие упражнений и их полезные темы сохраняли интерес к курсу на протяжении всего курса". "Курс был хорошо организован, с множеством интересных тем и разными методами обучения. Акцент на разговорной речи хорошо перемежался с обучением грамматике".

Подытоживая опыт составления и проведения краткосрочной программы с учетом метода целевых заданий, отметим следующее:

1. Как упоминалось ранее, большинство литературы, посвященной TBLT, говорит о том, что метод TBLT не применим для студентов низких уровней. Наш опыт показал, что при минимальном знании языка этот метод все-таки можно использовать благодаря клишированности элементов, составляющих коммуникацию на уровне "выживания". Если рассматривать обучение языку в рамках TBLT, с учетом механических отработок на предварительном этапе нам представляется такая задача доступной и осуществимой, так как студент вырабатывает навык благодаря постоянному повторению формы в клишированном виде наподобие методов, предлагающих работать, например, по схеме "стимул – действие".

2. Фокус TBLT находится на коммуникативном задании, которое отвечает прагматике краткосрочных курсов: у студента есть предсказуемый ими и преподавателем набор ситуаций, в которые он попадает за время своего обучения (например, знакомство, поиск адреса, совершение покупок, использование транспорта, решение проблем, выражение своих предпочтений и т.д.). Его цель – быстро научиться коммуникативно выживать в данных ситуациях, за счет практики именно коммуникативных ситуаций студент быстрее адаптируется к новым коммуникативным условиям.

3. Краткосрочность курсов позволяет наиболее точно и ёмко отобрать нужный материал. Во время отбора студент становится соорганизатором курса, подсказывая преподавателю, в каких коммуникативных ситуациях он постоянно оказывается в языковой среде. По мере освоения языковой среды и языковых трудностей, студенты сталкивались с набором ситуаций, характерной именно для их поездки. Например, группе студентов надо было пойти в спортзал в кампусе и получить информацию о наличии абонементов. Группа студентов, проживавших в семьях, столкнулась с ситуацией использования связки ключей

для открывания всех входных дверей и кодовых замков. Студенты, проживающие в семьях, были вынуждены научиться объяснять принимающей стороне, когда они вернуться домой вечером и когда им предстоит ужинать. Студенты, живущие в общежитии, разнообразили свой коммуникативный опыт ситуациями объяснения с дежурной по этажу о времени отбытия из общежития, вопросов по работе стиральной машины на этаже. Все эти примеры дополнительных внеурочных ситуаций были осмыслены методически, представлены студентам и отработаны в аудитории. Как видно из этих примеров, наполняемость модуля может варьироваться и расширяться за счет дополнительных ситуаций. Это положительно сказывается на мотивации студента. Как отмечалось ранее, краткосрочные курсы выступают динамичной, гибкой системой, которая способна адаптироваться под нужды студентов. Применяя принцип открытой архитектуры курса, мы даем преподавателю и студенту возможность коллаборации, что повышает мотивацию студента работать над языком в аудитории и не бояться применять язык вне аудитории.

Chapter 10

Task-based peer interaction in Russian as a second/foreign language classes

Dmitrii Pastushenkov

Chapter summary

Task-based peer interaction is an important element in many communicative and TBLT classrooms. Research has shown that peer interaction can benefit second language development and is often viewed as less stressful than teacher-student interaction. Therefore, task-based peer interaction can be a valuable addition to Russian classes. This chapter includes a discussion of prior peer interaction research and how some of the learners' individual differences may affect the effectiveness of communicative tasks. Drawing upon the author's experiences teaching and researching Russian as a foreign language in various environments, the chapter concludes with the description of peer interactive activities that Russian instructors may adopt in their classes. The activities are aimed for use in Russian classes in immersion programs, K–12 settings, and at a university level.

Краткое содержание главы

Групповые задания являются важным элементом в коммуникативном и задачном подходах к обучению иностранным языкам. Исследования показали, что взаимодействие между студентами может способствовать усвоению иностранного языка и часто является менее стрессовым для студентов, чем взаимодействие с учителем. Взаимодействие с другими студентами на основе задач может быть ценным дополнением к урокам русского языка. Данная глава включает в себя анализ исследований на тему взаимодействия студентов и некоторых индивидуальных различий, которые могут повлиять на эффективность коммуникативных задач. Глава основана на опыте автора в преподавании и исследованиях в области русского языка как иностранного в различных учебных заведениях и включает описание интерактивных задач, которые преподаватели русского языка могут использовать в своих занятиях. Задачи предназначены для использования на уроках русского языка в программах языкового погружения, школах и университетах.

DOI: 10.4324/9781003146346-10

Introduction

Peer interaction has become an essential element in many communicative and task-based second and foreign language (L2) classrooms (Loewen & Sato, 2018; Philp et al., 2014; Sato & Ballinger, 2016). Various researchers have suggested that task-based peer interaction can foster learners' focus on lexis (Pastushenkov et al., 2020) and form (Philp et al., 2010; Swain & Lapkin, 1998). Despite the rich insight provided by previous peer interaction research, these studies have primarily focused on more commonly taught languages such as English (e.g., Loewen & Isbell, 2017; Loewen & Wolff, 2016) and French (e.g., Philp et al., 2010; Swain & Lapkin, 1998, 2000). Less is known about how learners of Russian and other Less Commonly Taught Languages engage in a peer dialogue while working on communicative tasks. The present chapter discusses task-based peer interaction from both theoretical and pedagogical standpoints. It includes information about prior peer interaction research and the role of learners' peer familiarity and first language (L1) use in interactive tasks. The chapter concludes with the description of communicative activities (consensus task, conversation, spot-the-difference task, interview activity, and the role-playing game "Mafia") for Russian as a L2/FL classes at different proficiency levels.

Peer interaction in second/foreign language classrooms

Research has shown task-based peer interaction can facilitate L2/FL development (Philp & Iwashita, 2013) and learners often view it as less stressful than teacher-student interactions (Sato, 2013). Peer communicative tasks create a platform where learners can experiment with the language, as they tend to be less afraid to make mistakes (Philp et al., 2014). Peer interaction is a source of modified interactional input and peer feedback (Philp & Iwashita, 2013; Sato, 2013), and engaging in task-based peer interaction gives learners the opportunity to receive linguistic input, a key component to language development (Gass, 2017). Task-based peer interaction also gives learners more time to process linguistic input and output (Loewen & Sato, 2018). As a result of communication breakdowns, such tasks often involve negotiation of meaning, an essential tenet to the interaction hypothesis (Long, 1996). Moreover, task-based peer interaction promotes learners' production of the FL in a form of language-related episodes (LREs), a more explicit form of attention to the language (Loewen & Isbell, 2017; Pastushenkov et al., 2020).

LREs have often been central units of analysis as they capture learning-in-progress of peers engaging in a dialogue to improve and/or better understand the language (Swain & Lapkin, 1998). LREs have been defined as "any part of a dialogue where the students talk about the language they are producing, question their language use, or correct themselves or others" (Swain & Lapkin, 1998, p. 326). They indicate that learners pay attention to certain linguistic items, negotiate their meaning, and attempt to better understand what their interlocutors are saying (Philp et al., 2010). Such discussions can focus on any language aspects such as vocabulary, grammar, and pronunciation (Loewen & Wolff, 2016) and thus have been viewed as beneficial for L2/FL development (Kaivanpanah & Miri, 2017; Philp et al., 2010). Production of LREs in peer interaction can be achieved through communicative tasks such as spot-the-difference, consensus, and conversation (Loewen & Isbell, 2017), and role-playing games such as "Mafia" (Pastushenkov & Pavlenko, 2020), all of which are discussed in detail in the next sections of the chapter.

The role of peer familiarity and first language background/use in peer interaction

A primary reason why learners (even those from similar backgrounds and the same school cohorts) often achieve drastically different results in learning a L2/FL pertains to their individual differences. Considering that there are a countless number of factors (cognitive, affective, environmental, etc.) that shape the acquisition process, individual differences have become a central topic of Second Language Acquisition (SLA) research (Dörnyei, 2013). However, it is simply impossible to control for all the factors that may affect peer interaction in a language classroom (Sato & Ballinger, 2016). Additionally, previous SLA studies on individual differences have mostly focused on more commonly taught languages such as English, French, and Spanish. Undeniably, more research on peer interaction in L2/FL Russian is needed. Despite these limitations, some of the individual differences that may be applicable to Russian classes (and that teachers can control) include the following: having a shared or different L1 background in a pair/group (Loewen & Isbell, 2017); L1 use during peer interaction (Storch & Aldosari, 2010); L2 proficiency (Dao & McDonough, 2017); and peer familiarity (Philp et al., 2010). Pastushenkov et al. (2020) addressed several questions that we as language teachers (ESL teachers at that time) had with regards to learners' individual differences: should we separate friends and students who speak the same L1; should we let our students use their L1 while they work on communicative tasks; how much L1 is acceptable in L2/FL task-based peer interaction; and if students switch to their L1, what do they use it for? Based on our findings, there are strategies that teachers can adopt to make communicative tasks more effective. As Philp and Iwashita (2013) pointed out, "peer talk may be most beneficial when all participants are actively involved" (p. 366).

Peer familiarity and shared/different first language background in peer interaction

Pastushenkov et al. (2020) found evidence that peer familiarity (how well interlocutors knew each other) positively affected both task scores and production of LREs in short interactive pair work. The familiar classmates were accustomed to each other's working routines and worked productively, which is consistent with other studies (Poteau, 2017). As for having a shared or different L1 in short interactive peer work, Pastushenkov et al. (2020) found no significant differences between these types of pairs. However, having a shared or different L1 background in a pair may have influenced the familiar and unfamiliar pairs differently. The authors suggest that teachers might want to "avoid placing unfamiliar peers from different L1 backgrounds together, or at least make their students switch to give them a chance to work with other familiar students, including those from the same L1 background" (p. 13). While these findings need to be replicated with Russian language learners, there is empirical evidence suggesting that learners' language use changes depending on how well they know their interlocutors in peer interaction (O'Sullivan, 2002; Philp et al., 2010; Plough & Gass, 1993). Therefore, interlocutor familiarity is an important variable that teachers of Russian as a FL can take into consideration in their instruction practices. One possible strategy that my colleagues from STARTALK and I used in our classes was to assign numbers to desks in a classroom. When students entered the classroom, they picked up a number from a "sorting hat" (we often used a *shapka-ushanka* for these purposes) and took a seat at the desk with the same number, so the students would work with different partners every lesson and get to know each other better.

First language use in peer interaction

L1 use in an L2 classroom is another complicated issue (Macaro & Lee, 2013; Mak, 2011), with some scholars arguing in favor of target language-only policies, while others saying that L1 use is inevitable and we as teachers need to find ways how to use it effectively (Shvidko et al., 2015). Undeniably, L1 use has some benefits in task-based peer interaction. For example, Swain and Lapkin (1998, 2000) found that students using their L1 in interactive tasks often employed it to help them complete these tasks rather than discuss something else. In line with these findings, other researchers have argued that L1 use can help learners (specifically, those at lower proficiencies) manage tasks and discuss the language, including new vocabulary (Storch & Aldosari, 2010). Some students and teachers favor the inclusion of L1 in L2 classes (Brooks-Lewis, 2009; Macaro & Lee, 2013). Recently, the idea of *translanguaging* (García et al., 2016), or employing one's entire linguistic repertoire, came into the spotlight suggesting that different language resources can be effectively adopted in a classroom. However, L1 use in peer interaction may get out of hand and can possibly become detrimental to learning unless controlled by the instructor, as illustrated in the study by Pastushenkov et al. (2020). While working on a spot-the-difference task, the pairs sharing the same L1 used it 27 percent of the time during the five-minute task. The researchers found evidence that the amount of L1 use negatively correlated with the frequency of LREs (large effect size $R = -.73$, $p = .02$) and task scores (large effect size $R = -.68$, $p = .02$). In other words, the more students used their L1, the less LREs they produced and the lower their scores were. However, the pairs stayed on task the entire time and switched to their L1s only to manage the task and discuss vocabulary. Conforming to previous studies (Brooks-Lewis, 2009; Storch & Wigglesworth, 2003), this finding suggests that L1 use can be beneficial as long as it is intentional; however, to promote effective peer interaction, it should probably be limited (but not prohibited).

Peer interaction in communicative tasks

In this section of the chapter, I would like to discuss five task-based peer interactive activities that can be used in Russian as a Foreign Language (RFL) classes. The consensus, conversation, and spot-the-difference tasks were adapted from the studies by Loewen and Wolff (2016) and Loewen and Isbell (2017). I developed the interview activity for the Russian STARTALK program at Kent State University and California State University, Northridge. I also used the Russian role-playing game "Mafia" in STARTALK and at Michigan State University. The description of the "Mafia" game is based on a chapter that was originally prepared for an ESL teaching context (Pastushenkov & Pavlenko, 2020).

Table 10.1

Title of the task: Consensus task

Task goal/s, setting of instruction: In this task, students need to choose the best candidate to study abroad in Russia. This task is appropriate for advanced levels in a university setting.

Learner needs analysis: This task involves reading, interaction, and analytical decision-making, which are skills that advanced learners are looking to deepen. This activity could also help interested students apply for scholarships to study abroad in Russia.

Type of task: peer interaction/focused

Can-do statements:

1 I can understand the main message and interpret its supporting details on the topic of character qualities and their correspondence with a set of given requirements.
2 I conduct a critical exchange in Russian and come to an agreement with a partner.
3 I can express and defend my opinion and point of view, and present a convincing argument in Russian.
4 I can use academic vocabulary to describe someone's characteristics and qualities in Russian.

Assessment/s used:

- An informal Q/A exchange is used to continuously check for understanding.
- The students deliver a presentation about why they chose the candidate for a more formal summative assessment. The teacher can include specific points that the students need to address in their presentation (discuss the candidates' educational background, work experience, etc.). To successfully complete the task, the students need to address each category.

In a consensus task, teachers give students different pieces of information about a real-world situation. The students need to find the best candidate for a fellowship to study in Russia. Each student in a pair gets a separate sheet of information about the candidates (Appendix A). This consensus task is more appropriate for advanced learners of Russian and should be implemented in pairs. As a pre-task, teachers may introduce useful vocabulary and grammatical constructions to help students model their responses. Teachers can also ask their students questions about what qualities make a good candidate for a fellowship. As a post-task, teachers can ask why students chose their candidate. The task itself can take up to 15 minutes (the pre- and post-tasks can take up to 20–30 minutes).

Conversation tasks elicit more naturalistic peer interactions, as students are given less information than in consensus tasks. In this conversation task, peers discuss their favorite things in several categories (Appendix B). Like in the consensus task, students receive a sheet with the topics (teachers can prepare two or more lists with topics presented in different orders). The students are instructed to switch turns when asking questions. Finally, they are asked to discuss things that they had in common and those that were different. As opposed to the consensus and spot-the-difference tasks, the participants will not have to come to an agreement.

Table 10.2

Title of the task: Conversation Task

Task goal/s, setting of instruction: In this task, students practice basic grammar and vocabulary (what I/you like) in a peer dialogue. This activity is appropriate for beginner through intermediate levels, in K–12 or university settings.

Learner needs analysis: Sharing information about one's interests is an essential skill for all learners of Russian.

Type of task: peer interaction/focused

Can-do statements:
1 I can identify the general topic and some basic information in familiar and everyday contexts by recognizing practiced or memorized words, phrases, and simple sentences in Russian spoken and written texts.
2 I can communicate in spontaneous spoken conversations in Russian on very familiar and everyday topics, using a variety of practiced or memorized words, phrases, simple sentences, and questions.
3 I can orally express my preferences and dislikes on familiar topics.
4 I can compare and contrast my preferences and dislikes with those of a classmate.

Assessment/s used:
- An informal Q&A exchange is used to assess students' needs and understanding
- The students are required to ask questions about each category (любимый/ любимая книга, фильм, музыкальный жанр, музыкант, etc. [favorite book, film, music genre, musician, etc.]). A checklist of categories is provided.
- The teacher asks additional clarification and comprehension questions throughout the task cycle.

This conversation task may be used with all proficiency levels; however, it is more appropriate for high beginner and low intermediate learners. This task can be used in pairs or in small groups. The task should take approximately ten minutes. As a pre-task, teachers can introduce or review useful vocabulary on the topic and ask their students questions about their favorite things. As a post-task, teachers can ask their students to share the similarities and differences they found.

Table 10.3

Title of the task: Spot-the-Difference Task
Task goal/s, setting of instruction: The goal of this task is to practice vocabulary and grammar related to the topic "inside the house" in a peer dialogue. This task is appropriate for intermediate levels in K–12 or university settings. **Learner needs analysis:** The example from this chapter (Appendix C) can be used in a lesson about "inside the house." This task teaches to ask clarification questions, which is an important skill for all learners of Russian. **Type of task:** peer interaction/unfocused **Can-do statements:** 1 I can participate in spontaneous spoken conversations on familiar topics, creating sentences and series of sentences to ask and answer questions about an objects' location in Russian. 2 I can understand the main idea and some pieces of information on familiar topics from sentences and series of connected sentences within spoken texts in Russian. 3 Given an image of a room, I can use descriptive language to explain the image's contents. 4 I can formulate questions to find out where something is from my partner. **Assessment/s used:** A low-stakes assessment is recommended: it may be helpful to go over the differences that the students found to ensure comprehension and accuracy.

In this task, each student in a pair sees one of two similar pictures. These pictures include differences that the students need to find by interacting with each other without seeing each other's picture. An example of a spot-the-difference task is shown in Appendix C (Pavlenko, 2020). The students need to identify as many differences between the two pictures as possible. Examples of spot-the-difference and other communicative tasks can be found online or retrieved from the IRIS digital repository (Marsden et al., 2016). Spot-the-difference tasks have been widely used in interaction research (e.g., Loewen & Isbell, 2017; Loewen & Wolff, 2016; Pastushenkov et al., 2020). In these tasks, no linguistic information is usually provided to students. "Spot-the-difference" tasks are appropriate for intermediate students and should be implemented in pairs. The task itself should take no more than five minutes. As a pre-task, teachers can introduce or review useful vocabulary on the topic "inside the house." As a post-task, the teacher can ask students to list the differences that they found.

Table 10.4

Title of the task: Interview Activity

Task goal/s, setting of instruction: This task's goal is to practice interview skills in Russian, and is appropriate for beginner-advanced levels in a university setting.

Learner needs analysis: Many Russian learners plan to visit Russia and other Russian-speaking countries and some plan to become journalists and work abroad. Being able to interact with Russian speakers outside the classroom is an important skill to have.

Type of task: interaction/presentation, focused/unfocused

Can-do statements:

1. I can formulate interview questions to find out information of my own interest from a speaker of Russian.
2. I can participate in spontaneous conversations on familiar topics, creating sentences and series of sentences to ask and answer a variety of questions during an interview with speakers of Russian.
3. I can communicate information, make presentations, and express my thoughts about familiar topics, based on what I learned interviewing speakers of Russian.

Assessment/s used:
The teacher should observe each step in the task (interview preparation, interview, and presentation). Assessing every component separately is recommended.

In this interview activity, students work in small teams (up to five students) and conduct interviews with Russian speakers (Appendix D). This activity can be implemented using online conferencing tools (e.g., Skype, Zoom). For three teams, teachers should invite three speakers of Russian, so each team can interview one guest at a time and then switch. When I used this task with my STARTALK students, I put three laptops in different parts of the classroom, so teams could interview people from Russia via Skype without being interrupted. As a pre-task, teachers can ask their students to prepare questions. As a post-task, teachers can have their students prepare group presentations about the interviewees. I used this activity with beginner and intermediate learners. Teachers may choose specific topics for the interviews. For example, if the lesson's topic is Russian culture, it may be beneficial for the students to ask questions about Russian literature, movies, music, etc.

Table 10.5

Title of the task: Role-Playing Game "Mafia"

Task goal/s, setting of instruction: This task's goal is for students to engage in peer interaction through the popular Russian role-playing game "Mafia." This activity is recommended for intermediate/advanced learners in a university setting.

Learner needs analysis: Students consistently express excitement at learning more about Russian culture, and "Mafia" is one of the most popular role-playing games in Russia and an excellent platform for peer and teacher-student interaction.

(Continued)

160 Dmitrii Pastushenkov

Table 10.5 (Continued)

Title of the task: Role-Playing Game "Mafia"

Type of task: interaction, unfocused

Can-do statements:

1 I can maintain spontaneous conversations and contribute to discussions across various timeframes on familiar, as well as unfamiliar, concrete topics, using a series of connected sentences and probing questions during an interactive role-playing game.
2 I can understand the main message and supporting details on a wide variety of familiar and general interest topics across various time frames from complex, organized texts that are spoken during an interactive role-playing game.

Assessment/s used:

The teacher acts as the host in the game. During the game, the teacher asks clarification questions and gives feedback as necessary.

This activity was adapted for RFL classes from Pastushenkov and Pavlenko (2020). "Mafia" is appropriate for intermediate and advanced learners of Russian (Appendix E). Its goal is to promote peer interaction while engaging in active listening, speaking, and practicing new vocabulary. To implement this game in a classroom, teachers will need a deck of playing cards to assign roles. Teachers can prepare their own cards as well. In this interactive role-playing game, students need to figure out who is in the Mafia. The Mafia are the informed group of players, as they know who the other Mafia members are. The other group of players, the Civilians (Doctor, Detective, and Other Citizens), do not know who the Mafia members are. The teacher participates as the host. Depending on the number of players, one game can take up to 30 minutes. Before the game, it is crucial to explain the rules to the students and possibly introduce useful vocabulary (students can prepare their own phrases and sentences too). Some of the helpful words and phrases are: *злой/злая, раздражённый/раздражённая, нервный/нервная, энергичный/энергичная, подозрительный/подозрительная, он/она много говорит/мало говорит, я думаю, что он/она Мафия, потому что, в прошлом раунде он голосовал против*. Doing a practice round is very helpful. Right before the game, the teacher/host places the cards face down in front of the students. The students then select their cards without showing them to anybody. The roles are the following: Mafia (aces; three students); Detective (jack; one student; Doctor (queen; one student); and Other Civilians (number cards depending on the number of students).

Lessons learned, challenges, and practitioner's reflection

As a proponent of TBLT, I put an emphasis on real-world communicative tasks integrated with grammar and vocabulary support, scaffolding, peer interaction, and authentic materials. However, even with grammar and vocabulary support, some of the tasks discussed in this chapter may not work for every Russian teacher and learner. Task-based peer interaction requires active participation in the learning process. However, students sometimes choose not to participate in communicative activities. Some of them may be overwhelmed with the classes they take, the complexity of Russian grammar, are simply shy, or simply prefer to do grammar exercises from a Russian textbook. I believe that it is important to try communicative activities more than once, so your students can develop familiarity with the tasks. For example, I used the interview activity three weeks in a row (on Wednesdays) when I worked in STARTALK. I invited different interviewees and discussed different topics with the students.

Even though explicit grammar instruction is something that proponents of communicative teaching and TBLT would probably avoid, I strongly believe that there is a place for detailed rule explanations and grammar tables when teaching morphologically rich languages such as Russian, specifically outside immersion settings when students do not get as many opportunities for receiving linguistic input and producing output. Based on my experience, it may be helpful to draw learners' attention to certain grammatical forms. Students sometimes copy their classmates' mistakes in peer interaction, and teacher intervention in these instances could be beneficial. However, giving explicit rule explanations and grammar tables is not always necessary. For example, textual enhancement is a very effective technique when teaching grammar. Teachers can simply highlight suffixes or prefixes in the examples and models of dialogues. English is a morphologically "impoverished" language, and native speakers of this language sometimes ignore the complex Russian morphology. By using textual enhancement in examples and models, teachers can draw their students' attention to certain grammatical forms without doing extra grammar drills.

In this chapter, I discussed some learners' individual differences that may have an impact on the effectiveness of task-based peer interaction. In a nutshell, it is important to give students the opportunity to work with different partners. L1 use may also get out of hand. However, I would not recommend using just Russian, especially with beginner learners. Switching to English may be helpful sometimes.

Language proficiency is an important factor to consider. The tasks described in this chapter (consensus task, conversation, spot-the-difference task, interview activity, and a role-playing game "Mafia") do not work for every curricular level. Of course, teachers can adapt the tasks if necessary (for example, go over an example of a spot-the-difference with the students before they work on their own). Teachers can also talk about their own favorite things (movies, books, etc.) before the students complete the conversation task. I think it also helps build a sense of community in a Russian classroom. Overall, examples and modelling are very helpful for interactive tasks. These are essential elements of TBLT. As for the "Mafia" game, the students often come up with their own words and phrases. Based on my experience, it is very helpful to play "Mafia" once or twice to allow the students and teacher to understand what the rules of it are and start enjoying it. The students may also want to switch to their L1 during the game (sometimes they get excited and it can be difficult to express emotions in Russian). My rule for the game was that we only play in Russian. Also, based on one of the reviewers' comments, the words "kill" or "send to jail" may be omitted. Neither I nor my students have ever had any issues with these words. It is just a game, but if you think that your students may react to the words like "kill" or "send to jail" negatively, you may use some other words or give your students a warning before you play the game. Based on my experience, the students really enjoy playing "Mafia."

I would also like to mention that Russian language teaching in the United States (in my opinion) is often more focused on explicit grammar instruction and grammar drills: some of the students who came to my classes from other Russian courses sometimes were not accustomed to communicative activities. Therefore, it is important to try interactive activities more than once.

Appendix A
Instructions for the consensus task

Инструкции

В этой задаче вам нужно выбрать лучшего из трёх кандидатов на стипендию. Победитель поедет на обучение в Тверской Государственный Университет. Каждый из вас получит карточку с разной информацией о трёх кандидатах. Сначала вам нужно прочитать информацию о стипендии, а потом информацию о кандидатах. Потом вам нужно обсудить эту информацию с вашим партнёром (не показывайте вашему партнёру листок с информацией). После обсуждения вам нужно выбрать, кто получит стипендию на обучение в России.

Требования стипендии

Ваше правительство придаёт большое значение образованию и решило отправить молодых людей в Россию для обучения в Тверском Государственном Университете. Только один студент получит стипендию для оплаты университетских взносов и расходов на проживание в течение одного года. Кандидатам не обязательно свободно говорить по-русски. Если кандидаты не говорят свободно по-русски, они должны пройти курс русского языка как иностранного в России перед началом обучения в университете. Правительство хочет, чтобы молодые люди получили опыт за границей а затем вернулись домой, чтобы продолжить изучение России и русского языка.

Как вы думаете, кто из трёх кандидатов должен получить стипендию?
Победивший кандидат: _____

Информация о кандидатах на стипендию *(1)*

Кандидат 1: Альберт	Кандидат 2: Джина	Кандидат 3: Джулия
Пол: мужской	Возраст: 20 лет	Пол: женский
Коэффициент интеллекта: 110	Иногда пропускает занятия в университете	Коэффициент интеллекта: 85
Много работает (учится по 8 часов в день)	Сложное детство: родители много работали и проводили мало времени дома	Учится на "тройки"
Хобби: американский футбол, был капитаном школьной футбольной команды	Хорошо знает музыку и играет на музыкальных инструментах. Занималась с учителем музыки из России.	Есть подруга в Украине
Ездил в Россию как турист, когда ему было 15 лет	Дядя и тётя живут в России	Родители не хотят, чтобы она училась в России
	Уровень знания русского языка: средний	Свободно говорит по-русски

Информация о кандидатах на стипендию *(2)*

Кандидат 1: Альберт	Кандидат 2: Джина	Кандидат 3: Джулия
Возраст: 18 лет	Пол: женский	Возраст: 19 лет
Отличные оценки по всем предметам	Коэффициент интеллекта: 140	Её отец дипломат
Любит русскую культуру	Обычно получает "пятёрки", но получила "двойку" за итоговый экзамен в прошлом семестре, так как была на вечеринке с друзьями	Много путешествовала, так как её отец дипломат
Мечтает быть профессиональным футболистом, но хочет изучать бизнес в университете	Была арестована в 14 лет за кражу телефона	Любит помогать бедным людям. Получила награду за помощь беженцам
Уровень знания русского языка: начинающий	Никогда не была в России	Хочет изучать международные отношения
	Хочет изучать искусство в будущем	

Appendix B
Instructions for the conversation task

Инструкции

Что любит ваш одноклассник? Почему он любит это? Что вы оба любите/не любите?

Образец:

- Какая у тебя любимая книга?
- Моя любимая книга "Преступление и Наказание". А какая у тебя любимая книга?
- Моя любимая книга "Война и Мир".
- Мы оба любим американские фильмы.
- Мы оба не любим рэп музыку.

Любимый/любимая/любимое	Мой одноклассник	Я
Книга		
Фильм		
Еда		
Музыкальный жанр		
Музыкант		
Домашнее животное		
Ресторан		
Актёр/актриса		
Город		
Предмет в школе		

Что вы оба любите/не любите?

Appendix C

Example of a "spot-the-difference" task (Pavlenko, 2020, illustrations used with permission)

Инструкции

У вас есть две картинки. На этих картинках, как минимум, 10 отличий. Вам необходимо найти как можно больше отличий, но не показывать свои картинки друг другу.

Figure 10.1

Task-based peer interaction 167

Figure 10.2

Appendix D
Instructions for the interview activity

Инструкции

Вам нужно провести интервью с людьми из России. Вы будете работать в команде (3–5 человек) и общаться с вашими собеседниками по очереди. Перед интервью вам необходимо подготовить вопросы для ваших собеседников. Тема интервью сегодня: _____. После интервью у вас будет время подготовить презентацию о ваших собеседниках.

Appendix E

Instructions for the role-playing game "Mafia" (after the students pick up their cards)

Инструкции

Ночь

1. Ведущий говорит: "Все закрывают глаза. Наступает ночь".
2. Ведущий говорит: "Мафия просыпается".
3. Мафия открывает глаза. Им нужно выбрать одного человека и "убить", ничего не сказав. В первую ночь Мафия приветствует друг друга и не убивает никого.
4. Ведущий говорит: "Мафия сделала свой выбор. Мафия засыпает". (Мафия закрывает глаза).
5. Затем Ведущий говорит: "Доктор просыпается".
6. Доктор может указать на любого человека и спасти его или её. Например, если мафия "убила" кого-то, но Доктор указал на этого человека, он или она в безопасности. Также Доктор может спасти самого себя, но только один раз за игру.
7. Ведущий говорит: "Доктор засыпает. Детектив просыпается".
8. Детектив может указывать на любого человека. Ведущий кивает, если человек, которого выбрал Детектив, находится в Мафии, а это значит, что Детектив будет знать, кто в Мафии.
9. Ведущий говорит: "Детектив засыпает. Город просыпается", и все открывают глаза.

День

1. Ведущий говорит: "Прошлой ночью . . . убили . . ." Какие твои последние слова . . .? В настоящей игре люди, которых "убивают", больше не участвуют в игре. На уроках русского языка мы отправляем их в "больницы", чтобы они могли участвовать в обсуждениях. Их можно "навестить", чтобы все продолжали играть.
2. Студенты обсуждают результаты и свои наблюдения. Они говорят о том, кто, по их мнению, может быть в Мафии.

После обсуждения студенты голосуют за человека, который, по их мнению, является членом Мафии. Этот человек отправляется в "тюрьму". В настоящей игре люди, которых отправили в "тюрьму", больше не участвуют в игре. На уроках русского языка мы посещаем их в "тюрьме", чтобы они могли участвовать в обсуждении. Студенты не голосуют в первый день.

Chapter 11

Kommunalka

Virtual space as a platform for task-based learning

Evelina Mendelevich

Chapter summary

Since task-based language teaching (TBLT) became a more mainstream approach to teaching second/foreign languages, virtual spaces have attracted scholars' and teachers' attention as potentially effective platforms for task-based/supported language learning and teaching. Most of the current studies on the use of virtual worlds and virtual role-play have focused on 3D virtual worlds, rich simulation games, and, most recently, virtual and augmented reality technologies. While ripe with potential for language teaching and learning, these platforms are often impractical in a classroom setting because they require a steep learning curve and/or sophisticated technology. Drawing on the best practices of traditional scenario-based role-play and the insights emerging from the study of simulation games and 3D virtual worlds in the context of TBLT, this chapter proposes a technologically simpler alternative by introducing *Kommunalka*, a virtual-space project based on Google Sites designed to advance vocabulary acquisition and retention in Intermediate learners by converting textbook activities into scaffolded pedagogical tasks. This chapter describes the structure and set up of the online space, converting typical textbook assignments into tasks designed to engage students with new vocabulary through role-play and contextual learning, and discusses the role of avatars in increasing student engagement and creativity both in and outside of the classroom.

Краткое содержание главы

Со становлением TBLT (task-based language teaching) как одного из основных подходов к обучению иностранным языкам, виртуальные пространства все больше привлекают внимание исследователей и преподавателей как потенциально эффективные платформы для обучения языкам на основе коммуникативных заданий. Большинство последних исследований использования виртуальных миров и виртуальных ролевых игр в этом контексте посвящены таким новейшим разработкам как виртуальные 3D-миры, многофункциональные игры-симуляторы, а также технологии

DOI: 10.4324/9781003146346-11

виртуальной и дополненной реальности (VR/AG). Несмотря на то, что эти платформы обладают существенным потенциалом для обучения и изучения иностранных языков, они часто непрактичны в использовании на занятиях из-за технических требований и сложных технологий, требующих долгого осваивания. Опираясь на методику использования ролевых игр в обучении иностранным языкам и результаты исследований виртуальных миров и игр-симуляторов в контексте TBLT, эта статья предлагает технологически-упрощенный вариант виртуального пространства, который может быть с легкостью использован на уроках РКИ. В данной статье представляется проект "Коммуналка" – виртуальное пространство, созданное на платформе Google Sites с целью активизации и усвоения новой лексики студентами на среднем этапе изучения русского языка. В данной главе описывается создание и структура онлайн-пространства, приводятся примеры заданий, способствующих активизации лексико-грамматического материала с помощью ролевой игры и контекстуального обучения, а также обсуждается роль аватаров в повышении активности, вовлеченности и творческого подхода учащихся.

Background

Students who have successfully completed first-year Russian typically join Intermediate I courses in our program at the Novice High level, or as ACTFL defines it, "they are able to express themselves within the context in which the language was learned, relying mainly on practiced material" (*ACTFL Proficiency Guidelines*, 2012, p. 14). To reach Intermediate Level, students need to demonstrate the "ability to create with the language when talking about familiar topics related to their daily life" and to be "able to recombine learned material in order to express personal meaning" (*ACTFL Proficiency Guidelines*, 2012, p. 7). However, motivating students to expand their vocabulary and its application is often more challenging than getting them started in the first place, partly because they have already found a narrow comfort zone in the form of well-memorized phrases and rehearsed monologues that allow them to exchange basic information on personal topics. In most cases, little changes in the lives and circumstances of students as they transition from first-year to second-year Russian: they have the same relatives who have the same occupations, the same schedule and living conditions, the same hobbies and interests, and so they continue to use the same limited vocabulary applicable to their present situations. This becomes especially apparent during information-exchange activities found in many language textbooks (i.e., "discuss what instruments you play or used to play;" "ask your partner what they usually do on weekends, have for breakfast," etc.). Such communicative tasks often fall short of their aim of activating target vocabulary in one of two ways: students either have remarkably boring and uneventful lives (they don't eat breakfast, and they spend their whole weekends studying at the library), or on the opposite spectrum, they try to be so precise that they keep reaching for a dictionary (or instructor, or online translators) instead of deploying the available linguistic tools to negotiate meaning. In the end, many high-frequency items do not enter their active vocabulary simply because students do not find meaningful application for them.

Role-play situations have the potential to overcome the limitations of information-exchange activities by providing the context (characters, setting, conflict) for vocabulary application independent of students' backgrounds and personal experience and encouraging them to experiment and take linguistic risks. As Henry (1995) notes, "One of the great advantages to role-play situations is that they encourage students to create with the language, that is, to recombine learned elements to fit the situation at hand" (p. 10), especially if a "role play situation is not a play script that requires strict adherence to a set dialog on the part of its actors, but rather a scenario that can be played out in a number of different ways" (p. 6). Because of its dynamic and transactional nature, role-play comes closer to a meaningful communicative act as it requires participants to "attend not only to their own behavior (linguistic and otherwise), but also to that of their interlocutors" and to focus on communication rather than the form of the utterances (Henry, 1995, p. 6). Moreover, role-play activities present an excellent opportunity for introducing elements of everyday Russian life, including culture-specific vocabulary, and for comparison and contrast of Russian cultural norms and sociolinguistic behavior with what those students bring from their own cultural backgrounds (Henry, 1995, p. 10).

Ultimately, however, the success of any role-play, like that of other communicative activities, hinges on student engagement and motivation to carry out the task. As a "rehearsal of a real-life event" (Henry, 1995, p. 6), transactional role-play situations, such as asking for directions, placing an order, or renting an apartment, may provide sufficient motivation for students planning a trip to Russia. Often, however, this approach "fails to provide sufficiently compelling social, emotional, and environmental stimuli that would motivate learners to participate actively in target language situational practice" because "traditional instructional settings do not produce the equivalent real-world consequences" (Blasing, 2010, p. 109).

A task-based approach to role-play, on the other hand, with its focus on achievable outcomes, can make up for this deficiency, particularly when integrated with virtual space technologies that can serve as a platform for situational learning. Broadly defined, a virtual space is a computer network-facilitated platform or environment where people can interact and/or collaborate (Sköld, 2012). The term can thus serve as an umbrella for such diverse platforms as 3D virtual worlds like *World of Warcraft* or *Second Life*; 2D learning platforms like *Moodle*; as well as internet forums, wikis, and other collaborative sites. In this chapter, I would like to present a simple virtual space project called *Kommunalka* (a Virtual Communal Apartment),[1] designed for Intermediate Russian courses at New York University (NYU) with the goal of increasing learner engagement and providing students with a platform for contextual learning and application of new vocabulary. As a semester-long project, *Kommunalka* can be thought of as a "maxi-task," "a collection of sequenced and integrated tasks that all add up to a final project" (Nunan, 2004, p. 133), thus addressing one of the potential problems with a task-based program identified by Nunan, namely, "that it may consist of a seemingly random collection of tasks with nothing to tie them together" (p. 25).

For this project, students choose a Russian-speaking city to explore throughout the semester using Google Maps and other free, simple tools, and create fictional Russian-speaking personas to "inhabit" their shared virtual world (Table 11.1).

Table 11.1 Kommunalka brief description

Title of the task: *Kommunalka*: a Virtual Communal Apartment
Task goal/s, setting of instruction: This project was designed for university-level Intermediate Russian courses with the goal of increasing learner engagement (both in class and at home) and providing students with a platform for contextual learning and application of new vocabulary.
Learner needs analysis: As per ACTFL Proficiency Guidelines, and from my classroom observations, to reach Intermediate Level, students need to demonstrate the "ability to create with the language when talking about familiar topics related to their daily life" and to be "able to recombine learned material in order to express personal meaning." The collaborative virtual space of Kommunalka provides an opportunity for contextual learning and application of new vocabulary.
Type of task: As a semester-long project, *Kommunalka* can be thought of as a 'maxi-task,' "a collection of sequenced and integrated tasks that all add up to a final project" (Nunan, 2004, p. 133). Some of these tasks include focused and unfocused tasks, and opinion and reasoning gaps.
Can-do statements: Within a virtual space: • Students can state their viewpoint about familiar topics and give some reasons to support it, using common opinion phrases and connecting words. • Students can interact with others to meet their needs in a variety of daily situations, by making requests for information and asking follow-up questions. • Students can exchange preferences, feelings, or opinions and provide basic advice on a variety of familiar topics. • Students can connect sentences in a narrative format to tell a story about the life, activities, events, and other social experiences of their avatars. • Students can compare practices related to everyday life and personal interests in their own culture and Russian culture.
Assessments used: A combination of low-stakes formative assessments and high-stakes summative assessments has been used for this project. Throughout the semester, the instructor provided feedback on low-stakes online posts and highlighted errors in grammar and usage which students then had to correct to earn full credit. At the end of each unit, students wrote a high-stakes essay bearing a heavy grade load with the opportunity for a subsequent revision.

By navigating the daily life of a Russian city through the eyes of native speakers whose age, occupation, family, and living conditions differ from their own, students actively explore culture, history, and living language while activating their expanding vocabulary and new grammatical constructions in a realistic, experiential way. The following sections will describe the structure and setup of *Kommunalka*, present sample tasks, and discuss how this project in general and the individual tasks that comprise it fit within the framework of TBLT and reflect the seven principles for planning task-based lessons set out by Nunan (2004); namely, scaffolding, task dependency, recycling, active learning, integration, reproduction to creation, and reflection (pp. 35–38). Finally, I will reflect on what I learned from implementing this maxi-task and discuss the place of simulation games and 3D virtual worlds within the context of second language acquisition in general and task-based language teaching in particular.

Technical requirements and initial setup

Among the many available Web 2.0 tools, Google Sites, an intuitive webpage creation tool that supports collaboration between different editors, is one of the most accessible and easy to use. While lacking the visual appeal of 3D virtual environments, Google Sites provides a collaborative virtual space that is easy to set up and maintain and can serve as an effective platform for learner-centered, task-based collaborative learning. The choice of Google Sites narrows the technical requirements for this project to internet-connected computers or personal devices and Google accounts for all participants. Access to a classroom internet-connected computer with a projector is helpful but not required, given that many students today have at least one internet-connected personal device in class.

Before the start of the semester, the instructor creates a new Google Site[2] for the class and prepares a blueprint of the virtual communal apartment by creating a set of (mostly blank) pages as follows. The 'Home' page will later be filled with the details about the apartment's location, i.e., city, address, and the street view image of the building chosen by the class during one of the opening tasks discussed in the next section. Another essential area of the site is a common space where students (or rather their virtual Russian personas) can interact with each other. The most fitting space for this purpose in a communal apartment is, of course, the kitchen. Finally, the space needs blank personal pages to function as private rooms (their number should correspond to the number of participants, but pages can always be added or deleted with just a few clicks if students join or drop the class) (Table 11.2).

Instructors can choose the level of interaction they want to have with their students within the apartment: for example, they may choose full interaction and set aside one room (page) for their persona; they may decide to be a silent presence such as домовой, who may occasionally interfere with the apartment's life; or provide task directions while remaining entirely outside of role-play. Other pages, such as "газетный киоск" [news stand], "кинотеатр" [movie theater], "книжная

176 Evelina Mendelevich

Figure 11.1 Sample apartment areas/rooms

полка" [bookshelf], "почтовый ящик" [mailbox] can be created for a variety of purposes either during the initial setup or later in the semester. A page titled "Рабочий стол" [Desk] is useful for posting assignments and resources, so that students do not have to navigate between multiple course sites while completing homework assignments.

Once the site is published, the instructor sends invitations to students. A critical step at this stage is to grant students editing privileges, thus allowing them to post and edit the site content. This completes the initial setup.

Getting started: the setting

On the first day of classes, the instructor introduces students to the virtual space project and its role in addressing course objectives and learning outcomes (this information should also be clearly explained in the syllabus). Students are then presented with their first task: to choose a city within a Russian-speaking country to serve as a setting for their virtual life – a place they would love to visit or explore throughout the semester – and to persuade their classmates to endorse their choice. At home, students prepare to make their case by researching and collecting the necessary information on Russian cities. This is a good warm-up activity since the task is within students' linguistic abilities, especially if they made presentations on Russian cities in elementary Russian and thus possess some basic vocabulary and facts to work with.

As expected, in the beginning, most students follow the presentational format and recycle vocabulary and forms learned in elementary Russian. To successfully carry out the task, however, students must engage in a debate with their classmates to secure the majority of the votes for their city. During this in-class activity, the instructor does not take part in the debate (remaining outside the circle or even leaving the room) to encourage students to address each other as their audiences in order to move away from a presentational format to an authentic, purpose-driven exchange. As a result, instead of simply displaying their control of facts, vocabulary, or grammatical structures to the instructor, the focus shifts to communicating ideas for a meaningful purpose. As Brown and Bown (2014) point out, "because competing positions evolve during the course of a debate, learners must pay careful attention to ongoing exchanges" and negotiate meaning (pp. 11–12). In addition, debate forces learners to step outside their comfort zone, recombine learned forms and vocabulary and "push their linguistic competence to its limit as they attempt to express their ideas" (Swain, 1993, p. 162). The debate is followed by a vote, giving the task a clear, achievable, non-linguistic outcome.

The second opening task, although similar in format, requires students to engage with a different but related set of vocabulary. Using Google Maps and other internet resources, students must choose a specific location within the city to serve as their virtual home for the semester. Students are instructed to find the relevant information about their chosen city's neighborhoods, taking into account financial considerations, accessibility of public transportation, local attractions, and other potential advantages that make a particular address more desirable.

As in the previous task, students must reach an agreement by debating the pros and cons of their choices. This time, however, a visual element is added to the discussion, as students support their arguments using the street view feature of Google Maps, often prompting an interesting discussion of the differences and similarities between Russian and American cities. As students realize that the outcome of the debate will have an impact well beyond a single class, they demonstrate higher motivation and engagement, grow more animated, and use gestures and facial expressions to supplement their verbal message, which has been shown to increase vocabulary retention by proponents of connectivity theory (Macedonia & Klimesch, 2014).

Getting started: characters

Once the address is chosen, the instructor updates the home page of the site with a photograph of the city, a map, and the street view image of the building (Figure 11.2).

The participants are ready to move in! But first, they need to create a Russian-speaking persona, or avatar, whose point of view will guide their actions and interactions in their virtual life. Using Russian-speaking avatars encourages students to explore Russian culture and everyday life more deeply, and writing from the point of view of a fictional character can be both liberating and fun. In contrast, students whose adopted persona closely reflected their own character and identity (i.e., an expatriate or an American student in Russia) were less likely to exhibit creativity and take risks with subsequent tasks. One way to avoid this is to create a number of "template" roles, i.e., an old man/woman, a young mother, a professor, a factory worker, an artist, etc., and have students choose between them. It is also important to introduce students to the history and concept of communal apartments[3] and to emphasize the fact that their residents – persons and families of different ages, backgrounds, occupations, and social statuses – are obliged to live with each other under one roof, making this experience very different from living with roommates. A *Virtual Museum of Communal Living* from Colgate University (http://kommunalka.colgate.edu/) is a great resource for this. It also hosts an excellent collection of short video clips from Soviet movies and

Figure 11.2 Sample homepage

post-Soviet interviews with residents of communal apartments that can supply prototypes for students' adopted personas.

Students create their avatars in several stages: in class, they complete a questionnaire with basic information such as name, age, gender, occupation, marital status, etc. At home, they "move in" to their rooms by customizing their pages with photographs and other relevant images and a brief biographical narrative based on their in-class questionnaire. This assignment builds on what students already can do with the language (namely, "writing about myself") while encouraging them to use a wider range of vocabulary as they are not constrained by personal facts. At the same time, because students write for each other rather than for the instructor, they are more likely to utilize the target vocabulary and avoid the urge to overuse the dictionary. Throughout the course, they continue to develop their characters by adding specific details about their childhood, family, daily schedule, and other personal topics typically covered in Second-Year Russian courses (Figure 11.3).

Figure 11.3 Sample personal page with biographical details

Virtual space and vocabulary development

Upon completing the first three tasks (ideally within the first two weeks), students will have established the setting and characters and set the stage for a semester-long role-play that is comparable to simulation games in that the choices they make in subsequent tasks shape the narrative they collectively create. The instructor's role from this point on is to provide focused tasks that students can complete within this context. According to Ellis et al. (2020), "a focused task must satisfy the general criteria for a task but is designed to orientate learners to the use of a particular linguistic feature – typically but not necessarily a grammatical structure" (p. 12). In this section, I will present sample tasks focused on the development of vocabulary commonly covered in Intermediate Russian courses and textbooks. Topics focused on form will be discussed in the following section.

During the unit covering appearance, character traits, and personal relationships, students further develop their avatars by describing their personality on their personal pages. A list of target vocabulary and constructions that includes new topic-specific lexical items along with expressions and connectors learned in previous lessons promotes recycling of high-frequency items and gives students the opportunity to use them across a wide range of contexts. Although students are not limited to the list, they may be required to use a certain number of items from each category (connectors, adjectives, verbs). Where appropriate, grammatical context (i.e., case government) is also presented as part of the list to encourage students to focus on meaning while simultaneously paying attention to form. This also reminds students that if they choose to look up additional words in the dictionary, they must be aware of the grammatical baggage they carry.

The written psychological portrait itself is not the end-goal of the task, however. To fit within the framework of TBLT, a task must require students to *do* something with the language they produce. Hence, during the next stage, which can take place in class, online, or both, students must get to know their "neighbors" and determine what sort of relationships their avatar would have with them (Figure 11.4). In other words, rather than simply exchange information, students must overcome a reasoning gap by attending to the contents of and drawing conclusions from the information they receive from their "neighbors." Based on this information, participants write gossip posts about their neighbors in the "Kitchen" area of *Kommunalka*. This was one of the most popular activities with our students: "It really made the apartment seem like a real place and brought the charecters [sic] to life," one student commented in the survey, and another appreciated that "it gave [them] a chance to review all of [their classmates'] pages and create relationships with them."

The next example illustrates both the challenges of a traditional communicative approach to certain topics and the way a virtual space can be used to address them through a task-based approach. The communicative goals of one of the textbook lessons are "Discussing getting married and divorced" and "Planning a festive event" (i.e., a wedding). With traditional instruction, most assignments in this

Задание № 11. Сплетни. Характер и отношения.

A kitchen is a place for gossip (сплетни). On the kitchen page, talk about your neighbors and your relationships with them. Be sure to say something about every resident (read their pages before).

Опишите (describe) ваши отношения с соседями по квартире. Вы похожи или разные? С кем у вас хорошие отношения? С кем вы ссоритесь и почему? Use оба and и..., и.... where possible.

Наша лексика (стр. 15-16)

во-первых, во-вторых, в третьих…	ненавидеть + *инфинитив*
слишком	Обожать *кого? что?*
конечно	волноваться, нервничать (impf.)
может быть	похож(а) *на кого?*
например	ссориться/поссориться *с кем?*
кроме того	врать/наврать *кому?*
наверное	бояться *кого? чего?*
больше всего	помогать/помочь *кому?*
похожи	Уметь
разные	смеяться
По-моему	соглашаться /согласиться *с кем/чем*
	Вести себя (веду, ведёшь, ведут)
привычка (вредная привычка)	молчать

- Сильный
- Весёлый, жизнерадостный
- Грустный
- воспитанный/невоспитанный
- нежный/грубый
- заботливый
- глупый/неглупый, умный, образованный

- Разговорчивый, открытый, общительный
- Спокойный, тихий, молчаливый
- самостоятельный/несамостоятельный
- скромный/нескромный
- Смелый
- Трудолюбивый
- уверенный в себе/неуверенный в себе
- честный/нечестный

Figure 11.4 Sample task with accompanying vocabulary list

lesson, including those aligned with TBLT, elicited very low engagement and motivation among American students who did not find the stories and the tasks associated with these topics relatable. However, when the same topics were presented in the context of *Kommunalka*, student engagement and motivation to use the language increased dramatically, resulting in creative, purposeful application of target vocabulary and exploration of cultural norms and traditions. Sample tasks for this lesson include choosing a tenant (or tenants) to be married and interviewing them about the qualities they look for in a spouse; finding a match using authentic dating and romance ads; planning a wedding by choosing actual venues (ZAGS, church, restaurant) and researching Russian wedding traditions; and finally "gossiping" in the kitchen, with each character giving an account of the wedding from their point of view. These interrelated tasks can be used to expose students to a variety of input: textbook text and dialogs, personal dating ads, official web pages, and videos that illustrate Russian wedding traditions.

Over the course of the semester, numerous textbook assignments can be converted into tasks linked to the virtual space and its tenants. Depending on the unit, students can use their avatars to shop at online Russian stores, rent a *dacha*, find a restaurant for a meeting or a date taking into account the menu, location, price, and dietary needs of their partner, hire (or apply for a job as) a housekeeper using Avito.ru, a Russian classified advertisements website, report their neighbors to the police for stealing, or use the online "lost and found" services. The possibilities are endless, especially now that many museums, theaters, and other cultural institutions offer rich online programming following the COVID-19 lockdowns, and one can go on virtual tours, stream famous theatrical productions, or explore the scenery surrounding Lake Baikal without leaving home.

Form-focused tasks

Using a virtual space as a context in which students can apply the skills and knowledge targeted in a particular lesson or unit, instructors can adapt textbook activities or supplement them with virtual space tasks without making drastic changes to the syllabus or course design. For example, following the review of imperative forms in Unit 1 of the Intermediate Russian textbook *В пути* (Kagan et al., 2006), students watched a video about the importance of rules in a communal apartment from the *Virtual Museum of Communal Living* collection, read sample notes posted on bulletin boards of actual communal apartments, and based on what they learned about their neighbors, wrote their own apartment rules that ranged from basic ("Не шумите после десять [sic] часов!" to absurd "Не убивайте животных на кухне!" (the latter addressing an avatar of Dagestani origin who brought up sheep to slaughter in Moscow during one of the exchanges).

Other ideas for form-focused tasks include asking students to "furnish" their rooms by choosing items in online Russian furniture stores and "placing" them in their rooms using Russian verbs of position and positioning, or comparing themselves to other neighbors using comparative and superlative forms of adjectives. When working with verbs of motion and/or constructions expressing location/destination/origin, students can be asked to map and report the actions and movements of their avatars throughout the day using the My Google Maps tool – or to spy on their neighbors and report their actions and movements to others.

Virtual space and cultural literacy

Virtual space also serves as an effective platform for the application of cultural knowledge. For example, students will need to decide how various characters would address each other depending on their age and/or status, learn how

Russians give directions, and why they often choose monuments as meeting points. Reading Russian news also becomes more engaging when students have to respond to them from the point of view of their characters and think about how various current events might affect them. Because the project involves work with a variety of authentic materials, learners get exposed to a range of registers, including online slang and abbreviations, which further promotes multiliteracy.

Lessons learned: observations and student feedback

The pairing of the task-based approach with the use of virtual space in Intermediate Russian classes resulted in positive outcomes in student vocabulary acquisition and usage. Students often used the target vocabulary as a source of ideas and inspiration for character development and original stories. During classroom debates and online interactions, students manipulated the language as they sought a balance between creating rich and entertaining posts and memorable characters on the one hand, and the need to be understood by others on the other, opening frequent opportunities for negotiation of meaning during classroom exchanges. Over time, students began to associate specific words or phrases with individual characters – their own and others' – and these associations helped them recall the vocabulary in different contexts. In addition, the interactive nature of most tasks exposed students to alternative usages of familiar words and expressions through their classmates' posts, which further reinforced retention.

At the end of the semester, participants completed a short survey. Student feedback was very positive, and learners' self-evaluations confirmed the instructor's observations. Thus, for example, many respondents stated that using avatars and applying the language in the situational context of the virtual space allowed them to use a wider range of vocabulary and registers than they would have used in traditional writing assignments:

- "I think it forced me to use vocab I wouldn't normally use because I was writing from the perspective of my avatar."
- "When being asked to speak or write about yourself, it is more difficult to use varied vocabulary because people tend to be shy and not like to talk about themselves in detail, so this assignment avoided that problem."
- "I was able to use a wider variety of language because I wasn't limited to the same personal information."
- "There was a lot of vocabulary that I learned that was not in any of the units in the textbooks the realities of life in russia [sic] and how language is used in a household setting."

Students also reported feeling more engaged and motivated to complete the assignments and appreciated the opportunity for creative expression ("I was more engaged and enjoyed the assignments because it allowed me to be creative;" "I felt more engaged and would look forward to writing something about my character. I think it allowed me to be more creative with my writing").

Several comments highlighted the positive effect of the collaborative aspect of the project ("It encouraged me to read about my classmates [sic] posts which helped me expand my vocabulary when writing my posts;" "It was also helpful to see how other classmates used vocabulary and sentence constructions;" "It also improved my grammer [sic] abilities, looking at other posts was a helpful tool for this"). Students appreciated learning more about Russian culture and history through *Kommunalka* ("I learned about life in communal apartment buildings;" "I enjoyed seeing the additional music and pop-culture posts people made;" "It also helped incite interesting conversations in class that otherwise would not have happened").

TBLT principles and project design

In recent decades, TBLT has become a more mainstream approach to language teaching and has shown great potential to engage learners in purposeful, meaning-focused language use. Nevertheless, redesigning entire Russian courses, particularly at lower levels, to make them fully task-based remains problematic, as many of the challenges for implementing TBLT as the structuring principle for Russian curriculum outlined by Comer (2007) persist today (pp. 192–193). Still, converting individual assignments into task-based activities can help increase student engagement and motivation to use the language without requiring drastic changes to existing curriculum or materials. Using a virtual space like *Kommunalka* as a platform for task-based learning facilitates this process while providing structure and coherence throughout the semester. Instructors who seek to make existing materials more aligned with the task-based approach will benefit from Comer's (2007) checklist outlining the basic criteria for a task as summarized here:

1 A task is something the learners do with the target language, and that engagement can involve productive and/or receptive skills.
2 A task involves some kind of "gap," i.e., an information gap, a reasoning gap, or an opinion gap.
3 A task has a purpose.
4 Learners engage in communication to achieve an outcome or objective.

(Comer, 2007, p. 183)

In addition, Nunan's seven principles for planning task-based lessons were used in the design and implementation of the virtual space project as follows:

1 **Scaffolding**. The first three tasks rely on previously learned material but encourage students to use it in a different format. For subsequent tasks,

students are first introduced to new material (vocabulary, grammar) through textbook exercises and dialogs, thus ensuring that at the beginning of the learning process, learners are not expected to produce language that has not been introduced either explicitly or implicitly.

2 **Task dependency.** According to Nunan, "one task should grow out of, and build upon, the ones that have gone before" (p. 35). Not only does each task within the *Kommunalka* project build upon the previous ones, but individual tasks performed within a given unit often require that students complete them in stages or sub-tasks.

3 **Recycling.** Nunan argues that "recycling language maximizes opportunities for learning and activates the 'organic' learning principle" (p. 36). The tasks designed for this project were accompanied by vocabulary lists that included both old and new lexical items. This gave students the opportunity to "recycle" previously learned vocabulary and structures and use them in a variety of situations.

4 Virtual space tasks ensured that students were engaged in **active learning** both in class and at home as they had to *do* something with the language, be it persuading others, drawing conclusions from the information provided by their classmates, or using online classified ads to find products or services.

5 **Integration.** Nunan argues that "learners should be taught in ways that make clear the relationships between linguistic form, communicative function and semantic meaning" (p. 37). This principle was met by frequent reliance on focused tasks that required students to apply target constructions in a meaningful context.

6 In accordance with the "**reproduction to creation**" principle, students progressed from rehearsing textbook dialogs and using textbook texts as models to be innovative with the language by recombining previously learned vocabulary and structures to fit a given situation within their virtual world context.

7 **Reflection.** Throughout the semester, the instructor highlighted errors in grammar and usage and provided relevant feedback on student online posts which students then had to revise to earn full credit for the assignment. This gave students the opportunity to reflect on word usage and the interconnection between form and meaning. In addition, students reflected on what they had learned as a result of participating in the *Kommunalka* project at the end of the semester by completing a short anonymous survey. To further meet this principle, students can be given several opportunities throughout the semester (for example, at the end of each unit) to reflect on their progress and learning strategies, either by completing a survey or by writing a short reflection paper in English.

Challenges of and solutions to teaching Russian in the context of TBLT

One of the major challenges of teaching such a morphologically complex language as Russian lies in finding the right balance between effective grammar instruction and abundant opportunities for meaningful communicative practice. As Comer (2007) notes, the lack of focus on form in the "strong" interpretation of TBLT and other communicative approaches that rely solely on implicit or non-obtrusive grammar instruction represents "an especially thorny issue for Russian" (p. 190). Russian learners are required to master a great range of grammatical and syntactic structures before they can successfully communicate at the Intermediate level. Implicit grammar instruction may be effective in achieving this goal in immersion environments, such as study abroad or summer immersion programs. Most American college students, however, whose Russian classes typically meet no more than two to three times per week, do not have sufficient time and attention resources to make strong form-meaning connections based on communication and input alone and will require at least some explicit grammar instruction to master the rich complexity of Russian morphology. Moreover, different students achieve this mastery at different paces: while some are able to grasp form-meaning connections based on just a few examples, others require more extensive examples and explanations in English. Finally, as learners tend to make more grammatical mistakes when they venture out of their comfort zone, such as during spontaneous exchanges and creative language use, the instructor needs to be able to evaluate whether these errors are the result of learners' linguistic risk-taking or indicators of gaps in grammatical knowledge.

A flipped-classroom approach is an effective solution to this problem, as it allows for the adoption of TBLT practices without sacrificing in-depth grammar instruction. In a flipped-classroom model, students are introduced to key grammatical topics at home, where they can engage with the material at their own pace. For this project, a series of online video tutorials aligned with the existing textbook were recorded by the instructor over the summer. These mini-lectures were supplied with interactive self-graded online quizzes which helped students assess how well they understood the material. Students were required to complete these online grammar modules before class and were expected to know and be prepared to apply target forms during form-focused tasks. As illustrated earlier in this chapter, these tasks were an integral part of the *Kommunalka* project, keeping students engaged and focused on meaning and outcome but requiring them to use particular structures or forms. This approach reflects a "weak" interpretation of TBLT encapsulated in Nunan's definition of a task as "the deployment of grammatical knowledge to express meaning, highlighting the fact that meaning and form are highly interrelated, and that grammar exists to enable the language user to express different communicative meanings" (Nunan, 2004, p. 4). The combination of the flipped-classroom model and form-focused tasks thus offers a practical solution for instructors interested in adopting or trying a task-based approach but concerned about giving up traditional grammar instruction.

Virtual spaces in second language teaching and learning

With the emergence of new technologies, virtual spaces are becoming an increasingly common feature in education, with a growing number of scholars and teachers exploring their potential to engage learners in target language interaction through tasked-based instruction and situated learning. 3D virtual worlds and rich simulation games, in particular, have been seen to harness the potential of role-play for TBLT because they entail purposeful communication and can serve to contextualize target language use within narratives; and since they induce learners "to generate multiple connections between new vocabulary and episodic, emotive, motor-sensory, and linguistic memory networks" (Franciosi et al., 2016, p. 358), they are especially promising for vocabulary development. Studies show that when learners are provided with supplementary, form-focused activities (enabling tasks), and are given clear goals to accomplish, simulation games hold the potential to enhance vocabulary retention and transferability and generally improve learning outcomes (Miller & Hegelheimer, 2006; Franciosi et al., 2016; Franciosi, 2017). Thus, for example, Peterson (2010) argues that simulation games may support language acquisition through involvement in purposeful task-focused interactions and exposure to large amounts of target language input. Simulation games may also create an experiential learning environment where learners experience knowledge first-hand (Ang & Zaphiris, 2006) and can situate the meaning of words in terms of the actions, images, and dialogues that they relate to, showing how they vary across different contexts (Gee, 2005). Finally, they offer a more interactive, engaging, and meaningful real-world context, re-focusing students on communicating in the target language rather than being tested on the specifics relating to grammar, and provide an opportunity to learn from peers, which helps build a more supportive, encouraging, and less intimidating environment (Tsvetkova et al., 2009). As Franciosi et al. (2016) observe, "these possible effects are what communicative tasks in TBLT are designed to induce. Thus, theoretically, at least, simulation games are potentially beneficial tools for mediating communicative tasks that could support SLA" (p. 360). In addition, these studies report greater learner engagement and motivation to use the target language.

While most recent studies on the effects of virtual worlds and simulation games were conducted in the context of teaching English as a foreign language, Blasing (2010) examines the benefits of an online virtual world known as *Second Life* for advanced Russian students by approaching it through the prism of the National Standards for Foreign Language Education, concluding that "L2 interaction in a virtual world such as *Second Life* offers opportunities to address the learning goals of communicative language teaching by expanding beyond the bounds of traditional classroom instruction" (p. 102). While Blasing's study was not focused on role-play as such – advanced Russian students interacted primarily with native speakers – it provides valuable insights on the role of avatars in virtual spaces as a medium for increasing learner interaction and engagement. Participants in Blasing's study reported a strong appeal in the mediating force of the avatar, emphasizing the fact that "the avatar's name and appearance can act as a mask, permitting the user to try on a new identity, not only as an L2 speaker, but also as an entirely new persona" (p. 110). Notably, participants who chose to disguise their true identity (i.e., presenting themselves as a native Russian speaker, endowing the avatar with different personality traits and even sexual identity) demonstrated a heightened sense of freedom to experiment with the language and to take more linguistic risks (Blasing, p. 112). Among other benefits, Blasing reports that "interaction in the virtual environment promotes attention to linguistic accuracy along with cultural sensitivity" (p. 104) while allowing learners to "effectively interact with one another and practice their language skills in contextualized, content-rich environments even without the presence of native speakers" (p. 104).

Conclusion

While ripe with potential, 3D virtual worlds have their shortcomings. Blasing notes that "not all learners will have the linguistic proficiency to engage in spontaneous conversations with native speakers in *Second Life*, and not all instructors will have the skills or desire to create intricate learning spaces for their students" (p. 113). Likewise, Franciosi et al. (2016) conclude that while showing promise for second language teaching and learning, 3D environments are often impractical in a classroom setting because they require sophisticated technical capabilities, and learners must undergo a steep learning curve to operate the complex systems before they are able to begin learning the subject matter (p. 356).

This does not mean, however, that insights gained from these studies cannot be used to create an alternative virtual space that is easier for students to navigate and for instructors to implement within a classroom setting. Drawing on the best practices of traditional scenario-based role-play and the insights emerging from the study of simulation games and 3D virtual worlds in the context of TBLT, the virtual space project presented in this chapter offers a more practical alternative that teachers of Russian can implement in their courses with minimal technology and skill investment to achieve comparable benefits.

Notes

1 I would like to acknowledge Aline Baehler, whose presentation "Virtual Spaces and Places as Foundation for a New Learning Experience" at the NYU CAS Innovation in Language Teaching Conference (2016) inspired this project.
2 Creating a new Google Site takes only a few clicks and does not require any special knowledge in website design. Numerous tutorials are available online to guide those new to this tool.
3 Although a Virtual Space can be any space where learners' avatars can interact and collaborate with each other (a city or an apartment building), I designed our virtual space as a communal apartment for two reasons. First, this project was implemented in 2017,

which marked the 100th anniversary of the Bolshevik Revolution, with many talks and events planned across the university. The subject of communal apartments proved to be a helpful link to those discussions, as well as an introduction to some important but hard-to-grasp aspects of Soviet and post-Soviet daily culture and mentality. Second, and probably most important, is that this setting allows one to create a variety of engaging situations for contextual application of new vocabulary in which students use it for specific purposes as they interact with each other through their adopted personas.

Chapter 12

Developing global competence in an advanced Russian course

Snezhana Zheltoukhova

Chapter summary

This chapter explores the ways a task-based language teaching (TBLT) approach was applied to a higher-level L2 Russian class at an American liberal arts college. The pilot content-based course was taught in Spring 2019 and aimed at increasing the global competence of learners through academic discussions and creative projects based on Ilf and Petrov's travelogue *One-Storied America*. The innovative curriculum employed three pedagogic task types based on the classification of Willis (2004). This project discusses major course features and potential issues for the use of this approach in future application.

Краткое содержание главы

В данной главе описывается инновационный метод преподавания русского языка как иностранного, включающий в себя целевое задание как базис структуры курса и основного критерия оценивания прогресса учащихся. Основные выводы главы основываются на примере пилотного курса русского языка на продвинутом уровне, который преподавался в одном из колледжей США в течение весеннего семестра 2019 года и базировался на материалах произведения И. Ильфа и Е. Петрова "Одноэтажная Америка" а также одноименного телевизионного проекта В. Познера. В практической части главы читателю предлагается ознакомиться с примерами заданий пилотного курса, отзывами студентов и преподавателя. Глава будет полезна интересующимся применением метода в контексте обучения иностранному языку.

Introduction

In recent decades, the task-based language teaching (TBLT) approach has become one of the most significant and popular methods implemented in advanced-level second language (L2) classrooms (e.g., Ellis, 2006; Long, 2015). Task-based instruction greatly fits the curriculum of upper-level courses when learners

DOI: 10.4324/9781003146346-12

develop their argument through the use of paragraph-length oral and written discourse (ACTFL Proficiency Guidelines; American Council on the Teaching of Foreign Languages, 2012). However, certain pedagogical challenges arise when educators use the approach in a classroom while establishing connections between theory, research, and practice (East, 2017; Yen, 2016). This results in the current demand for TBLT teacher training materials or studies that focus on L2 Russian classrooms. This chapter offers a contribution to the existing body of practice-oriented narrative literature on TBLT in teaching an advanced Russian course.

I will reflect on my teaching experience of an advanced-level pilot course designed for fourth-year L2 Russian students at a private U.S. liberal arts college. Typically, the primary focus of upper-level task-based language courses is making meaning through the use of authentic language materials in order to create opportunities for students to discuss, present, and write about it. Assessment in such courses similarly addresses the balance between focus-on-form and focus-on-content teaching techniques. Frequently, L2 Russian language classes target authentic fiction texts, classical or contemporary literature, oftentimes narrowing the discussions to literary analysis. At the same time, non-fiction texts, talk shows, interviews, and documentaries are also useful material for newly designed courses due to the increased accessibility of various streaming services. Thus, the core of the learning materials for the course under discussion comprises of the travelogue by Il'yia Il'f and Evgenii Petrov *Odnoetazhnaia Amerika* (Ilf et al., 2013), and a contemporary documentary TV series of the same title by Vladimir Pozner (2008). The interdisciplinary approach of the course aims at the development of student global competence through a sociological and historical analysis of the two "Americas": the one that existed a century ago and a contemporary one vis-à-vis the Soviet Union and Russia. The main goal of this course is to help students "become literate about a text and not simply opinionated" (Swaffar & Arens, 2005), in which students strive to become strong readers and confident listeners; in other words, to acquire the cognitive strategies and linguistic resources necessary to comprehend and interpret a written or video-recorded non-fiction work rather than engaging with a language per se.

Global competence in content-based language learning curriculum

Language educators regard global competence as a critical component of 21st century higher education, which plays a central role in any university curriculum (Reaching Global Competence, 2014). It is defined as a profound understanding of international phenomena of all sorts, including the "ability to learn and work with people from diverse linguistic and cultural backgrounds, proficiency in a foreign language, and skills to function productively in an interdependent world community" (National Education Association, 2010, p. 1). Due to ever-expanding opportunities for prolonged intercultural communication both inside and outside one's home country, study opportunities, and work prospects in different cultural environments, language programs have been placing increased emphasis on competencies that prepare students for global citizenship. The ACTFL World-Readiness Standards for Learning Languages (National Standards in Foreign Language Education Project, 2015) stress the importance of integrating cultural knowledge into the curriculum with a focus not merely on accumulating a variety of culture-specific facts, but rather on understanding the interconnections of values and beliefs as a matrix for all cultural practices and products. Thus, the pilot course curriculum represents the integration of a TBLT approach with content-based advanced-level language instruction. Focusing on global competence requires negotiation of meaning, and thus implicitly promotes language acquisition (Blake, 2013).

Throughout the course, students learned to integrate knowledge acquired from multiple resources into meaningful output. According to Met's continuum of content and language integration (1998), courses range from the most content-driven (total immersion classes) to the most language-driven (language classes with frequent use of content aimed to serve as grammar illustrations). The more proficient the students, the more courses tilt towards the content-driven end. Multiple bilingual K–12 programs in Canada and Spain develop exclusively content-driven courses paying minimum attention to the form of the language (Cenoz, 2015; Swain, 1996). Similarly, in American higher education, some world language programs such as French, Spanish, Italian, or German offer a variety of academic subjects taught in the target language with assessment mainly based on content (see Lyster and Ballinger (2011) or Schulz (1998) for some examples of such programs). However, this is not typical for less commonly taught world languages including Russian due to the scarcity of scholarly literature on the topic (exceptions include Leaver (1997) and Brown et al. (2009)). Therefore, Russianists always need to find the balance between language and content in teaching, such as various practices that Lyster (2007) describes in aimed at integrating both form-focused and content-based approaches.

Pedagogical task

Over the years, prominent SLA theoretical researchers provided multiple definitions of tasks, which sometimes differ significantly. Moreover, practitioners and empirical researchers have illuminated more facets of this complex concept. However, there is certainly an array of basic task-based principles that could be drawn from the literature. As Nunan (2004) summarized:

> While these definitions vary somewhat, they all emphasize the fact that pedagogical tasks involve communicative language use in which the user's attention is focused on meaning rather than grammatical form. This does not mean that form is not important.
>
> (p. 4)

This quote emphasizes the distinction between focus-on-formS and focus-on-form teaching approaches, as described in Long (1991). While the focus-on-formS principle prioritizes the acquisition of individual language elements such as verbal paradigms, focus-on-form "entails a prerequisite engagement in meaning before attention to linguistic features can be expected to be effective" (Doughty & Williams, 1998, p. 3). The core characteristic of the task should be a primary focus on meaning rather than grammar. Moreover, the outcome of the task should not necessarily be directly connected to language practice. In other words, the main focus of the TBLT approach is the use of language rather than knowledge of the language.

I used the feature mentioned earlier and the following four characteristics of a task as the basic theoretical underpinning of my course design (see Ellis, 2003; Comer, 2007; Nunan, 2012):

1   A task involves real-world examples of language use. An instructor should strive to formulate an activity in a way that could be found in the real world, for example, writing a blog on a recent spring break road trip.
2   A task targets cognitive processes, such as classifying, reasoning, evaluating, analyzing information, and so forth. Linguistic scaffolding should be provided in various degrees depending on the topic and class level.
3   A task has a purpose other than the target language specifics. As the course on the travelogue encompassed the knowledge of literature, sociology, history, and anthropology, one of the course objectives was to enhance students' global competence.
4   A task involves a communicative outcome beyond the use of language for its own sake, such as agreeing on a plan for a new local museum or a collaborative advertising text.

Additionally, the design of the task-based curriculum involved consideration of the following eight universal methodological principles of task-based instruction adapted from Long (2016): use task as a unit of analysis; promote learning by doing; provide rich input; focus-on-form approach (vs. focus-on-formS approach); provide implicit negative feedback in the form of recasts; acknowledge learner syllabi and developmental processes; promote cooperative collaborative learning; individualize instruction. Table 12.1 connects the main task characteristics (Ellis, 2003; Comer, 2007; Nunan, 2012) with the guiding methodological principles for the course (Long, 2016).

The course in focus featured a text-driven approach applied to written, spoken, or visual text-based materials. Importantly, the tasks were driven by potential engagement with the texts rather than pre-chosen teaching points (Tomlinson, 2018). The underlying principles of creating a task for the course included vast exposure to the target language; critical thinking stimulation; analysis and research conducted in the language-in-use. The first step of working with a text would be to read and react by responding to the text with observations (cognitively) and reactive comments (affectively).

Table 12.1 Pedagogical task framework

Task characteristics	Methodological principles
1. Focus on meaning	• Provide rich input • Focus-on-form • Implicit negative feedback
2. Real-world examples of language use	• Promote learning by doing
3. Task targets cognitive processes	• Individualize instruction • Acknowledge learner developmental processes
4. Purpose other than language specifics	• Use task as a unit of analysis
5. Communicative outcome	• Promote collaborative learning

The amount of explicit and implicit grammar explanations, drills, and other traditional practice activities vary depending on the particular goals of each language course. Empirical research has provided evidence that task-based instruction proves to be as effective at promoting L2 development as the traditional approach, while students demonstrated positive attitudes towards both tasks and grammar-oriented approaches (Mackey et al., 2013). Pedagogical tasks are valued for abundant opportunities for implicit negative feedback[1] on grammatical forms, which is conducive to improved language competency, while drills are appreciated for their role in "alleviating anxiety and increasing confidence" (Mackey et al., 2013, p. 81). In her review of the studies on the form-focused part of task-based and content-based instruction, Spada (2016) concludes that language-focused instruction positively contributes to L2 learning, when integrated into TBLT. Therefore, the course adopted a mixed focus-on-meaning and focus-on-form approach where the language instructor considered both innovative pedagogic tasks and more language-oriented exercises.

In terms of designing appropriate learning materials, a typical goal of grammar-in-context approaches is usually a high frequency of target linguistic elements in the materials. For instance, a recent study by Comer (2019) on the frequency of lexical items across beginning Russian textbooks calls for the development of "better graded reading texts which learners can use to build their receptive vocabularies" (p. 112). However, for task-based instruction, it is crucial "to identify topics that allow L2 learners to reflect on their L1 and L2 knowledge base (i.e., existing schemata) in new and illuminating ways" (Blake, 2013, p. 44). Thus, it appears crucial for instructors to carefully choose a range of authentic[2] engaging materials among those available to students.

Long (2016) notes that tasks tend to differ largely depending on a particular group of learners, making textbooks with no additional materials insufficient for TBLT. Thus, I refrained from using textbooks for the course. Instead, abundant input was obtained through authentic resources, while I developed the pedagogical tasks and used form-focused scaffolding exercises with the students. As previously mentioned, the main content resource was Ilf and Petrov's road memoir from 1935 accompanied by travelogues *"Odnoetazhnaia Amerika" of Vladimir Pozner* and *"Odnoetazhnaia Amerika" of Brian Kahn* (OA).[3] Both authors use quotation marks in the titles pointing out the primacy of the original text (Ilf et al., 2013). The video resource is a 16-episode documentary of Vladimir Pozner (2008) featuring Ivan Urgant and Brian Kahn. Each episode loosely corresponds to a particular part of the original travelogue as Pozner's main goal was to repeat Ilf and Petrov's iconic trip across America in 1935. The travelogue consists of 47 chapters (each chapter is roughly ten pages long). Pozner and Kahn's travel memoirs are 17 and 14 chapters respectively (each chapter is approximately 10–20 pages long). Each of the 16 episodes of the documentary is 44 minutes long. This unique compilation of materials provided students with the opportunity to learn about various facets of life in the U.S. through the eyes of foreigners (Ilf & Petrov) as well as Americans (Solomon Trone portrayed as Mr. Adams in the original travelogue, Vladimir Pozner, and Brian Kahn). The major connection between the three resources is abundant cross-citation that allows for vocabulary recycling in the format of a written text and video.

Pilot course description

Table 12.2 briefly introduces the course's overarching task and is followed by a more detailed description of the course design. This part of the chapter focuses on the student cohort, course goals, learning outcomes, assessment, typology of tasks, and my reflections as the course creator and practitioner.

Table 12.2 Task introduction table

Title	American Phenomena from a Variety of Perspectives
Task goals and educational setting	The overarching task goals for the students are: • to produce new and original work based on the text and video course materials • to design a project proposal • to collaborate while searching for information and reporting Instructional setting: university course, advanced language proficiency level
Learner needs analysis	Questionnaires and informal in-class conversations throughout the semester targeted learners' L2 Russian future needs, their learning background, and academic interests.
Type of task	Pedagogical tasks, form-focused tasks, information gaps

(*Continued*)

Table 12.2 (Continued)

Title	American Phenomena from a Variety of Perspectives
Can-do statements	• I can conduct an informational interview and report what I have learned • I can present a structured argument in written and oral forms (an essay and a presentation) • I can participate fully and effectively in a debate by expressing my opinion and using appropriate language to try to persuade others • I can interpret and infer meaning from a range of sources in different modalities (written text and video) • I can interact and negotiate with my peers to resolve matters while working on collaborative tasks
Assessment	Debates, presentations, and interviews were assessed summatively through content-based rubrics and checklists.

Students

The students in the fourth year of college language classes are usually of drastically diverse backgrounds and language levels. Some learners took six or seven semesters of Russian language, which equals roughly 268 contact hours, while others added a semester-long study abroad to those hours; yet others belong to the cohort of heritage students placed in the fourth year based on the reading placement test. Consequently, student language skills usually range from Intermediate Mid to Advanced High (ACTFL, 2012). The pilot course had three students, two of them heritage students (Advanced Mid) and an L1 English speaker who had spent a semester in Russia and reached at least Advanced Low[4] in speaking by the beginning of the course. The small size of the pilot group was perfect for applying a TBLT approach that emphasizes individualized instruction (Long, 2016). Third- and fourth-year students have two and a half contact hours per week, totaling 34 contact hours per semester.

Course content and learning outcomes

The participants of the course covered five parts of *One-Storied America* following my original idea to devote roughly three weeks to each unit. I assigned text segments and documentary episodes for each unit, while the actual topics of pedagogical tasks were collaboratively created during class discussions of the readings by all course participants. Unit 1 (Chicago and Dearborn) topics included American roads, the car industry, Henry Ford, and the purpose of museums. Unit 2 (Santa Fe) topics included the U.S. Army, Native Americans, and the Grand Canyon as a natural wonder. Unit 3 (California) topics included Hollywood as art, the problems faced by immigrants, and the Stanford and Silicon Valley phenomenon.

Unit 4 (New Orleans and Washington, D.C.) discussions included racial injustice and American democracy, while Unit 5 (New York) topics included the penitentiary system and life in small towns vs. big cities (then and now). The abundance of potential topics to discuss and research added flexibility to the course, making it possible to adapt the content and tasks to the particular learning needs of each student group.

Learning outcomes and course objectives could be roughly classified as content-based, task-based, and language-related (focus-on-form) outcomes. The main criterion for the course outcomes is the degree the learners interact with content material for content acquisition and their ability to discuss, present, and write about it. Additionally, the course's content-related outcomes were based on the following general dimensions for the global competence construct: first, "the willingness to perceive social phenomena from perspectives of people from a foreign culture," then "awareness of the similarities and/or differences between one's own and a foreign culture," and the "ability to articulate one's own perspective to other people of a different culture" (Li, 2012, p. 130).

In the course syllabus, I presented the task-based outcomes in conformity with the five core characteristics of the task and eight corresponding methodological principles (Table 12.1). The learning outcomes of in-class discussions and debates include persuading others, supporting opinions, hypothesizing, and advocating a position at length. All of these facets allow learners to use language as a tool rather than an object. The overarching learning outcome of student community outreach projects and collaborative work is that students can participate in goal-oriented communication that resembles real-life activities.

In terms of language-related outcomes, the main goal was to increase learner speaking, writing, reading, and listening skills with particular emphasis on opinion phrases and collocations, participles, indirect speech, complex sentences, punctuation rules, and verbal aspect.

Assessment

Following the methodological principle of using a task as a unit of analysis, the grading criteria did not specify any target forms or structures. Instead, the main focus of rubrics was on content. For instance, oral research presentations were evaluated based on the quality of material, presentation, and PowerPoint slides. Debates were evaluated in connection with specific can-do statements listed in the task guidelines. Specifically, task guidelines and rubrics varied largely throughout the semester depending on particular pedagogical sub-tasks. The guidelines were distributed in class in advance with an opportunity for Q&A interaction in L1 English to minimize confusion and misunderstanding. The final course grades were based on the following:

   25 percent – Debates (five debates, one at the end of every course unit).
   20 percent – Individual research (an essay and a presentation).

15 percent – Semester-long group project (community outreach project: an interview with local Russian-speaking community members based on Vladimir Pozner's list of questions.)

40 percent – Participation grade including 20 in-class discussions of assigned readings, close translations, transcripts, and in-class collaborative tasks.

Assessment points notably did not include vocabulary or grammar quizzes. Students appreciated that, mentioning in informal oral evaluative remarks that it made them feel more competent in their language knowledge and inherently more motivated. Moreover, there were no assessment points assigned to homework for each class, as the output was integrated into the class performance and evaluated by the participation grade.

Course tasks

TBLT-related literature provides various classifications of pedagogical tasks (e.g., Ellis, 2006; Long, 2015; Willis, 2004). Below is a list of major task categories (Willis, 2004) applied in the pilot classroom. The classification was modified to fit the purpose of the course and includes some categories described by Leaver and Kaplan (2004).

Information-gap tasks. The main idea of information-gap pedagogical tasks is for learners to obtain certain information with the help of communicative interaction in order to fulfill the task. The outcome could be a flowchart, a survey, or a collaborative report. During the pilot course, information-gap tasks, while being dispersed throughout the semester, were perceived positively due to higher levels of involvement and informality of pair work. The abundance of course material allowed for individualized teaching, when students were assigned individual homework and then paired accordingly for in-class information-gap tasks. The three students of the course usually worked as a single group on the following 'jigsaw puzzle'-type activity: while one student watched a documentary episode, another one read the corresponding chapter by Pozner, and the third student read the corresponding chapter by Kahn. In class, students compared their findings and offered their opinions on the social issue discussed in the episode.

Another example of a larger information-gap project was comparing how various interviewees of Pozner reacted to his list of questions throughout the series. In almost every episode, Pozner would repeatedly ask people what it meant to be an American citizen or what they were most proud of, and what their biggest worries as Americans were. Moreover, there were other questions he posed more than once and students usually received a take-home task to add a question they heard in the assigned episode to the collaborative "question list" in Google docs. As a result, the class compiled a list of nine questions by the end of the semester. As a community project based on this information, students conducted interviews with the local Russian community members and presented their findings in class. This pedagogical task targeted the real-life skill of interviewing and conveying a point of view in the form of a journalistic report.

Cognitive tasks. Cognitive tasks typically target major cognitive processes ranging in complexity and creativity from simpler elements such as listing, brainstorming, or reading, to more sophisticated creative projects. Instructors usually have a great deal of flexibility with tasks based on the cognitive processes as those could "be designed around any theme or topic, selected to suit learners' lexical and discourse needs, whether general or specialist" (Willis, 2004, p. 23). Smaller cognitive pedagogic tasks oftentimes include matching or finding similarities and differences in pictures. Students used the photos that Ilf took for 11 short photo-essays to be published in the Soviet magazine *Ogonëk* in 1936. The photographs were reproduced in an English-language photo book *Ilf and Petrov's American Road Trip: The 1935 Travelogue of Two Soviet Writers* (2007). The main volume of OA used in the course also includes a collection of 42 color photographs that Ivan Urgant took during the trip. Those two resources of historic photographs allowed for designing engaging pedagogical tasks aimed at the cognitive challenge of "comparing and contrasting" (Willis, 2004, p. 22).

In the course, the more challenging cognitive tasks included in-class debates. Discussions as a task in an L2 Russian language classroom allow learners to use the target language "as a vehicle for communicating ideas for a meaningful purpose – persuading others, rather than viewing language merely as an object of study" (Bown et al., 2019, p. 36), which follows the main principle of the TBLT approach. Moreover, skillful debating requires an advanced competency level knowledge of the language and is a useful asset in a workplace or academic environment in the target-language country. The travelogue by Pozner has a number of transcripts of conversations on the road between Pozner, Urgant, and Kahn. These serve as input materials for pedagogical tasks in the form of debates. Students chose the debate topics based on their preliminary in-class discussions of the assigned materials. The five debate topics included: Thomas Edison vs. Nikola Tesla; Henry Ford: Hero or Villain; Capital Punishment; Hollywood: Then and Now; and California Controversies. For linguistic scaffolding, the student handouts would usually include a glossary that aimed to help the students with some lexical forms. Additionally, opinion words and collocations, as well as connectors that allow speakers to convey their position, were marked in bold so that students could briefly analyze and use them in their commentary (see the Appendix for a handout on one of the debate topics).

One of the outcomes of the course was an opportunity for each student to conduct individual research based on Ilf and Petrov's initial interest in various phenomena. The final product included an essay and a PowerPoint presentation during the final week. For example, one student's research revealed what happened to the iconic A&P stores, which impressed Ilf and Petrov so much. Another student's essay was devoted to the legendary actress Mae West, who was just briefly mentioned in the travelogue.

"Push the performance" exercises. The main purpose of this group of tasks is to refine advanced speakers' language use. Therefore, they relate to focus-on-form to a greater degree than the earlier-mentioned two categories. Particularly, they aim to force learners "to avoid the kinds of strategic competence, such as compensation strategies, that allow students to deal with everyday situations comfortably at lower levels of proficiency" (Leaver & Kaplan, 2004, p. 54). As a result, such tasks help students to attain nuance and precision of advanced and superior levels of speaking and writing. Each student self-recorded their presentation and analyzed it with me during individual debriefings. The procedure of watching the recording either alone or with the instructor proved to be uncomfortable for most of the students, yet highly effective in terms of self-awareness. Other kinds of "Push the Performance" tasks required students to create a three-minute transcription of the TV documentary episode as well as Russian-to-English translations of short paragraphs from OA. Finally, a useful regular in-class task was an informal spontaneous discussion of the topics in that week's chapter, which students found more engaging in contrast to a more traditional approach based on predetermined questions. Such discussions allowed for a more authentic interaction among students while training the skill of unplanned talk. By the end of the semester, these short informal warm-up discussions became an essential part of the curriculum included in the TBLT syllabus as a participation grade.

Integrated use of the authentic text and video materials: sample task

Choosing and combining the materials for the classwork presented an exciting and challenging task for the author due to multiple cross-references and citations of the original work in the documentary and the two accompanying texts. While *One-Storied America* states Ilf and Petrov's opinions, Pozner's book often provides arguments for and against those points of view, and the documentary adds visual and audio support to the arguments. Brian Kahn's book adds yet a different angle to the main topics of the narrative, enriching the unusual discussion through time and place. As a result, students have a chance to visualize what they are reading while forming their own opinions on certain social phenomena in the U.S.A. then and now, the Soviet Union, and the modern Russian-speaking world. The materials for each pedagogical task or chain of tasks could require viewing a whole episode of the TV documentary and reading of a larger text (i.e., two or three chapters of *One-Storied America* targeting an overarching theme of the episode).

As an example of a larger chunk of material would be Chapter 15 "Dearborn" and Chapter 16 "Henry Ford" of *One-Storied America* were assigned as preparatory materials accompanied by Episode 3 of the TV documentary, Chapter 4 "Sic Transit Gloria Mundi" of Pozner's book, and the chapter titled "River Rouge" of Kahn's book. The first take-home pedagogical task related to this compilation of input was to read Chapters 15 and 16 and write observations and comments in a free writing style for 15–20 minutes. The guidelines specified that the object of the task was the holistic meaning of the text, not the language. Then in class, students shared their notes[5] in an informal discussion to mitigate the stress of being evaluated. The instructor usually followed the discussion with further tasks rooted in the topics that students had found more engaging. An example of a text-driven collaborative task-based project guided students to skim the two chapters and find detailed descriptions of the national historic landmark The Henry Ford, which constitutes the Museum of American Innovation, Greenfield Village, the factory, and Edison's Menlo Park complex. Then students participated in a role-play where they needed to create a proposal for a local museum and present it to the local authorities to seek funding.

Close reading of certain passages proved to be as fertile in terms of student engagement and learning as the larger amount of input. As an example of a close-reading task, the class was asked to reread a passage where Ilf and Petrov describe the genuinely excited reaction of two Americans whom they had asked to show them the road to Cleveland. The ironic style of the excerpt instigated a fruitful discussion on what is considered polite or acceptable behavior today. Using Google docs, students created a collaborative list of the generalizations abundantly present throughout the text including, for instance, Ilf and Petrov's observation that Americans are prone to extremes: "В области температур американцы склонны к крайностям. Работают в чересчур натопленных помещениях и пьют чересчур холодные напитки. Все, что не подается горячим, подается ледяным. Середины нет. [In the matter of temperatures Americans are inclined to extremes. They work in overheated dwellings and drink overcooled drinks. Everything not offered piping hot is offered ice-cold. There is no middle ground] (Translated by Charles Malamuth) (OA, Ilf et al., 2013, p. 188). Learners reacted to the observation, providing supporting arguments based on anecdotal evidence.

Some reflections on the course

As a practitioner, I was mostly satisfied with the course outcomes as all three students demonstrated progress in language and content acquisition throughout the semester. However, I encountered several issues during the implementation of the task I will seek to avoid in the future. First, I frequently had to "play by ear" with my language and content scaffolding as the in-class discussions could go in any direction. Moreover, due to time constraints, we could not examine all the materials available during the semester. Thus, I stayed alert for topics that would interest students in the readings and modified the curriculum accordingly. Answering the course evaluation question on how to improve the course, one student summarized this challenge as follows: "*Having a more organized layout of the class, both weekly and overall for the semester. Every class it seemed like we did not accomplish what was expected, and so then things would change on the fly and that was hard to plan for.*" In the future, I will plan in-class discussions according to the initial informal exchange of student opinions on the chapter contents.

I believe this approach will strengthen the overall course framework and prove to be fruitful in terms of student level of engagement and motivation.

The second challenge of the pilot course was to find L1 Russian participants for the interview project, which required the collaborative efforts of the instructor, the students, and the local academic community. Another idea of implementing this task would be to devote one of the final classes of the course to the topic of being an American citizen and a global citizen at the same time. Students would then interview their peers and prepare a five-minute video on the overarching topic of global citizenship/local awareness. The interviews could be conducted in English to expand the potential pool of interviewees while the final presentation would be in Russian. However, I will encourage students to find Russian-speaking participants for consistency in terms of language learning.

Challenges of teaching L2 Russian

To summarize the particular challenges I faced while creating and implementing the task, I will point out a number of interconnected issues relevant to teaching L2 Russian in general. A major challenge of the preparatory phase for Russian teachers is the scarcity of learning materials. "For Russianists, TBLT remains a theoretical construct that has yet to be enhanced with sample lesson plans, textbooks, teacher training materials, and other instantiations of the theory" (Comer, 2007, p. 182). However, the situation has improved since the ACTFL world-readiness standards were published for Russian with many language-specific learning scenarios (National Standards in Foreign Language Education Project, 2015). A major challenge of the active task phase for students and teachers is to find a balance between focus on form and focus on content. The TBLT approach encourages students to use a variety of available tools needed for task completion including dictionaries, online resources, and communication with peers instead of the tailored textbook-style materials. At the same time, teaching intricate Russian morphology remains "an especially thorny issue for Russian in terms of implementing TBLT within a model of implicit or non-obtrusive grammar instruction" (Comer, 2007, p. 190). Coming from a grammar-oriented background, students might feel overwhelmed with the amount of authentic input and require more scaffolding. In this course, students regularly asked for extra worksheets and handouts on punctuation and grammar, while our in-class discussions included spontaneous language-oriented teaching episodes. Finally, a major challenge of the post-task phase for the teacher is providing feedback according to the task guidelines and rubrics that do not feature specific grammar points. It usually took me more time to provide meaningful feedback at multiple stages of the larger course tasks (i.e., essays, presentations, and the interview project) as I focused on ways to improve the content and delivery method rather than the language per se.

Another limitation that applies to a variety of less commonly taught languages including Russian is the low number of students in advanced level courses. As I had three students in the OA course, it was rather problematic to create debate teams. We alternated the scenarios with one person arguing against the other two or each student defending their own randomly assigned position. I believe this task would be more effectively implemented in a classroom of at least four participants. Thus, I intend to replace this learning activity with a more individualized one should I have a group of fewer than four students in the future. For the same reason, all three students worked on one interview project. As the final report needed viewers, I invited members of the university Russian club to the presentation. Due to the fact that most of the guests had a lower level of Russian, the Q & A part was limited.

Conclusion

The TBLT approach provides higher-level language students with unique opportunities to develop global competence while simultaneously honing their target language skills, as this chapter describes. The course on OA was successful in terms of student language use within the five goal areas of the World-Readiness Standards – Communication, Cultures, Connections, Comparisons, and Communities – targeted by pedagogical tasks throughout the semester. Each course unit made students work regularly in five language modalities (reading, listening, speaking, writing, and cultural awareness). Practical ideas implemented in the course might be applied in any world language classroom regardless of the course level or focus.

However, TBLT remains an innovative approach that requires certain theoretical expertise, access to practical examples, and significant time investment on the part of the instructor, who needs to create a course practically from scratch (Long, 2016). During this journey, teachers may experience challenges with making course materials engaging and modifying them for each particular group of students. Planning and integrating language scaffolding continues to depend entirely on the teacher as researchers' suggestions differ. The class size is another issue to be considered when designing a TBLT course. For my course, student group work proved to be effective, but having more students in a class would also mean a larger variety of interests to attend to while shaping the curriculum. Thus, acknowledging the limitations of this work, the suggestion for beginner practitioners would be to start with partial implementation of task-based instruction and move into deeper exploration of the benefits of TBLT.

Appendix

Student Worksheet. Debates on Capital Punishment

1. Давайте перечитаем отрывок из заметок В. Познера (стр. 555):

    Познер: **Я считаю**, что главное право, которое есть у человека, это право на жизнь. Для меня, в принципе, государство не имеет права убивать человека.

    Кан: **Я считаю**, что некоторые военные преступления, имеющие отношение к геноциду, заслуживают смертной казни. **Я считаю**, что некоторые виды насильственных, особо жестоких преступлений требуют того, чтобы была возможность убить того, кто отнял чужую жизнь. Единственное, что смогло **поколебать мою позицию**, это интервью с монахиней Хелен Крейджиан, которая сказала, что мы совершаем ошибки, что <u>присяжные заседатели</u> иногда ошибаются. **А если** мы используем смертную казнь, **то** мы лишаем жизни и невинных людей. Это неизбежно. И я ничего на это **не смог возразить**.

    Ургант: **Я правильно понимаю, что** вам человек, которого вы интервьюировали в камере смертников, сказал, что у него был самый простой, плохой адвокат, и большинство из тех людей, которые сейчас находятся в камере смертников, они все были с плохими адвокатами, то есть с теми, которых им предоставило государство, и не было у них нормальных адвокатов, хороших, потому что у них просто не было денег. **Получается** – <u>неравноправие</u>. **И получается**, что <u>рычаг</u> опять во всей этой истории – это деньги. **И в обратную сторону** это может работать – виновный человек, имеющий хорошие деньги и хорошую защиту, может избежать этого наказания. **То есть получается**, что, **по крайней мере**, по этому показателю демократия находится <u>в загоне</u> страшном.

    Кан: **Я не верю**, что во многих странах мира равноправие находится на таком же уровне, как в Америке. У нас в большинстве штатов есть отлаженная система <u>государственных защитников</u>. Мы прошли долгий путь, чтобы защитить права от нарушений <...>

Познер: Но я говорил только об одном – о смертной казни. И когда ты говоришь, что есть люди, которые заслуживают смерти . . . я бы хотел, чтобы что-то ужасное и неотвратимое убило их. Они заслужили умереть от страшной формы рака. **Я бы хотел** этого, **но считаю**, что мы, как люди, не имеем права отнимать жизнь у другого человека, мы совершаем узаконенное убийство. Хотим мы этого или нет.

- Присяжные заседатели – обычные люди, которые выносят приговор обвиняемому в суде
- неравноправие – когда у людей нет равных прав. Антоним – "равноправие"
- рычаг – (здесь) двигатель; то, что играет решающую роль
- в загоне – (сленг) в тупике; нет выхода
- государственные защитники – "бесплатные" адвокаты, за которых обвиняемый не платит

Каким образом выражает свою позицию каждый участник дискуссии?

Notes

1 Implicit negative feedback is the interlocutor's indication that the previous sentence was erroneous by rephrasing or repeating the problematic part rather than providing an overt correction.
2 Here and further, authentic materials are defined as "documents written *by* native speakers *for* native speakers" (Brown et al., 2009, p. 427).
3 The volume lists multiple authors including Ilya Ilf, Evgenii Petrov, Vladimir Pozner, Ivan Urgant, and Brian Kahn on the title page alongside the title *Odnoetazhnaia Amerika x 2*. Here and further, the book is abbreviated as OA to stand out among other editions.
4 The assessment was based on unofficial oral proficiency interviews (OPIs) conducted by the instructor, who is a certified OPI tester in Russian.
5 The practice is similar to various real-life academic sessions based on transcripts or other data forms.

Chapter 13

TBLT in Russian classrooms
Reflections on practice and future directions

Wendy Whitehead Martelle and Svetlana V. Nuss

Chapter summary

This chapter summarizes practitioners' reflections and lessons learned in implementing task-based language teaching (TBLT) in the context of L2 Russian classrooms. It reviews the aspects of how tasks, authenticity, and cultural awareness are interconnected; as well as the intertwined nature of tasks, learner-centeredness, and motivation; and brings forward the challenges of teaching L2 Russian in a task-based setting. We particularly discuss issues of the definition of task through the lens of practitioners, what assessment can look like in a TBLT-based L2 Russian classroom and how it should be conducted, along with other practical matters of teaching Russian in general and particularly through tasks. We add a fourth *real issue* for TBLT instruction (Long, 2016), and bring forward the institutional support available to teachers as an essential *real issue* the language teaching profession is facing in general (not Russian-specific). The chapter also offers some practical advice gleaned from the experience of implementing TBLT in the L2 Russian context along with the candid reflections of the challenges encountered. Then, we offer remaining questions and future directions that may help inform future scientific inquiry. The chapter ends with a call to teachers of L2 Russian to (a) shift their instruction by making it more learner-centered, holistically meeting needs of the diverse L2 Russian students; (b) recognize their power to better support students by attending to the teacher's own professional development; and (c) change the professional and societal – both implicit and explicit – discourse of the field of Russian language study from the current narrative of *difficulties* of learning Russian to that of *success and possibilities* for learners to attain high levels of proficiency, which can be achieved by consciously shaping a more learner-friendly and responsive environment.

Краткое содержание главы

Данная глава посвящена анализу практики применения целевого задания при обучении русскому языку как иностранному (РКИ), второму или унаследованному вне языковой среды. Рассматриваются вопросы

DOI: 10.4324/9781003146346-13

взаимовлияния целевого задания, понимания русской культуры и аутентичности как процесса так и материалов обучения; анализируются связи между целевым заданием, мотивацией и личностно ориентированным обучением, где обучающийся и его интересы, умения и цели во многом определяют учебный процесс. Отдельно рассматриваются особенности организации образовательного процесса овладения русским как иностранным при помощи метода целевого задания. Определение целевого задания рассматривается с точки зрения практики его применения в РКИ, в частности, обсуждается оценка языковых компетенций и способы ее проведения. К трем *главным проблемам теории и практики метода целевого задания*, определенных М. Лонгом (Long, 2016), мы добавляем *вопрос профессиональной поддержки*, которую учитель/преподаватель получает от организации работодателя. В главе суммируется опыт авторов-участников сборника в применении целевых заданий в различной образовательной среде (в частности, программы бакалавриата университета, частная школа, краткий курс во время посещения страны изучаемого языка, интенсивное погружение) от начального до продвинутого уровней языковой компетенции и намечаются горизонты новых исследований. В целом, глава утверждает (а) необходимость организации обучения с учетом социальных и лингвистических потребностей обучаемого, в том числе делая обучение более разнообразным и активным; (b) учитель/преподаватель – важнейший фактор успеха обучения; активная личностная позиция профессорско-преподавательского состава в овладении новыми педагогическими приемами определяет степень профессиональной подготовки педагога и его умение на практике вывести обучаемых на новый уровень языковой компетенции; (c) необходимость вывести профессиональный дискурс РКИ из доминирующего сегодня тона *трудности в овладении русским языком* в *успех и удовлетворение личным успехом* изучающих русский язык, уверенное овладение новыми уровнями компетенций. Это может быть достигнуто путем целенаправленного переформатирования среды обучения и концентрирования внимания педагогического сообщества РКИ на обучающихся и *их*, а не наших, целях, потребностях и предпочтениях. РКИ, вместе с современным обществом, переживает один из поворотных моментов своего развития. Хочется надеяться, что в этот раз цикличные процессы реорганизации общества привнесут так давно назревшие и уже действующие в некоторых реалиях перемены и в мир обучения русскому как иностранному и сделают их более массовыми и активными.

Practitioners newly introduced to TBLT may become intrigued by the ideas and discussions surrounding it. However, some teachers might get overwhelmed by how much time it takes to design and implement tasks in the classroom. Or, they may feel that in order to implement TBLT, their syllabus needs to be entirely task-based or *systemic*, where the instruction of all units is delivered via tasks exclusively (see Nuss & Whitehead Martelle, Chapter 1, for the discussion of terms *systemic* and *incremental*).

The strength of this volume is that it showcases multiple ways of incorporating tasks into the classroom's workflow. Some practitioners use task-based instruction systemically (Nimis et al., Chapter 8; Smirnova Henriques et al., Chapter 7; Zheltoukhova, Chapter 12), while many others create individual tasks designed to complement other classroom activities. This underscores the value of TBLT as a highly flexible, not an "all or nothing," approach. Based on our experience, in the context of L2 Russian instruction, tasks can be as short or as long as the instructor wants them to be. They can take 15 minutes or an entire class period – incremental TBLT; or they can comprise a 3-week unit or an entire semester – systemic TBLT. Tasks can act as the nuclear piece to anchor a unit, or they can be ancillary or optional activities.

When teachers choose to implement task-based instruction, they face a series of instructional decisions:

- what role tasks will play in their instructional setting,
- what purpose the use of task/s will serve and what needs of a particular cohort of students would be met through task/s,
- what instructional goals would be achieved via task/s, among other considerations, which would, in turn, help to determine how much time in the course will be devoted to task/s, along with other resulting instructional decisions.

Because of the extensive planning and pedagogical foresight involved in task-based instruction, the role of the teacher in TBLT cannot be minimized or relegated to the role of "manager" or "facilitator" (as suggested by Swan, 2005, p. 391); rather, the instructor plays a crucial role – that of strategic planning in determining what tasks and activities are relevant and useful for their instructional setting. The level of the teacher's professional preparedness to take on this kind of practice comes into play here as well. By their very nature, tasks can invite spontaneous developments, including questions from students about language functions. This places on the teacher greater pedagogical demands than those found in the more traditional classroom: when a group is following a textbook, any language structure-related questions are answered as they arise, with explanatory texts readily available. In contrast, during task-based instruction, students' questions may arise spontaneously, placing the urgency of response solely on the teacher's foresight and linguistic and pedagogical preparedness.

The chapters presented in this collection thus – directly or indirectly – speak to the issue of the role of the teacher, taken up by Long (2016) in his *In Defense of Tasks and TBLT*. The role of the teacher is prominent in all chapters of the volume without exception. This lends support to Long's claims of teacher responsibilities as being more demanding in a task-based context than those of a textbook-based. For example, given the frequency of morphology-based errors in L2 Russian learner production, as teachers provide corrective feedback, they need to quickly determine where on the acquisition continuum a particular error is. In the case of task-based instruction, this information is crucial, as it leads to the fundamental decisions of instructional design. They also have to respond to spontaneously arising focus on form discussions, often without explanatory texts to rely upon or time to research answers to questions like *why neuter is used* in мне *было* пять лет [I was 5 years old] that do take deeper knowledge of Russian language structures. It is easy to see that task-based instruction takes high language expertise, pedagogical savviness, and professional courage to venture into the world of teaching without a textbook and brings the teacher's role to the forefront, affording issues of praxis, practice, and teacher agency a central role in TBLT discourse.

In editorial conversations with authors shaping this volume, we asked them to reflect on the challenges of teaching Russian as a Foreign Language (RFL) through tasks and in doing so look beyond the case endings, verbs of motion, and aspect – features that notoriously dominate conversations of the challenges in the instruction of RFL regardless of the methodology employed. Some authors responded to this request directly in their chapters, others chose to address it in personal communication. Interestingly, while all of the authors could easily refrain from mentioning aspect, case, and verbs of motion per se, most of them anchored challenging aspects of their teaching practices in the rich morphology of the Russian language and described their views on challenges of teaching L2 Russian in their relationship to and through the lens of morphology acquisition.

The main themes emerging from responses were learner-, teacher-, and environment-related and all had Russian morphology underpinning their explanatory context and elaborations: (a) individual learner differences, to include students' previous learning experiences; (b) variability of instruction, such as learner interactions and instructional modes, materials curation and creation; (c) feedback and its quantity, quality, timing, and volume, particularly in relation to what features to address, when, and to what degree; (d) form-meaning mapping and how it is affected by cognitive and other resources; (e) balance of content and form; (f) the role of assessment and the teacher's ability to estimate student growth; (g) the importance of a learner-centered environment and the need for students to feel successful in learning, as well as in the degree of their proficiency in communication; (h) institutional and professional support for teachers.

This closing chapter therefore brings together some of the practitioners' observations and reflections on task design and implementation and share certain themes that have surfaced from their experiences working with TBLT in an RFL setting, including how the notion of "task" is entangled with the concepts of culture, authenticity, learner-centered approaches, and motivation. We will also address what has emerged as some of the more pressing challenges of task-based instruction in RFL. This chapter then concludes with remaining questions, as well as future directions for task-based instruction of Russian.

Lessons learned in implementing TBLT

The contributors in this volume adopt different definitions of "task" as an anchor to inform their task design and implementation. Several chapters cite Ellis (2003), others draw on Comer (2007), while other contributors refer to Long (2015), Nunan (2004, 2012), Skehan (1998), Willis (2004), Lee (1995), or Richards (2006). Although many of these definitions share common characteristics (see Nuss & Whitehead Martelle, Chapter 1 for a more detailed overview), practitioners, on the one hand, struggle with the wide-ranging and seemingly unlimited discussion on how a task can be defined within TBLT and on the other, appreciate this flexibility. One contributor reflected that "the most revealing and challenging was to discover the overwhelming number of different ways of understanding tasks that can be found in TBLT literature . . . [which] makes it difficult to define the boundaries of so-called TBLT" (M. Bondarenko, personal communication, December 28, 2020), while another "felt empowered by the realization that we can tailor TBLT to our unique needs, and there are no obstacles to use TBLT with any learner" (V. Kogan, personal communication, December 28, 2020).

Despite the many definitions and interpretations of what a "task" is, we wish to highlight the importance of designing and using tasks to suit both the instructional situations and learners' needs. However, because TBLT affords the instructor a great deal of freedom in course design, we echo a word of caution raised by Nunan (2004); namely, that a program intended to be task-based "may consist of a seemingly random collection of tasks with nothing to tie them together" (p. 25). In other words, if an instructor is considering the use of tasks and/or the implementation of a task-based syllabus in their teaching context, it is imperative that the units and activities have an overarching goal and purpose, and that they do not come across as a collection of random activities.

In relation to how tasks are defined, chosen, and implemented in the Russian language classroom, many of the volume's contributors noted connections between their implementation of tasks and the concepts of authenticity, cultural awareness, learner-centeredness, and motivation in language learning. Each of these themes is discussed in the following sections.

Tasks, authenticity, and raising cultural awareness

Authenticity has been examined from a variety of perspectives within language learning: texts and materials, tasks, and participants in communicative situations (Breen, 1985; Widdowson, 1998; Mishan, 2005; Gilmore, 2007; Rilling & Dantas-Whitney, 2009). In terms of text/materials, Morrow (1977) provides a foundational definition of an authentic text as "a stretch of real language, produced by a real speaker or writer for a real audience and designed to convey a real message of some sort" (p. 13). Many of the volume's chapters highlight how authentic materials (such as demographic data, menus, maps, websites, role-playing games, various types of literature) can be integrated into a variety of RFL learning situations (traditional classrooms, intensive and immersion contexts, study abroad contexts) with beginner, intermediate, and advanced proficiency levels. As a result of using more authentic materials in their instructional design of tasks compared to teaching with textbooks, several contributors observed that in contrast to

> the contrived materials of traditional textbooks . . . [a]uthentic materials, particularly audio-visual ones, offer a much richer source of input for learners and have the potential to be exploited in different ways and on different levels to develop learners' communicative competence.
>
> (Gilmore, 2007, p. 103)

Another component of authentic materials in language learning relates to who has created the materials. Often, materials created by native speakers have been privileged, where "both teachers and students often regard 'native-speakers' as being the ideal model and therefore an example of authenticity" (Pinner, 2014, p. 22). We, in line with Pinner (2014) and Gilmore (2007), argue that the term *authenticity* can be broadened to include materials/texts produced by learners, who are themselves "real" users of the language. Novikov and Vinokurova's contribution (Chapter 4) provides a compelling illustration of this broadened concept of authenticity by integrating a corpus of learner language within a task-based approach.

Many contributors notice that incorporating authentic materials in task design leads to an increase in students' cultural awareness and adds to the aspect of cultural knowledge featured in a number of the tasks' intended learning outcomes (for example, Mendelevich, Chapter 11; Nimis et al., Chapter 8; Kogan & Bondarenko, Chapter 6; Smirnova Henriques et al., Chapter 7). However, in addition to the use of authentic materials and tasks, some contributors note that certain interactions with their students reveal cultural differences, which lead to an increase in cultural awareness for both teachers and learners. For example, Vinokurova observes that a challenge "has been predicting students' interests and the kind of vocabulary that they would need in order to complete a certain task" because, for instance, she and her students "envision small talk at a dinner party in completely different ways – be it because of cultural differences or because of differing interests and background knowledge" (personal communication, July 31, 2020). In communicative approaches to language teaching, East (2012) notes that intercultural aspects of language learning are often neglected and treated as separate from language learning, but that TBLT could offer a potential entry point for developing and reflecting on intercultural awareness. Several contributions in this volume can serve as a foundation for starting conversations about intercultural awareness in teaching Russian through tasks, and we suggest the interaction of cultural awareness and TBLT to be a potentially rich avenue for future research.

Tasks, learner-centeredness, and motivation

A number of contributors raise another topic that concerns the intertwined ideas of learner-centeredness and motivation. Motivation has received substantial attention in the field of second language acquisition, with areas of focus on developing a framework in defining motivation (Gardner & Lambert, 1972; Dörnyei, 1990; Tremblay & Gardner, 1995), understanding motivation in the classroom (Dörnyei, 1994, 2001; Dörnyei & Ushioda, 2011; Ushioda, 2008), as well as how motivation interacts with such concepts as attitudes (Gardner, 1985), identity (Dörnyei & Ushioda, 2009), and autonomy (Ushioda, 2014).

Within a TBLT framework, several contributors notice increased levels of student motivation as a result of engaging with the tasks. For instance, Esser notes that the video assignments are ideal for distance learning as they spark a new level of engagement in the absence of face-to-face interactions and afford "creative freedom" in which the students are given a chance to express themselves and an opportunity to "use Russian productively" (Chapter 5). Mendelevich (Chapter 11) also observes that students reported "feeling more engaged and motivated to complete the assignments and appreciated the opportunity for creative expression" while they engaged in the tasks through virtual space. Regarding the connection between motivation and technology, it is important to bear in mind that the use of technology in and of itself "does not result in automatic motivational increases in teachers or learners" (Stockwell, 2013, p. 170), and should not replace or be an alternative to pedagogical practices, including task design and implementation.

Kositsky (Chapter 3) shares another observation connecting TBLT and motivation; namely, that framing the task as a game has the potential to increase student motivation. This observation is in line with previous research on the potentially positive impact of games within a language learning context and their ability to lead to increased student motivation (McFarlane et al., 2002; Calvo-Ferrer, 2017). From the contributions mentioned earlier (Esser, Mendelevich, Kositsky), we offer the connection between tasks and games, including play and creativity (as explored by Cook, 2000; Maybin & Swann, 2007; and Cho & Kim, 2018), as another fruitful path for future research within Russian language learning contexts.

Smirnova Henriques et al. (Chapter 7) presents another connection between TBLT and motivation: that TBLT is a good fit for the learning contexts in the Russian language schools in Brazil because the students "are frequently motivated by the idea to travel to Russia and are excited for speaking Russian in the situations that imitate the real-life activities" (personal communication, August 29, 2020). Similarly, Burvikova and Stremova (Chapter 9) identify the collaboration between instructors and students as a motivating factor to use the language in authentic interactions outside the classroom:

> Применяя принцип открытой архитектуры курса, мы даем преподавателю и студенту возможность коллаборации, что повышает мотивацию

студента работать над языком в аудитории и не бояться применять язык вне аудитории.

By applying the principle of open architecture design, the teacher and the student are given the chance for collaboration, which increases the motivation of the student to work on the language in the classroom and not to be afraid to use the language outside the classroom.

(personal communication, September 29, 2020)

Further, Nimis et al. (Chapter 8) prefer the term "investment" over "motivation" to reflect their students' language learning commitment within a full immersion setting through such tasks as completing a simulated immigration process, creating cooking videos, or producing a TV series.

From the examples highlighted in this section, we see a connection between motivation and authenticity, described and outlined in Gilmore (2007), and further developed by Pinner (2016), who identifies a "dearth" of empirical studies related to authenticity and motivation and calls for more qualitative and mixed-methods studies to develop an "understanding of people as individuals within contextualized social settings" (pp. 86–87).

Besides authenticity, most of the contributions that highlight or mention the concept of motivation demonstrate how learner-centeredness plays a key role in their task-based instruction. In the design of the tasks, not only are the learners' needs considered – they largely define the context and content of instruction, where learners are given opportunities for creative expression, the learners' intentions and goals are taken into account, and the tasks are primarily meaning-focused and aligned in accordance with the learners' proficiency levels. Additionally, some contributions (notably, Smirnova Henriques et al., Chapter 7; Burvikova & Stremova, Chapter 9) highlight learner-centeredness in the sense that the students themselves can come up with ideas on tasks that are relevant to their needs and interests.

Teaching L2 Russian in a task-based setting: challenges, remaining questions, and future directions

In addition to the call for more empirical research exploring the connections between TBLT, motivation, and authenticity in the foregoing sections, many of the volume's contributors shared, through editorial conversations or through the reflections in their chapters, what questions still remained for them and ideas for future research. Several themes emerged from these conversations and reflections, which we share in what follows.

What is a task, anyway? For both new and experienced teachers who are interested in diversifying their instruction with task-based approaches, it may be a challenge to fully understand what a task is and what is entailed in the design and implementation of TBLT (Littlewood, 2004; Erlam, 2016). As mentioned at the beginning of this chapter, a myriad of definitions and a considerable amount of research on TBLT can make it overwhelming to decide where to start. It seems relevant, therefore, to mention that many of the contributors in this volume were introduced to TBLT in professional development workshops or graduate and undergraduate courses related to language teaching and learning (but mostly in the field of teaching EFL, ESL, or in professional development unrelated to language teaching). This could partially explain the variety of definitions used by the contributing authors as an anchor for their implementation of TBLT. Although the definitions were from different sources, there were shared principles among the definitions (for an overview, see Nuss and Whitehead Martelle, Chapter 1). For the RFL practitioners who are keen to try TBLT but are unsure where to start, the contributions in this volume provide wide-ranging yet accessible starting points for implementing a task-based approach.

How and what to assess? Assessment within task-based settings has been identified as a potential challenge for educators interested in implementing TBLT (Ellis, 2017; Long, 2016; Norris, 2016), and although there are some resources on task-based language assessment (e.g., Bachman, 2002; Norris, 2016), some educators may still find it difficult to decide on what, how, and when to assess within a TBLT context. In fact, several contributors in this volume highlighted challenges of task-based language assessment in relation to implementing it within the L2 Russian context. Zheltoukhova (Chapter 12) found it difficult during the post-task phase to provide feedback on tasks and rubrics that do not include specific grammatical features. She also noted that giving students quality and timely feedback was one of the most time-consuming aspects of task-based instruction of Russian. Mendelevich (Chapter 11) highlights a particular challenge for the instructor to be able to ascertain whether student errors are the result of linguistic risk-taking or a developmental gap in their grammatical knowledge. Finally, Novikov shared a tension in which students may be "presented with conflicting ideas as to what their grade is dependent on: the successful completion of tasks or the memorization of grammatical structures" (personal communication, July 31, 2020). Although assessment-related challenges may be a source of difficulty and uncertainty for teachers considering the implementation of TBLT, the chapters of this volume provide some direction by illuminating possible areas of concern and ways some teachers chose to address them. Several of the assessments shared in this volume's chapters show the possibilities of implementing assessments that go beyond the "traditional" pencil-and-paper tests. Additionally, task-based assessment tools described here not only provide feedback to students, but can also be used to inform future task design.

Russian-specific research. This volume's contributions provide a valuable source of pedagogical accounts for how TBLT can be implemented in a variety of RFL settings and proficiency levels. These chapters, however, are not empirical studies, and we encourage more empirical research to be carried out on TBLT within RFL settings. One possibility is to conduct replication studies of those previously done in more commonly taught languages like English and Spanish. We also suggest empirical studies that gauge the efficacy of TBLT at different proficiency levels in RFL: specifically, designing and implementing TBLT on a systemic level for novice and beginning-level learners of RFL.

One specific theme that frequently emerged in this volume's chapters and in our editorial conversations with the contributors relates to the tension between form and meaning: *how* and *when* to implement grammatical instruction within TBLT in a RFL setting. As outlined in Chapter 2 of this volume (Nuss), Russian morphology is complex. Because students are accustomed to learning Russian grammar explicitly and deductively, Zheltoukhova (Chapter 12) observes that some students may be overwhelmed with the amount of authentic input, which results in requests for more support in the form of extra worksheets, handouts, and/or tables on punctuation and grammar. Consequently, we suggest future investigations related to the Morphological Complexity Index (MCI; Brezina and Pallotti, 2019 – for a brief discussion of its value for teaching Russian through tasks, see Nuss, Chapter 2, as well as Nuss and Whitehead Martelle, Chapter 1). Such research studies could provide insight into more inductive approaches to teaching Russian grammar in which "instructors can facilitate students' observation and explicitly show ways of generalization in order to help develop learners' understanding of how Russian words are built and how meaning forms through elements and structures of Russian grammar" (Nuss, Chapter 2). Future research into this area could offer more understanding into how instructors can train students to detect patterns while simultaneously teaching the learners not to overgeneralize. Another possible direction for future research, as proposed by Mendelevich (Chapter 11), is to investigate how the combination of flipped classroom models and form-focused tasks can address the tension between form and meaning in RFL. As a whole, research studies that examine the interplay of deductive and inductive approaches to teaching grammar within a TBLT framework would be a welcome addition to the field of Russian language pedagogy.

Practical matters of teaching RFL. We found it illuminating to ask the contributing authors for their input related to the practical implementation of TBLT in RFL settings, and in this section we outline some themes that emerged to further support practitioners interested in TBLT for RFL. As a whole, contributors expressed a strong interest in using "blueprints" for task design and clear directions for task implementation.

The contributors were primarily interested in the "how-to":

- how to determine language objectives, adapt the ACTFL Can-Do statements, create tasks, and assess students' performance;
- how to design or choose materials for TBLT units;
- how to design group-based interactive tasks in face-to-face and online settings;
- how to implement and sequence different kinds of tasks (unfocused and focused);

- if, how, and when to use the L1 during the task cycle; and
- how to identify the role that explicit grammar instruction can play in TBLT – what language structure(s) should be explicitly taught, when, and to what extent.

Sharing such materials through research studies, publications, and databases would be of great use to practitioners not only of RFL, but of any language with a complex morphology.

Secondly, although none of the contributors specifically mention teacher action research (TAR; Mills, 2018; Herr & Anderson, 2015) as their approach to crafting the chapter's narration, each of the authors in the present volume engaged in planning, implementing, and reflecting in their teaching contexts. Future TAR studies could be useful to share with teachers new to TBLT, and we encourage teachers of Russian to use TAR more actively as a way of formalized reflection and sharing of knowledge and pedagogical expertise.

An added dimension: Institutional support. The scale and fidelity of task implementation – on the level of syllabus (systemic) vs. individual task increments – would depend on a number of conditions, a primary one being institutional support and professional development. Consider the following:

- How much institutional support does the teacher have and how much professional development and scaffolding of instruction is available?
- How much paid time is available for research, planning, curation/creation of materials, implementation, and reflection on practice? To what degree is a teacher supported during each of these stages?
- How much does the teacher know about TBLT and its research base? How many publications does the teacher have access to or have to buy? Is the guidance available for the teacher to choose a comfortable starting point among those publications?

We therefore raise the question of the level of institutional commitment to TBLT instruction. Such institutional commitment would play into the teachers' decisions in determining both the scale of implementation – whether tasks are used systemically or incrementally in programming (see Chapter 1 of this volume for a more specific discussion of the terms *systemic* and *incremental* use of tasks), and the fidelity of implementation of task-based instruction.

Thus, in addition to the three main *issues* with tasks and TBLT outlined by Long (2016): task complexity criteria, task-based assessment and the transferability of task-based abilities, and in-service teacher education for TBLT, we see a fourth – pragmatics of implementation – which takes into account to what degree the teacher is supported by the workplace. This question, of course, transcends the narrow lens of one approach to language teaching, however well-researched and well-developed it may be. Professional development for teachers of Russian as a foreign language has inherent challenges, including large class sizes and rare

Russian-specific methodological support at public schools. At the university level, more challenges include increasing adjunct workloads, practically non-existent sustainable ways of professional growth for both adjunct and full-time faculty, and very little to no paid opportunities for mastery of teaching skills or research, to mention just a few.

Concluding thoughts

Task-Based Instruction for Teaching Russian as a Foreign Language embodies ideations of what task-based instruction may look like in L2 Russian contexts. Tasks here are used both as episodes of instruction in a Russian language course – incrementally – and as a TBLT-based syllabus – systemically – and provide a starting point and a solid foundation upon which teachers of L2 Russian may choose to build their own task-based instruction.

The final beneficiaries of this volume are learners of Russian scattered around the globe in a multitude of settings and modes of learning. In this respect, the volume represents a collective pedagogical effort to orchestrate a more student-friendly environment by centering our collective pedagogy on the learner and making instruction of Russian not only more effective, but also more holistic. This kind of learning environment takes into account learners' needs and abilities and makes learning Russian more fun and less of a challenge and cannot be fostered without empowering the practitioners who teach the Russian language.

Applied linguistics has made many advances in the way we teach FLs, however, instructors of Russian often feel like they spin their wheels when they try to implement the kind of instruction their colleagues who teach English as a FL appear to use with such ease and grace. Thus, the inspiration for this volume comes from the desire to make the study of Russian more approachable, to make its teaching more learner-centered, and to shake up the notion that Russian is a 'difficult language to study' for people with a non-Slavic linguistic background.

A lot has changed in pedagogy, indeed, in the last two years alone. Teaching and learning reflect societal changes, sometimes spearheading them and other times lagging behind. It should come as no surprise that, with task-based practices gaining ground in the teaching of L2 Russian and with all the COVID-19 pandemic-induced changes in education and global society, we may be witnessing a new cycle in the pedagogy of teaching the Russian language. It is our hope that this new cycle will be more centered on the learners, their needs, and aspirations.

References

ACTFL, American Council on the Teaching of Foreign Languages. (2011). *21st century skills map: World languages*. Partnership for 21st Century Skills. Retrieved from ERIC: https://eric.ed.gov/?id=ED519498

ACTFL, American Council on the Teaching of Foreign Languages. (2012). *ACTFL proficiency guidelines 2012*. Retrieved June 10, 2020, from www.actfl.org/sites/default/files/pdfs/public/ACTFLProficiencyGuidelines2012_FINAL.pdf

ACTFL, American Council on the Teaching of Foreign Languages. (2016). *Assigning CEFR ratings to ACTFL assessment*. Retrieved from www.actfl.org/sites/default/files/reports/Assigning_CEFR_Ratings_To_ACTFL_Assessments.pdf

Ahmadian, M. J. (2012). Task repetition in ELT. *ELT Journal, 66*(3), 380–382.

Ahmadian, M. J., & Tavakoli, M. (2011). The effects of simultaneous use of careful online planning and task repetition on accuracy, complexity, and fluency in EFL learners' oral production. *Language Teaching Research, 15*(1), 23–49.

Aksel, A., & Gürman-Kahraman, F. (2014). Video project assignments and their effectiveness on foreign language learning. *Procedia – Social and Behavioral Sciences, 141*, 319–324.

Almutairi, N. D. (2016). The effectiveness of corpus-based approach to language description in creating corpus-based exercises to teach writing personal statements. *English Language Teaching, 9*(7), 103–111.

Anderson, J. R. (1983). *The architecture of cognition*. Cambridge, MA: Harvard University Press.

Ang, C. S., & Zaphiris, P. (2006). Developing enjoyable second language learning software tools: A computer game paradigm. In Z. Panayiotis & Z. Giorgos (Eds.), *User-centered computer aided language learning* (pp. 1–21). Hershey, PA: IGI Global.

Antonova, V. E., Nakhabina, M. M., & Tolstykh, A. A. (2018). *Tipovye testy po russkomu jazyku kak inostrannomu. Elementarnyi uroven'. Obshchee vladenie* (Типовые тесты по русскому языку как иностранному. Элементарный уровень. Общее владение) [Examples of tests in Russian as a foreign language. Elementary level. General proficiency]. St. Petersburg, Russia: Zlatoust.

Antonova, V. E., Nakhabina, M. M., Tolstykh, A. A., & Kurlova, I. V. (2019). *Tipovye testy po russkomu jazyku kak inostrannomu. Basovyi uroven'. Obshchee vladenie* (Типовые тесты по русскому языку как иностранному. Базовый уровень. Общее владение) [Examples of tests in Russian as a foreign language. Basic level. General proficiency]. St. Petersburg, Russia: Zlatoust.

Arefiev, A. (2019). Sotrudnichestvo Rossii i Portugalii v oblasti obrazovaniya i vzaimnoe izuchenie iazykov (Сотрудничество России и Португалии в области образования и взаимное изучение языков) [Cooperation between Russia and Portugal in the education field and mutual learning of languages]. In A. Nikunlassi & E. Protassova (Eds.). *Russian language in the multilingual world* (pp. 123–133). Slavica Helsingiensia 52. University of Helsinki. Retrieved from https://blogs.helsinki.fi/slavica-helsingiensia/slavica-helsingiensia-52/

Assis. I. G. (2014). *Guerra em Surdina: a ficção de Boris Schnaiderman entre a política e a poética* [M.S. Thesis. Universidade Federal de Uberlândia]. Repositório Institucional – Universidade Federal de Uberlândia. Retrieved from https://repositorio.ufu.br/bitstream/123456789/11872/1/GuerraSurdinaFiccao.pdf

Baayen. H.. Wurm. L. H.. & Aycock. J. (2007). Lexical dynamics for low-frequency complex words: A regression study across tasks and modalities. *The Mental Lexicon. 2*(3). 419–463.

Bachman. L. (2002). Some reflections on task-based language performance assessment. *Language Testing. 19.* 453–476.

Baehler. A.. & Hall. Z. (2016. November 11). *Virtual spaces and places as foundation for a new learning experience* [Conference presentation]. NYU CAS Innovation in Language Teaching Conference. New York. NY.

Behan. L.. Turnbull. M.. & Spek. J. (1997). The proficiency gap in late immersion [extended French]: Language use in collaborative tasks. *Le journal de l'immersion, 20*(2). 41–42.

Belz. J.. & Vyatkina. N. (2008). The pedagogical mediation of a developmental learner corpus for classroom-based language instruction. *Language Learning & Technology. 12*(3). 33–52.

Benati. A. (2017). The role of input and output tasks in grammar instruction: Theoretical. empirical and pedagogical considerations. *Studies in Second Language Learning and Teaching. 7*(3). 377–396. https://doi.org/10.14746/ssllt.2017.7.3.2. Retrieved from https://files.eric.ed.gov/fulltext/EJ1155604.pdf

Benson. P. (2007). Autonomy in language teaching and learning. *Language Teaching. 40.* 21–40.

Benson. P. (2011). *Teaching and researching autonomy* (2nd ed.). New York: Routledge.

Benson. P. (2012). Learner-centered teaching. In J.C. Richards. & A. Burns (Eds.). *The Cambridge guide to pedagogy and practice in second language teaching* (pp. 30–37). Cambridge. U.K.: Cambridge University Press.

Beyersmann. E.. Wegener. S.. Nation. K.. Prokupzcuk. A.. Wang. H.-C.. & Castles. A. (2021). Learning morphologically complex spoken words: Orthographic expectations of embedded stems are formed prior to print exposure. *Journal of Experimental Psychology: Learning, Memory, and Cognition. 47*(1). 87–98. https://doi.org/10.1037/xlm0000808

Biber. D.. Conrad. S.. & Reppen. R. (1998). *Corpus linguistics: Investigating language structure and use.* Cambridge: Cambridge University Press.

Bird. S. (2010). Effects of distributed practice on the acquisition of second language English syntax. *Applied Psycholinguistics. 31.* 635–650.

Blake. R. J. (2013). *Brave new digital classroom: Technology and foreign language learning.* Washington. DC: Georgetown University Press.

Blasing. M. T. (2010). Second language in second life: Exploring interaction. identity and pedagogical practice in a virtual world. *The Slavic and East European Journal. 54*(1). 96–117. Retrieved from www.jstor.org.proxy.library.nyu.edu/stable/23345003

Blik. E. C. (2015). Ispol'zovanie metoda kommunikativnykh zadanii v obuchenii studentov angliiskomu iazyku (Использование метода коммуникативных заданий в обучении студентов английскому языку) [Application of the communicative task-based approach in English language teaching]. *Pedagogicheskoe obrazovanie v Rossii. 2.* 68–72. Retrieved from https://cyberleninka.ru/article/n/ispolzovanie-metoda-kommunikativnyh-zadaniy-v-obuchenii-studentov-angliyskomu-yazyku

Bolitho, R., Carter, R., Hughes, R., Ivanič, R., Masuhara, H., & Tomlinson, B. (2003). Ten questions about language awareness. *ELT Journal*, *57*(3), 251–259.

Bondarenko, M. (in press). Open architecture design meeting cognitive architecture: Spiral-like design for teaching inflectional languages at elementary levels. In A. R. Corin, C. Campbell, & B. L. Leaver (Eds.), *Open architecture curricular design: Courses and concepts*. Washington, DC: Georgetown University Press.

Bondarenko, M., & Kogan, V. (in preparation). Rethinking task complexity at a low proficiency level. Manuscript in preparation.

Boulton, A., & Cobb, T. (2017). Corpus use in language learning: A meta-analysis. *Language Learning*, *67*(2), 348–393.

Bown, J., Bown, T., Christiansen, C., Dudley, S., Gibbons, S., Green, J. (2007). Now I know my АБВ's: A comparison of inductive and deductive methods of teaching on the acquisition of the Cyrillic alphabet. *Russian Language Journal*, *57*, 89–107.

Bown, J., Smith, L. C., & Talalakina, E. V. (2019). The effects of an EFL and L2 Russian teletandem class: Student perceptions of oral proficiency gains. *Journal of Language and Education*, *5*(3), 33–55. https://doi.org/10.17323/jle.2019.8953

Brasil. Secretaria de Educação Fundamental. (1998). *Parâmetros curriculares nacionais: terceiro e quarto ciclo do ensino fundamental: língua estrangeira*. Retrieved from http://portal.mec.gov.br/seb/arquivos/pdf/pcn_estrangeira.pdf

Breen, M. (1985). Authenticity in the language classroom. *Applied Linguistics*, *6*(1), 60–70.

Breen, M. (1989). The evaluation cycle for language learning tasks. In R. Johnson (Ed.), *The second language curriculum* (pp. 187–206). Cambridge: Cambridge University Press.

Brezina, V., & Pallotti, G. (2019). Morphological complexity in written L2 texts. *Second Language Research*, *35*(1), 99–119.

Brooks, P. J., Kempe, V., & Donachie, A. (2011). Second language learning benefits from similarity in word endings: Evidence from Russian. *Language Learning*, *61*(4), 1142–1172. https://doi.org/10.1111/j.1467-9922.2011.00665.x

Brooks-Lewis, K. A. (2009). Adult learners' perceptions of the incorporation of their L1 in foreign language teaching and learning. *Applied Linguistics*, *30*(2), 216–235. https://doi.org/doi10.1093/applin/amn051

Brown, A. H., & Green, T. D. (2019). *The essentials of instructional design: Connecting fundamental principles with process and practice* (4th ed.). New York: Routledge.

Brown, N. A., Bown, J., & Eggett, D. L. (2009). Making rapid gains in second language writing: A case study of a third-year Russian language course. *Foreign Language Annals*, *42*(3), 424–452.

Brown, T., & Bown, J. (2014). *Teaching advanced language skills through global debate: Theory and practice*. Washington, DC: Georgetown University Press.

Bryfonski, L., & McKay, T.H. (2017). TBLT implementation and evaluation: A meta-analysis. *Language Teaching Research, 23*(5), 603–632.

Bygate, M. (1996). Effects of task repetition: Appraising the developing language of learners. In J. Willis & D. Willis (Eds.), *Challenge and change in language teaching* (pp. 136–146). Oxford: Macmillan.

Bygate, M. (2001). Effects of task repetition on the structure and control of oral language. In Bygate, M., Skehan, P., & Swain, M. (Eds.), *Researching pedagogic tasks: Second language learning, teaching and testing* (pp. 23–48). Harlow, U.K.: Longman.

Bygate, M. (Ed.). (2018). *Learning language through task repetition*. Amsterdam and Philadelphia: John Benjamins.

Bygate, M., & Samuda, V. (2005). Integrative planning through the use of task repetition. In R. Ellis (Ed.), *Planning and task performance in second language* (pp. 37–74). Amsterdam: John Benjamins.

Bygate, M., Skehan, P., & Swain, M. (Eds.). (2001). *Researching pedagogic tasks, second language learning, teaching and testing*. Harlow: Longman.

Calvo-Ferrer, J. R. (2017). Educational games as stand-alone learning tools and their motivational effect on L2 vocabulary acquisition and perceived learning gains. *British Journal of Educational Technology, 48*(2), 264–278.

Campbell, C. (2018). Introduction to proceedings of the actualizing open architecture in the classroom (May, 2016). *Dialogue on Language Instruction, 28*(1), 27–28. Defense Language Institute Foreign Language Center.

Carson, E., & Kashihara, H. (2012). Using the L1 in the L2 classroom: The students speak. *The Language Teacher, 36*(4), 41–48.

Castro, T. (2005). *Fale russo* (Vol. 1). São Paulo, Brazil: Editora Plátano Ltda.

Castro, T. (2006). *Fale russo* (Vol. 2). São Paulo, Brazil: Editora Plátano Ltda.

Castro, T. (2007). *Fale russo* (Vol. 3). São Paulo, Brazil: Editora Plátano Ltda.

Castro, T. (2008). A interferência fonética durante a formação das habilidades auditiva e de pronúncia no aprendizado de LE. *Organon, 22*(44–45), 151–170. https://doi.org/10.22456/2238-8915.39658

CEFR. (2018). *Common European framework of reference for languages: Learning, teaching, assessment*. Council of Europe. Companion volume with new descriptors. Council of Europe. Language policy programme. Retrieved from www.coe.int/lang-cefr

Cenoz, J. (2015). Content-based instruction and content and language integrated learning: The same or different? *Language, Culture and Curriculum, 28*(1), 8–24. http://doi.org/10.1080/07908318.2014.1000922

Chambers, A. (2015). The learner corpus as a pedagogic corpus. In S. Granger, G. Gilquin, & F. Meunier (Eds.), *The Cambridge handbook of learner corpus research* (pp. 445–464). Cambridge: Cambridge University Press.

Chan, J. S., Wade-Woolley, L., Heggie, L., & Kirby, J. R. (2020). Understanding prosody and morphology in school-age children's reading. *Reading and Writing, 33*(5), 1295–1324. https://doi.org/10.1007/s11145-019-10005-4

Cho, H., & Kim, H. K. (2018). Promoting creativity through language play in EFL classrooms. *TESOL Journal, 9*(4), 1–9.

Cho, J., & Slabakova, R. (2014). Interpreting definiteness in a second language without articles: The case of L2 Russian. *Second Language Research, 30*(2), 159–190. https://doi.org/10.1177/0267658313509647

Chong, S. W., & Reinders, H. (2020). Technology-mediated task-based language teaching: A qualitative research synthesis. *Language Learning & Technology, 24*(3), 70–86.

Clifford, R. (2016). A rationale for criterion-referenced proficiency testing. *Foreign Language Annals, 49*(2), 224–234.

Coelho, T. (2018, June 24). Custos baixos e desafio cultural levam 500 brasileiros a buscarem diploma de medicina na Rússia. *G1*. Retrieved from https://g1.globo.com/educacao/noticia/custos-baixos-e-desafio-cultural-levam-500-brasileiros-a-buscarem-diploma-de-medicina-na-russia.ghtml

Comer, W. (2007). Implementing task-based teaching from the ground up: Considerations for lesson planning and classroom practice. *Russian Language Journal, 57*, 181–203. Retrieved from www.jstor.org.proxy.library.nyu.edu/stable/43669794

Comer, W. (2012a). Communicative language teaching and Russian: The current state of the field. In V. Makarova (Ed.), *Russian language studies in North America: New perspectives from theoretical and applied linguistics* (pp. 133–159). U.K.: Anthem.

Comer, W. (2012b). Lexical inferencing in reading L2 Russian. *Reading in a Foreign Language, 24*(2), 209–230.

Comer, W. (2014). Reading L2 Russian: The challenges of the Russian-English dictionary. *The Reading Matrix, 14*(2), 1–19.

Comer, W. (2019). Measured words: Quantifying vocabulary exposure in beginning Russian. *Slavic & East European Journal, 63*(1), 92–114.

Comer, W., & deBenedette, L. (2011). Processing instruction and Russian: Further evidence is IN. *Foreign Language Annals, 44*(4), 646–673.

Comer, W., & Murphy-Lee, M. (2004). Letter-sound correspondence acquisition in first semester Russian. *Canadian Slavonic Papers, 46*(1/2), 23–35.

Cook, G. (2000). *Language play, language learning*. New York: Oxford University Press.

Cope, B., & Kalantzis, M. (2009). "Multiliteracies": New literacies, new learning. *Pedagogies: An International Journal, 4*(3), 164–195.

Corin, A. R. (2020, February). *The challenge of the inverted pyramid. Open architecture and learning efficiency in achieving superior and distinguished levels of proficiency*. Paper presented at the AATSEEL, San Diego, U.S.A.

Corin, A. R. (2021). Foreign language learning efficiency. Transformative learning in an outcomes-based environment. In B. L. Leaver, D. Davidson, & C. Campbell (Eds.), *Transformative language learning and teaching* (pp. 51–60). Cambridge: Cambridge University Press.

Corin, A. R., Campbell, C., & Leaver, B. L. (Eds.). (2021). *Open architecture curricular design: Courses and concepts*. Washington, DC: Georgetown University Press.

Cotos, E. (2014). Enhancing writing pedagogy with learner corpus data. *ReCALL, 26*(2), 202–224.

Cotterall, S. (2008). Autonomy and good language learners. In C. Griffiths (Ed.), *Lessons from good language learners* (pp. 110–120). Cambridge: Cambridge University Press.

Council of Europe. (2018). *Common European framework of reference for languages: Learning, teaching, assessment*. Retrieved from https://rm.coe.int/cefr-companion-volume-with-new-descriptors-2018/1680787989

Coyle, Y., & Roca de Larios, J. (2014). Exploring the role played by error correction and models on children's reported noticing and output production in a L2 writing task. *Studies in Second Language Acquisition, 36*(3), 451–485.

Crookes, G. (1986). Task classification: A cross-disciplinary review. *Technical Report No.4*. Honolulú: Center for Second Language Classroom Research, Social Science Research Institute, University of Hawai'i at Manoa.

Cubillos, J., & Invento, T. (2019). Syllabus matters: The impact of course type on speaking gains abroad. *NECTFL Review, 83*, 41–56.

Dao, P., & McDonough, K. (2017). The effect of task role on Vietnamese EFL learners' collaboration in mixed proficiency dyads. *System, 65*, 15–24.

Darvin, R., & Norton, B. (2016). Investment and language learning in the 21st century. *Langage et Société, 157*(3), 19–38.

Davidson, D., Gor, K., & Lekic, M. (1996). *Russian stage I: Live from Moscow* (Vol. 1). Dubuque, IA: Kendall/Hunt Publishing Company.

deBenedette, L. (2020). Content, language and task in advanced Russian. In E. Denguh, I. Dubinina, & J. Merrill (Eds.), *The art of teaching russian* (pp. 187–210). Washington, DC: Georgetown University Press.

deBenedette, L., Comer, W. J., Smyslova, A., & Perkins, J. (2015). *Mezhdu Nami*. Retrieved from https://mezhdunami.org/

DeKeyser, R. (2007). Skill acquisition theory. In B. VanPatten & J. Williams (Eds.), *Theories in second language acquisition: An introduction* (2nd ed., pp. 94–112). New York: Routledge.

Dobrushina, N. R. (2005). Kak ispol'zovat' natsionalnyi korpus russkogo yazyka v obrazovanii? (Как использовать национальный корпус русского языка в образовании?) [How to use the Russian National Corpus in education]. In *Natsionalnyi Korpus Russkogo Yazyka: 2003–2005. Sbornik statei* (pp. 308–329). Moskva: Indrik.

Dolenga, M. (1948). *A língua russa*. Rio de Janeiro, Brazil: Editora Globo.

Dörnyei, Z. (1990). Conceptualizing motivation in foreign language learning. *Language Learning, 40*(1), 45–78.

Dörnyei, Z. (1994). Motivation and motivating in the foreign language classroom. *Modern Language Journal, 78,* 273–284.

Dörnyei, Z. (2001). *Motivational strategies in the language classroom*. Cambridge: Cambridge University Press.

Dörnyei, Z. (2013). *The psychology of second language acquisition*. Oxford: Oxford University Press.

Dörnyei, Z., & Ushioda, E. (2009). *Motivation, language identity and the L2 self*. Bristol, U.K.: Multilingual Matters.

Dörnyei, Z., & Ushioda, E. (2011). *Teaching and researching motivation* (2nd ed.). Harlow, U.K.: Pearson Education.

Doughty, C. J., & Long, M. H. (2003). Optimal psycholinguistic environments for distance foreign language learning. *Language Learning & Technology, 7*(3), 50–80.

Doughty, C., & Williams, J. (1998). Issues and terminology. In C. Doughty & J. Williams (Eds.), *Focus on form in classroom second language acquisition* (pp. 1–12). Cambridge: Cambridge University Press.

Drozdova, O. A., Zamyatina, E. V., Volodina, D. N., Zakharova, E. O., Ruchina, O. V., & Nepryakhin, A. F. (2015). Situational communication in teaching russian as a foreign language to beginner learners. *Procedia – Social and Behavioral Sciences, 215,* 118–126. https://doi.org/10.1016/j.sbspro.2015.11.584

Dubinina, N. A., Il'icheva, I. Y., Smirnova Henriques, A., Maznova, S., & Fomina, V. (2019). Testirovanie po russkomu iazyku kak inostrannomu v Brazilii: opyt podgotovki i provedeniia (Тестирование по русскому языку как иностранному в Бразилии: опыт подготовки и проведения) [Testing Russian as a foreign language in Brazil: The experience of exam preparation and implementation]. *Testologia, 13*(1), 37–40.

Dubinina, N., Smirnova Henriques, A., Maznova, S., Fomina, V., Mikheeva, Y., dos Reis, A., & Yermalayeva Franco, V. (2020). Survey of test of Russian as a foreign language: Participants' results in Brazil. *Testologia, 14*(2), 104–113.

Duffy, R. (2018, July 11). Canvas edges out blackboard in LMS market share. *Edscoop*. Retrieved from https://edscoop.com/canvas-edges-out-blackboard-in-lms-market-share/

Duran, G., & Ramaut, G. (2006). Tasks for absolute beginners and beyond: Developing and sequencing tasks at basic proficiency levels. In K. Van den Branden (Ed.), *Task-based language education: From theory to practice* (pp. 47–75). Cambridge: Cambridge University Press.

East, M. (2012). Addressing the intercultural via task-based language teaching: Possibility or problem? *Language and Intercultural Communication, 12*(1), 56–73.

East, M. (2017). Research into practice: The task-based approach to instructed second language acquisition. *Language Teaching, 50*(3), 412–424.

Edwards, C., & Willis, J. (2005). *Teachers exploring tasks in English language teaching.* New York: Palgrave Macmillan.

Ellis, N. (2005). At the interface: Dynamic interactions of explicit and implicit language knowledge. *Studies in Second Language Acquisition, 27,* 305–52.

Ellis, R. (1982). Informal and formal approaches to communicative language teaching. *ELT Journal, 36,* 73–78.

Ellis, R. (1997). *SLA research and language teaching.* Oxford: Oxford University Press.

Ellis, R. (2001). Non-reciprocal tasks, comprehension and second language acquisition. In M. Bygate, P. Skehan, & M. Swain (Eds.), *Researching pedagogic tasks, second language learning, teaching and testing* (pp. 49–74). Harlow, U.K.: Pearson Education.

Ellis, R. (2003). *Task-based language learning and teaching.* Oxford: Oxford University Press.

Ellis, R. (2006). The methodology of task-based teaching. *Asian EFL Journal, 8*(3), 19–45.

Ellis, R. (2009). Task-based language teaching: Sorting out the misunderstandings. *International Journal of Applied Linguistics, 19*(3), 221–246.

Ellis, R. (2017). Position paper: Moving task-based language teaching forward. *Language Teaching, 50*(4), 507–526.

Ellis, R. (2018). *Reflections on task-based language teaching.* Bristol, U.K.: Multilingual Matters.

Ellis, R., Skehan, P., Li, S., Shintani, N., & Lambert, C. (2020). *Task-based language teaching: theory and practice.* Cambridge: Cambridge University Press. https://doi.org/10.1017/9781108643689

Emidio, D. E. (2017). *Planejamento temático baseado em tarefas no ensino e aprendizagem do inglês na distância* [Ph.D. Thesis, Universidade Federal de São Carlos]. Repositório Institucional UFSCar. Retrieved from https://repositorio.ufscar.br/handle/ufscar/8829?show=full

Endresen, A., & Janda, L. A. (2020). Taking construction grammar one step further: Families, clusters, and networks of evaluative constructions in russian. *Frontiers in Psychology, 11,* Article 574353. https://doi.org/10.3389/fpsyg.2020.574353

Endresen, A., Zhukova, V., Mordashova, D., Rakhilina, E., & Lyashevskaya, O. (2020). Russkij Konstruktikon: novyi lingvisticheskii resurs, ego ustroystvo i spetsifika (Русский Конструктикон: новый лингвистический ресурс, его устройство и специфика) [The Russian constructicon: A new linguistic resource, its design and key characteristics]. *Computational Linguistics and Intellectual Technologies, Dialogue 2020 Proceedings.* https://doi.org/10.28995/2075-7182-2020-19-241-255

Erlam, R. (2016). 'I'm still not sure what a task is': Teachers designing language tasks. *Language Teaching Research, 20*(3), 279–299.

Erlam, R., & Ellis, R. (2018). Task-based language teaching for beginner-level learners of L2 French: An exploratory study. *Canadian Modern Language Review, 74*(1), 1–26.

Erlam, R., & Ellis, R. (2019). Input-based tasks for beginner-level learners: An approximate replication and extension of Erlam & Ellis (2018), *Language Teaching, 52*(4), 490–511.

Faez, F., Taylor, S., Majhanovich, S., & Brown, P. (2011). Teacher reactions to CEFR's task-based approach for FSL classroom. *Synergies Europe, 6,* 109–120.

Feryok, A. (2017). Sociocultural theory and task-based language teaching: The role of Praxis. *TESOL Quarterly, 51*(3), 716–727.

Foster, P., & Skehan, P. (1996). The influence of planning and task type on second language performance. *Studies in Second Language Acquisition, 18*(3), 299–323.

Franciosi, S. J. (2017). The effect of computer game-based learning on FL vocabulary transferability. *Journal of Educational Technology & Society, 20*(1), 123–133. Retrieved from www.jstor.org.proxy.library.nyu.edu/stable/jeductechsoci.20.1.123

Franciosi, S. J., Yagi, J., Tomoshige, Y., & Ye, S. (2016). The effect of a simple simulation game on long-term vocabulary retention. *CALICO Journal, 33*(3), 355–379. https://10.2307/90014365

Freynik, S., Gor, K., & O'Rourke, P. (2017). L2 processing of Arabic derivational morphology. *The Mental Lexicon, 12*(1), 21–50. https://doi.org/10.1075/ml.12.1.02fre

Fukuta, J. (2016). Effects of task repetition on learners' attention orientation in L2 oral production. *Language Teaching Research, 20*(3), 321–340.

Furniss, E. (2013). Using a corpus-based approach to Russian as a foreign language materials development. *Russian Language Journal, 63*, 195–212.

Furniss, E. (2016). Teaching the pragmatics of Russian conversation using a corpus-referred website. *Language Learning & Technology, 20*(2), 38–60.

Gagarina, N. (2009). Verbs of motion in Russian: An acquisitional perspective. *The Slavic and East European Journal, 53*(3), 451–470.

García, O., Johnson, J., & Seltzer, K. (2016). *The translanguaging classroom: Leveraging student bilingualism for learning*. Philadelphia, PA: Caslon.

Gardner, R. C. (1985). *Social psychology and second language learning: The role of attitudes and motivation*. London: Edward Arnold.

Gardner, R. C., & Lambert, W. E. (1972). *Attitudes and motivation in second language learning*. Rowley, MA: Newbury House.

Gass, S. M. (2017). *Input, interaction, and the second language learner* (2nd ed.). New York: Routledge.

Gass, S., M. A., Alvarez-Torres, M. J., Fernández-García, M. (1999). The effects of task repetition on linguistic output. *Language Learning, 49*, 549–581.

Gatbonton, E., & Segalowitz, N. (2005). Rethinking communicative language teaching: A focus on access to fluency. *The Canadian Modern Language Review La Revue canadienne des langues vivantes, 61*(3), 325–353.

Gee, J. P. (2005). Good video games and good learning. *Phi Kappa Phi Forum, 85*(2), 33–37.

Germain, C. (2017). *The Neurolinguistic Approach (NLA) for learning and teaching foreign languages, theory and practice*. Newcastle upon Tyne, U.K.: Cambridge Scholars Publishing.

Gilabert, R., & Castellví, J. (2019). Task and syllabus design for morphologically complex languages. In J. W. Schwieter & A. G. Benati (Eds.), *The Cambridge handbook of language learning* (pp. 527–549). Cambridge: Cambridge University Press. https://doi.org/10.1017/9781108333603.023

Gilmore, A. (2007). Authentic materials and authenticity in foreign language learning. *Language Teaching, 40*(2), 97–118.

Glazunova, O. I., Kolesova, D. V., & Popova, T. I. (2017). *Programma po russkomu iazyku kak inostrannomu* (Программа по русскому языку как иностранному) [Educational curriculum for Russian as a Foreign Language]. Russkiy iazyk. Kursy.

González-Lloret, M. (2016). *A practical guide to integrating technology into task-based language teaching*. Washington, DC: Georgetown University Press.

González-Lloret, M., & Ortega, L. (2014). Towards technology-mediated TBLT: An introduction. In M. González-Lloret & L. Ortega (Eds.), *Technology-mediated TBLT: Researching technology and tasks* (pp. 1–21). Amsterdam: John Benjamins.

Gor, K. (2015). Phonology and morphology in lexical processing. In J. W. Schwieter (Ed.), *The Cambridge handbook of bilingual processing* (pp. 173–199). Cambridge: Cambridge University Press.

Gor, K. (2017). The mental lexicon of L2 learners of Russian: Phonology and morphology in lexical storage and access. *Journal of Slavic Linguistics*, 25(2), 277–302. https://doi.org/10.1353/jsl.2017.0011

Gor, K., & Cook, S. V. (2018). A mare in a pub? Nonnative facilitation in phonological priming. *Second Language Research*, 36(1), 123–140. https://doi.org/10.1177/0267658318769962

Gor, K., & Long, M. H. (2009). Input and second language processing. In W. C. Ritchie & T. J. Bhatia (Eds.), *Handbook of second language acquisition* (pp. 445–472). New York: Academic Press.

Greenberg, G. (Дж. Гринберг) (1963). Kvantitativnyj podhod k morfologicheskoj tipologii jazykov (Квантитативный подход к морфологической типологии языков) [A quantitative approach to the morphological typology of language]. In V. A. Zvegentsev (Ed.), *Novoe v lingvistike (Новое в лингвистике), III* (pp. 60–94). Moscow: Progress (Прогресс).

Gromik, N. A. (2012). Cell phone video recording feature as a language learning tool: A case study. *Computers & Education*, 58, 223–230.

Groothuijsen, S., Bronkhorst, L., Prins, G., & Kuiper, W. (2020). Teacher-researchers' quality concerns for practice-oriented educational research. *Research Papers in Education*, 35(6), 766–787. https://doi.org/10.1080/02671522.2019.1633558

Hacking, J. F., & Tschirner, E. (2017). The contribution of vocabulary to reading proficiency: The case of college Russian. *Foreign Language Annals*, 50(3), 500–518.

Hamilton, H. E., Crane, C., & Bartoshesky, A. (2005). *Doing foreign language: Bringing concordia language villages into language classrooms*. London: Pearson/Merrill/Prentice Hall.

Han, Z. H. (2016). Research meets practice. Chinese as a second language (漢語教學研究 – 美國中文教師學會學報). *The Journal of the Chinese Language Teachers Association, USA*, 51(3), 236–251. https://doi.org/10.1075/csl.51.3.01han

Han, Z. H. (2020). Usage-based instruction, systems thinking, and the role of language mining in second language development. *Language Teaching*, 1–16. https://doi.org/10.1017/s0261444820000282

Harmer, J. (1982). What is communicative? *ELT Journal*, 36(3), 164–168.

Harmer, J. (1991). *The practice of English language teaching*. London and New York: Longman.

Harrison, D. (2011, January 12). Can blogging make a difference? *Campus Technology*. Retrieved from https://campustechnology.com/Articles/2011/01/12/Can-Blogging-Make-a-Difference.aspx?Page=1

Hattie, J., & Hamilton, A. (2020). *Real gold vs. fool's gold: The visible learning methodology for finding what works best in education*. Thousand Oaks, CA: Corwin.

Hawkins, R., & Chan, C. (1997). The partial availability of Universal Grammar in second language acquisition: The 'failed functional features hypothesis.' *Second Language Research*, 13, 187–226.

Hayes-Harb, R., & Hacking, J. (2015). The influence of written stress marks on native English speakers' acquisition of Russian lexical stress contrasts. *The Slavic and East European Journal, 59*(1), 91–109.

Heimann, K. S., & Roepstorff, A. (2018). How playfulness motivates: Putative looping effects of autonomy and surprise revealed by micro-phenomenological investigations. *Frontiers of Psychology, 9*, Article 1704.

Henry, K. (1995). Developing and testing sociolinguistic and grammatical competence through the use of role play situations. *Russian Language Journal/Русский Язык, 49*(162), 3–23. Retrieved from www.jstor.org.proxy.library.nyu.edu/stable/43675316

Herr, K., & Anderson, G. L. (2015). *The action research dissertation: A guide for students and faculty* (2nd ed.). Thousand Oaks, CA: SAGE.

Higa, B. S. (2015). *O instituto São Vladimir e a presença russa em Santos, pela voz dos imigrantes (1958–1968)* [Undergraduate thesis]. Universidade Católica de Santos.

Holec, H. (1981). *Autonomy and foreign language learning*. Oxford: Pergamon.

Howatt, A. (1984). *A history of English language teaching*. Oxford: Oxford University Press.

Ilf, I., & Petrov, E. (2007). *Ilf and Petrov's American road trip: The 1935 travelogue of two Soviet writers* (Wolf, E., Ed.). Princeton Architectural Press.

Ilf, I., Petrov, E., Pozner, V., & Kahn, B. (2013). *Odnoetazhnaia Amerika* (Одноэтажная Америка) [One-storied America]. Moscow: AST.

Isurin, L. (2013). Hits and misses in teaching Russian in the US: The perspectives of instructors, students, and enrollment. *Russian Language Journal/Русский язык, 63*, 25–49.

Janda, L. A., Kopotev, M., & Nesset, T. (2020). Constructions, their families and their neighborhoods: The case of durak durakom 'a fool times two'. *Russian Linguistics, 44*(2), 109–127. https://doi.org/10.1007/s11185-020-09225-y

Janda, L. A., & Tyers, M. F. (2018). Less is more: Why all paradigms are defective, and why that is a good thing. *Corpus Linguistics and Linguistic Theory, 17*, 109–141. https://doi.org/10.1515/cllt-2018-0031

Jefferson Education Exchange. (2019). *Educator voices on education research*. Retrieved from https://drive.google.com/file/d/1AnLli4KeRD8fkFc-HULM45b4_mnt3viR/view

Jing-Schmidt, Z., & Peng, X. (2018). Linguistic theories and teaching Chinese as a second language. In C. Ke (Ed.), *The Routledge handbook of chinese second language acquisition* (pp. 63–81). New York: Routledge. https://doi.org/10.4324/9781315670706-4

Johns, T. (1991). From printout to handout: Grammar and vocabulary teaching in the context of data-driven learning. *ELR Journal, 4*, 27–45.

Kagan, O., Miller, F. J., & Kudyma, G. (2006). *V puti: Russian grammar in context* (2nd ed.). Hoboken, NJ: Pearson Prentice Hall.

Kaivanpanah, S., & Miri, M. (2017). The effects of task type on the quality of resolving language-related episodes and vocabulary learning. *TESOL Journal, 8*(4), 920–942. https://doi.org/10.1002/tesj.311

Kanakina, V. P., & Goretskiy, V. G. (Канакина, В. П., & Горецкий, В. Г.). (2021). *Russkij jazyk. 1 klass. Uchebnik* (Русский язык. 1 класс. Учебник) [Russian. 1st grade. Textbook]. Moscow: Prosveshenie (Просвещение).

Kang, E. Y. (2020). Using model texts as a form of feedback in L2 writing. *System, 89*, Article 102196. https://doi.org/10.1016/j.system.2019.102196

Kempe, V., & Brooks, P. J. (2008). Second language learning of complex inflectional systems. *Language Learning, 58*(4), 703–746.

Kempe, V., Brooks, P. J., & Kharkhurin, A. (2010). Cognitive predictors of generalization of Russian grammatical gender categories. *Language Learning*, *60*(1), 127–153. https://doi.org/10.1111/j.1467-9922.2009.00553.x

Kempe, V., & MacWhinney, B. (1998). The acquisition of case marking by adult learners of Russian and German. *Studies in Second Language Acquisition*, *20*, 543–587.

Kirby, J. R., & Bowers, P. N. (2018). The effects of morphological instruction on vocabulary learning, reading, and spelling. In R. Berthiaume, D. Daigle, & A. Desrochers (Eds.), *Morphological processing and literacy development* (pp. 217–243). New York: Routledge. https://doi.org/10.4324/9781315229140-10

Kireev, M., Slioussar, N., Chernigovskaya, T., & Medvedev, S. (2018). Organization of functional interactions within the fronto-temporal language brain system underlying production and perception of regular and irregular Russian verbs. *International Journal of Psychophysiology*, *131*, S13.

Kireev, M., Slioussar, N., Chernigovskaya, T., Medvedev, S., & Shilin, P. (2019). *The age of acquisition effect in the processing of Russian inflectional morphology*. Paper presented at International Morphological Processing Conference. Retrieved from https://quantling.org/MoProc2019/docs/MoProc_2019.pdf

Kisselev, O., Dubinina, I., & Polinsky, M. (2020). Form-focused instruction in the heritage language classroom: Toward research-informed heritage language pedagogy. *Frontiers in Education*, *5*, Article 53. https://doi.org/10.3389/feduc.2020.00053

Klimanova, L., & Bondarenko, M. (2018). Problematizing the notion of the beginning L2 writer: The case of text-based telecollaboration. In J. Demperio, M. Deraîche, R. Dewart, & B. Zuercher (Eds.), *L'Enseignement-Apprentissage de l'Écrit/Current trends in the teaching and learning of written proficiency* (pp. 64–89). Éditeur: Université du Québec à Montréal, UQAM Press.

Kramsch, C. (2002). Beyond the second vs. foreign language dichotomy: The subjective dimensions of language learning, In K. S. Miller & P. Thompson (Eds.), *Unity and diversity in language use*. London: British Association of Applied Linguistics in Association with Continuum.

Kramsch, C. (2013). Afterword. In B. Norton (Ed.), *Identity and language learning: Extending the conversation* (2nd ed., pp. 192–201). Bristol, U.K.: Multilingual Matters.

Krashen, S. (1981). *Second language acquisition and second language learning*. Oxford: Pergamon.

Krasner, I. (2018). Open architecture approach to teaching Russian as a foreign language. *ACTR Letter*, *45*(2), 1–2, 4–5. Retrieved September 29, 2020, from www.actr.org/uploads/4/7/5/1/47514867/actr_vol.45_2_winter_2018.pdf

Kulikova, O. (2015). *Vocabulary learning strategies and beliefs about vocabulary learning: A study of beginning university students of Russian in the United States* [Doctoral dissertation, University of Iowa]. Iowa Research Online.

Lai, C., & Li, G. (2011). Technology and task-based language teaching: A critical review. *CALICO Journal*, *28*(2), 498–521. https://doi.org/10.11139/cj.28.2.498-521

Lambert, C., Kormos, J., & Minn, D. (2017). Task repetition and second language speech processing. *Studies in Second Language Acquisition*, *39*(1), 167–196.

Lambert, C., & Oliver, R. (Eds.). (2020). *Using tasks in second language teaching*. Bristol, U.K.: Blue Ridge Summit: Multilingual Matters. https://doi.org/10.21832/9781788929455

Lardiere, D. (2008). Feature-assembly in second language acquisition. In J. Liceras, H. Goodluck, & H. Zobl (Eds.), *The role of formal features in second language acquisition* (pp. 107–40). New York: Lawrence Erlbaum.

Lardiere, D. (2009). Some thoughts on the contrastive analysis of features in second language acquisition. *Second Language Research, 25*(2), 173–227.

Laverick, E. (2019). *Project based learning*. Alexandria, VA: TESOL International Association.

Lazareva, O. A. (2013). *Shkola testora* (Школа тестора) *[Tutorial for a language examiner]*. Moskva: Russkiy yazyk. Kursy.

Leal, T., & Slabakova, R. (2017). The relationship between L2 instruction, exposure, and the L2 acquisition of a syntax-discourse property in L2 Spanish. *Language Teaching Research, 23*(2), 237–258. https://doi.org/10.1177/1362168817745714.

Leaver, B. L. (1997). Content-based instruction in a basic Russian program. In S. B. Stryker & B. L. Leaver (Eds.), *Content-based instruction in foreign language education: Models and methods* (pp. 30–54). Washington, DC: Georgetown University Press.

Leaver, B. L., & Campbell, C. (2020). The shifting paradigm in Russian language pedagogy: From communicative language teaching to transformative language learning and teaching. In E. Dengub, I. Dubinina, & J. Merrill (Eds.), *The art of teaching Russian* (pp. 147–162). Washington, DC: Georgetown University Press.

Leaver, B. L., Davidson, D., & Campbell, C. (Eds.). (2021). *Transformative language learning and teaching*. Cambridge: Cambridge University Press.

Leaver, B. L., & Kaplan, M. A. (2004). Task-based instruction in U.S. government Slavic language programs. In B. L. Leaver & J. R. Willis (Eds.), *Task-based instruction in foreign language education: Practices and programs* (pp. 47–66). Washington, DC: Georgetown University Press.

Leaver, B.L., & Willis, J.R. (Eds). (2004). *Task-based instruction in foreign language education: Practices and programs*. Washington, DC: Georgetown University Press.

Lebedeff, T. B., & Facchinello, B. (2018). Vamos fazer um filme?! Uma experiência de Ensino de Línguas Baseado em Tarefas para aprender Libras. *ReVEL, 15*, 274–289. Retrieved from www.revel.inf.br/files/d6eec9b29337e847302cea5718873071.pdf

Lecouvet, M., Degand, L., & Suner, F. (2021). Unclogging the bottleneck: The role of case morphology in L2 acquisition at the syntax-discourse interface. *Language Acquisition*. https://doi.org/10.1080/10489223.2020.1860056

Lee, D., & Swales, J. (2006). A corpus-based EAP course for NNS doctoral students: Moving from available specialized corpora to self-compiled corpora. *English for Specific Purposes, 25*(1), 56–75.

Lee, J. F. (1995). Using task-based activities to restructure class discussions. *Foreign Language Annals, 28*(3), 437–446.

Lee, J. F. (2000). *Tasks and communicating in language classrooms*. Boston: McGrawHill.

Lekant, P. A. (Лекант, П. А.) (1988). *Sovremennyj russkij literaturnyj jazyk* (2nd ed.) (Современный русский литературный язык. 2е изд.) [Modern Russian literary language. 2nd ed.]. Moscow: Vysshaja shkola (Высшая школа).

Leminen, A., Smolka, E., Duñabeitia, J. A., & Pliatsikas, C. (2019). Morphological processing in the brain: The good (inflection), the bad (derivation) and the ugly (compounding). *Cortex, 116*, 4–44. https://doi.org/10.1016/j.cortex.2018.08.016

Levesque, K. C., Kieffer, M. J., & Deacon, S. H. (2018). Inferring meaning from meaningful parts: The contributions of morphological skills to the development of children's reading comprehension. *Reading Research Quarterly, 54*(1), 63–80. https://doi.org/10.1002/rrq.219

Li, Y. (2012). Cultivating student global competence: A pilot experimental study. *Decision Sciences Journal of Innovative Education, 11*(1), 125–143.

Littlewood, W. (1981). *Communicative language teaching.* Cambridge: Cambridge University Press.
Littlewood, W. (2004). The task-based approach: Some questions and suggestions. *ELT Journal, 58,* 319–326.
Loewen, S., & Isbell, D. R. (2017). Pronunciation in face-to-face and audio-only synchronous computer-mediated learner interactions. *Studies in Second Language Acquisition, 39*(2), 225–256. https://doi.org/10.1017/s0272263116000449
Loewen, S., & Sato, M. (2018). Interaction and instructed second language acquisition. *Language Teaching, 51*(3), 285–329. https://doi.org/10.5040/9781472542113
Loewen, S., & Wolff, D. (2016). Peer interaction in F2F and CMC contexts. In M. Sato & S. Ballinger (Eds.), *Peer interaction and second language learning: Pedagogical potential and research agenda* (pp. 162–184). Amsterdam: John Benjamins.
Long, M. (1983). Does second language instruction make a difference? A review of research. *TESOL Quarterly, 17,* 359–382.
Long, M. (1985). A role for instruction in second language acquisition: Task-based language teaching. In K. Hyltenstam, & M. Pienemann (Eds.), *Modelling and assessing second language acquisition* (pp. 77–99). Clevedon, U.K.: Multilingual Matters.
Long, M. (1991). Focus on form: A design feature in language teaching methodology. In K. De Bot, R. Ginsberg, & C. Kramsch (Eds.), *Foreign language research in cross-cultural perspectives* (pp. 39–52). Amsterdam: John Benjamins.
Long, M. (1996). The role of the linguistic environment in second language acquisition. In W. C. Ritchie & T. K. Bahtia (Eds.), *Handbook of second language acquisition* (pp. 413–468). New York: Academic Press.
Long, M. (1998). Focus on form in task-based L2 teaching, *University of Hawai'i Working Paper in ESL, 16*(2), 35–49.
Long, M. (2007). *Problems in SLA.* Mahwah, NJ: Lawrence Erlbaum Associates.
Long, M. (2015). *Second language acquisition and task-based language teaching.* Malden, MA: John Wiley & Sons.
Long, M. (2016). In defense of tasks and TBLT: Nonissues and real issues. *Annual Review of Applied Linguistics, 36,* 5–33.
Long, M., Gor, K., & Jackson, S. (2012). Linguistic correlates of second language proficiency: Proof of concept with ILR 2–3 in Russian. *Studies in Second Language Acquisition, 34*(1), 99–126.
Long, M., Jackson, S., Aquil, R., Cagri, I., Gor, K., & Lee, S.-Y. (2006). *Linguistic correlates of proficiency: Rationale, methodology, and content* [Technical report]. College Park, MD: University of Maryland.
Looney, D., & Lusin, N. (2018). *Enrollments in languages other than English in United States institutions of higher education, Summer 2016 and Fall 2016: Preliminary report.* New York: Modern Language Association of America. Retrieved January 2, 2021, from www.mla.org/content/download/83540/2197676/2016-Enrollments-Short-Report.pdf
Lopes Jr., J. A. (2014). *Aprendizagem da língua inglesa como segunda língua baseada em tarefas: uma proposta de trabalho com ciclo complexo* [M.S. Thesis, Universidade Federal de Pelotas]. Repositório UFPel. Retrieved from http://guaiaca.ufpel.edu.br/handle/ri/2721
Lubensky, S., Ervin, G., & Jarvis, D. (1996). *Nachalo: When in Russia . . .* Boston, MA: McGraw-Hill.
Lys, F. (2005). Using web technology to promote writing, analytical thinking, and creative expression in German. In B. L. Leaver & J. R. Willis (Eds.), *Task-based instruction in*

foreign language education: Practices and programs (pp. 228–250). Washington, DC: Georgetown University Press.

Lyster, R. (2001). Negotiation of form, recasts, and explicit correction in relation to error types and learner repair in immersion classrooms. *Language Learning, 51*(s1), 265–301.

Lyster, R. (2007). *Learning and teaching languages through content*. Amsterdam: John Benjamins.

Lyster, R., & Ballinger, S. (2011). Content-based language teaching: Convergent concerns across divergent contexts. *Language Teaching Research, 15*(3), 279–288.

Macaro, E., & Lee, J. H. (2013). Teacher language background, codeswitching, and English-only instruction: Does age make a difference to learners' attitudes? *TESOL Quarterly, 47*(4), 717–742. https://doi.org/10.1002/tesq.74

Macedonia, M., & Klimesch, W. (2014). Long-term effects of gestures on memory for foreign language words trained in the classroom. *Mind, Brain, and Education, 8*(2), 74–88. https://doi.org/10.1111/mbe.12047

Mackey, A. (2020). *Interaction, feedback and task research in second language learning*. Cambridge: Cambridge University Press.

Mackey, A., Fujii, A., Biesenbach-Lucas, S., Weger, H., Dolgova Jacobsen, N., Wright, L., Lake, J., Sondermann, K., Tagarelli, K., Tsujita, M., Watanabe, A., Abbuhl, R., & Kim, K. (2013). Tasks and traditional practice activities in a foreign language context. In K. McDonough & A. Mackey (Eds.), *Second language interaction in diverse educational contexts* (pp. 71–88). Amsterdam and Philadelphia: John Benjamins.

Magnani, M., & Artoni, D. (2015). Teaching learnable grammar in Russian as a second language: A syllabus proposal for case. In E. F. Quero Gervilla, B. Barros Garcia, & T. R. Kopylova (Eds.), *Trends in Slavic studies* (pp. 57–70). Moscow: Editorial URSS.

Mak, B. (2011). An exploration of speaking-in-class anxiety with Chinese ESL learners. *System, 39*(2), 202–214. https://doi.org/10.1016/j.system.2011.04.002

Manfra, M. M. G. (2019). Action research and systematic, intentional change in teaching practice. *Review of Research in Education, 43*(1), 163–196. https://doi.org/10.3102/0091732x18821132

Markina, E. (2017). Challenges in task design for learners of Russian with a low level of proficiency. *EPiC Series in Language and Linguistics, 2*, 82–91.

Markina, E. (2018). *Comparing focus on forms and task-based language teaching in the acquisition of Russian as a foreign language* [Ph.D. Thesis, Universitat de Barcelona]. Dipòsit Digital de la Universitat de Barcelona. Retrieved from http://diposit.ub.edu/dspace/handle/2445/130175

Marsden, E., Mackey, A., & Plonsky, L. (2016). Breadth and depth: The IRIS repository. In A. Mackey & E. Marsden (Eds.), *Advancing methodology and practice: The IRIS repository of instruments for research into second languages* (pp. 1–21). New York: Routledge.

Martel, J. (2016). Tapping the National Standards for thought-provoking CBI in K–16 foreign language programs. In L. Cammarata (Ed.), *Content-based foreign language teaching* (pp. 115–136). New York: Routledge.

Martin, C. (2020). Looking back, moving forward: Teaching and learning Russian in the United States in the post-Soviet Era. In E. Dengub, I. Dubinina, & J. Merrill (Eds.), *The art of teaching Russian* (pp. 23–48). Washington, DC: Georgetown University Press.

Maybin, J., & Swann, J. (2007). Everyday creativity in language: Textuality, contextuality, and critique. *Applied Linguistics, 28*, 497–517.

McDonald, J. (2006). Beyond the critical period: Processing-based explanations for poor grammaticality judgment performance by late second language learners. *Journal of Memory and Language, 55,* 381–401.

McFarlane, A., Sparrowhawk, A., & Heald, Y. (2002). Report on the educational use of games. *TEEM (Teachers Evaluating Educational Multimedia).* Retrieved from www.teem.org.uk/publications/teem_gamesined_full.pdf

McQuillan, J. (2020). The effects of morphological training on vocabulary knowledge: A reanalysis of Goodwin & Ahn (2013). *Language Issues, 1*(1), 19–38.

Mellone, K. D. (2018). *Tatiana Belinky: A história de uma contadora de histórias* [M.S. Thesis, Universidade de São Paulo]. Biblioteca Digital de Teses e Dissertações da USP. Retrieved from www.teses.usp.br/teses/disponiveis/27/27156/tde-20052009-165223/publico/1024815.pdf

Met, M. (1998). *Content-based instruction: Defining terms, making decisions.* Washington, DC: National Foreign Language Center.

Miller, M., & Hegelheimer, V. (2006). The SIMs meet ESL incorporating authentic computer simulation games into the language classroom. *Interactive Technology and Smart Education, 3*(4), 311–328.

Mills, G. E. (2018). *Action research: A guide for the teacher researcher* (6th ed.). New York: Pearson.

Miranda, Y. C. C., & Lopez, A. P. A. (2019). Considerações sobre a formação de professores no contexto de ensino de português como língua de acolhimento. In M. Freitas Silva (Ed.), *Língua de Acolhimento: experiências no Brasil e no mundo* (pp. 17–40). Belo Horizonte, Brasil: Mosaico Produção Editorial. www.letras.ufmg.br/padrao_cms/documentos/profs/luciane/capa_linguadeacolhimentoEBOOK%20DEFINITIVO.pdf

Mishan, F. (2005). *Designing authenticity into language learning materials.* Portland, OR: Intellect Books.

Montrul, S., Foote, R., Perpiñán, S. (2008). Gender agreement in adult second language learners and Spanish heritage speakers: The effects of age and context of acquisition. *Language Learning, 58*(3), 503–553.

Morrow, K. (1977). Authentic texts and ESP. In S. Holden (Ed.), *English for specific purposes* (pp. 13–17). London: Modern English Publications.

Nabei, T., & Swain, M. (2002). Learner awareness of recasts in classroom interaction: A case study of an adult EFL student's second language learning. *Language Awareness, 11*(1), 43–66.

National Education Association Policy Brief. (2010). *Global competence is a 21st century imperative.* Retrieved from www.nea.org/assets/docs/HE/PB28A_Global_Competence11.pdf

National Standards in Foreign Language Education Project. (2015). *World-readiness standards for learning languages.* Alexandria, VA: American Council on the Teaching of Foreign Languages.

Nesselhauf, N. (2004). Learner corpora and their potential for language teaching. In J. Sinclair (Ed.), *How to use corpora in language teaching* (pp. 125–152). Amsterdam: John Benjamins.

The New London Group. (1996). A pedagogy of multiliteracies: Designing social futures. *Harvard Educational Review, 66*(1), 60–93.

Norris, J. (2016). Current issues for task-based language assessment. *Annual Review of Applied Linguistics, 36,* 230–244.

Norton Peirce, B. (1995). Social identity, investment, and language learning. *TESOL Quarterly, 29*(1), 9–31.
Norton, B. (2000). *Identity and language learning: gender, ethnicity and educational change.* Harlow, U.K.: Pearson.
Norton, B. (2010). Identity, literacy, and english-language teaching. *TESL Canada Journal, 28*(1), 1. https://doi.org/10.18806/tesl.v28i1.1057
Nummikoski, M. (2011). *Troika: A communicative approach to Russian language, life, and culture.* Hoboken, NJ: John Wiley & Sons.
Nunan, D. (1988a). *The learner-centred curriculum: A study in second language teaching.* Cambridge: Cambridge University Press.
Nunan, D. (1988b). *Syllabus design.* Oxford: Oxford University Press.
Nunan, D. (1989). *Designing tasks for the communicative classroom.* Cambridge: Cambridge University Press.
Nunan, D. (1991). Communicative tasks and the language curriculum. *TESOL Quarterly, 25*(2), 179–195.
Nunan, D. (2004). *Task-based language teaching.* Cambridge: Cambridge University Press.
Nunan, D. (2006). Task-based language teaching in the Asia context: Defining "task." *Asian EFL Journal, 8,* 12–18.
Nunan, D. (2012). *Learner-centered English language education: The selected works of David Nunan.* New York: Routledge.
Nuss, S. (2020). K voprosu o teorii i praktike organizatsii raboty posredstvom tselevogo zadaniya (К вопросу о теории и практике организации работы посредством целевого задания) [Advancing task-based language learning & instruction: L2 Russian]. In *World without borders* (pp. 72–78). Pskov, Russia: Pskov University Press. (Print, in Russian)
Nuss, S., Whitehead Martelle, W., Zheltoukhova, S., Pastushenkov, D., & Siekmann, S. (2021). *Task-Based Language Teaching (TBLT): History, research, and reflection on practice.* PNCFL 2021 Conference Expert Panel.
O'Sullivan, B. (2002). Learner acquaintanceship and oral proficiency test pair-task performance. *Language Testing, 19*(3), 277–295. https://doi.org/10.1191/0265532202lt205oa
Ogilvie, G., & Dunn, W. (2010). Taking teacher education to task: Exploring the role of teacher education in promoting the utilization of task-based language teaching. *Language Teaching Research, 14*(2), 161–181.
Oliveira, R. S. (2015). Linha do tempo da didática das línguas estrangeiras no Brasil. *Non Plus, 7,* 27–38. https://doi.org/10.11606/issn.2316-3976.v4i7p27-38
Paas, F., & van Merriënboer, J. J. G. (2020). Cognitive-load theory: Methods to manage working memory load in the learning of complex tasks. *Current Directions in Psychological Science, 29*(4), 394–398.
Pais Marden, M., & Herrington, J. (2020). Design principles for integrating authentic activities in an online community of foreign language learners. *Issues in Educational Research, 30*(2), 635–654.
Pallotti, G. (2019). An approach to assessing the linguistic difficulty of tasks. *Journal of the European Second Language Association, 3*(1), 58–70. https://doi.org/10.22599/jesla.61
Paran, A. (2017). 'Only connect': Researchers and teachers in dialogue. *ELT Journal, 71*(4), 499–508.
Pastushenkov, D., Camp, C., Zhuchenko, I., & Pavlenko, O. (2020). Shared and different L1 background, L1 use, and peer familiarity as factors in ESL pair interaction. *TESOL Journal.* Article e538. https://doi.org/10.1002/tesj.538

Pastushenkov, D., & Pavlenko, O. (2020). Mafia: A role-playing game promoting peer interaction. In U. Nurmukhamedov & R. W. Sadler (Eds.), *New ways in teaching with games* (pp. 149–151). Annapolis Junction, MD: TESOL Press.

Pavlenko, O. (2020). *BEEtaminS* [Ridero eBook]. Retrieved from https://ridero.ru/books/beetamins/.

Peirce, G. (2018). Representational and processing constraints on the acquisition of case and gender by heritage and L2 learners of Russian: A corpus study. *Heritage Language Journal, 15*(1), 95–115.

Peterson, M. (2010). Computerized games and simulations in computer-assisted language learning: A meta-analysis of research. *Simulation & Gaming, 41*(1), 72–93.

Petukhova, M. E., Simulina, I. A., Kozhemyakova, E. A., & Grigoreva, E. A. (2020). Case system of the Russian language: Difficulties of mastering and experience of overcoming them. *International E-Journal of Advances in Social Sciences, 6*(16), 200–209.

Philp, J., Adams, R., & Iwashita, N. (2014). *Peer interaction and second language learning*. New York: Routledge.

Philp, J., & Iwashita, N. (2013). Talking, tuning in and noticing: Exploring the benefits of output in task-based peer interaction. *Language Awareness, 22*(4), 353–370. https://doi.org/10.1080/09658416.2012.758128

Philp, J., Walter, S., & Basturkmen, H. (2010). Peer interaction in the foreign language classroom: What factors foster a focus on form? *Language Awareness, 19*(4), 261–279. https://doi.org/10.1080/09658416.2010.516831

Pinner, R. (2014). The authenticity continuum: Towards a definition incorporating international voices. *English Today, 30*(4), 22–27.

Pinner, R. (2016). *Reconceptualising authenticity for english as a global language*. Tonawanda, NY: Multilingual Matters (Second Language Acquisition).

Pinto, J. (2018). Immersion learning activities: Developing communicative tasks in the community. *Theory and Practice of Second Language Acquisition, 4*(1), 23–48.

Plonsky, L., & Kim, Y. (2016). Task-based learner production: A substantive and methodological review. *Annual Review of Applied Linguistics, 36*, 73–97.

Plough, I., & Gass, S. (1993). Interlocutor and task familiarity: Effect on interactional structure. In G. Crookes & S. Gass (Eds.), *Tasks and language learning* (pp. 35–56). Clevedon, U.K.: Multilingual Matters.

Polinsky, M. (1997). American Russian: Language loss meets language acquisition. In W. Browne, E. Dornisch, N. Kondrashova, & D. Zec (Eds.), *Annual workshop on formal approaches to Slavic linguistics,* Michigan Slavic materials, vol. 39 (pp. 370–407). Ann Arbor: Michigan Slavic Publications.

Polinsky, M. (2008). Gender under incomplete acquisition: Heritage speakers' knowledge of noun categorization. *Heritage Language Journal, 6*(1), 40–71.

Polivanova, S. (2017, September 19). Nakanune ChM-2018 brazil'cy uchat russkiy iazyk (Накануне ЧМ-2018 бразильцы учат русский язык) [The 2018 World Cup approaches, Brazilians are studying Russian]. *Russkiy mir*. Retrieved from https://russkiymir.ru/publications/230673/

Ponomareva, L. D., Churilina, L. N., Buzhinskaya, D. S., Derevskova, E. N., Dorfman, O. V., & Sokolova, E. P. (2016). Russian national corpus as a tool of linguo-didactic innovation in teaching languages. *International Journal of Environmental & Science Education, 11*(18), 13043–13053.

Portin, M., Lehtonen, M., & Laine, M. (2007). Processing of inflected nouns in late bilinguals. *Applied Psycholinguistics, 28*, 135–156.

Potapova, N. (1961). *Breve manual da língua russa*. Moskva: Izdatel'stvo literatury na inostrannyh jazykah.

Poteau, C. E. (2017). *Pedagogical innovations in foreign language learning via interlocutor familiarity*. Newcastle, U.K.: Cambridge Scholars Publishing.

Poupore, G. (2005). Quality interaction and types of negotiation in problem-solving and jigsaw tasks. In C. Edwards, & J. Willis (Eds.), *Teachers exploring tasks in English language teaching* (pp. 242–255). New York: Palgrave Macmillan.

Pozner, V. V. (Producer). (2008, February 11–May 26). *Odnoetazhnaia Amerika* [Television broadcast]. Moscow, Russia: Pervyi Kanal.

Prabhu, N. S. (1987). *Second language pedagogy*. New York: Oxford University Press.

Puh, M. (2020). Estudos eslavos no Brasil: constituição de uma área. *Revista X, 15*(6), 674–697. http://doi.org/10.5380/rvx.v15i6.76848

Pylypiuk, N. (2004). Introduction: Teaching Slavic languages and cultures. *Canadian Slavonic Papers, 46*(1/2), 1–7.

Quintino, F., & Tonhati, T. (2017). Uma análise das autorizações de trabalho concedidas a estrangeiros pela Coordenação Geral de Imigração (CGIg 2011–2016). In L. Cavalcante, A. Tadeu de Oliveira, D. Araujo, & T. Tonhati (Orgs.), *A inserção dos imigrantes no mercado de trabalho brasileiro. Relatório anual 2017* (pp. 16–33). Observatório das Migrações Internacionais (OBMigra); Ministério do Trabalho/ Conselho Nacional de Imigração e Coordenação Geral de Imigração. Retrieved from http://obmigra.mte.gov.br/index.php/publicacoes-obmigra

Rahimi, S., Ahmadian, M., Amerian, M., & Dowlatabadi, H. R. (2020). Comparing accuracy and durability effects of jigsaw versus input flood tasks on the recognition of regular past tense /-ed/. *SAGE Open, 10*(2), Article 215824402091950. https://doi.org/10.1177/2158244020919505. Retrieved from https://journals.sagepub.com/doi/10.1177/2158244020919505

Rankin, T., & Whong, M. (2020). *Grammar: A linguists' guide for language teachers*. Cambridge: Cambridge University Press.

Ranta, L., & Lyster, R. (2018). Form-focused instruction. In P. Garrett & J. M. Cots (Eds.), *The Routledge handbook of language awareness* (pp. 40–56). New York: Routledge.

Rashtchi, M., & Etebari, F. (2018). Learning the English passive voice: A comparative study on input flooding and input enhancement techniques. *International Linguistics Research, 1*(1), 67–79. https://doi.org/10.30560/ilr.v1n1p67

Ravitch, L., & Marruffo, S. *Russian Homestay Simulation*. Retrieved January 21, 2021 from www.concordialanguagevillages.org/adult-programs/educator-programs/teacher-resources/startalk-curriculum-modules/russian

Razumovskaja, M., L'vova, S., & Kapinos, V. (Разумовская, М., Львова, С., Капинос, В.) (2020). *Russkij jazyk 6 klass* (*Русский язык 6 класс*) [Russian 6th grade]. Moscow: Drofa (Дрофа).

Reaching Global Competence. (2014, August). Retrieved from www.actfl.org/sites/default/files/news/GlobalCompetencePositionStatement0814.pdf

Reppen, R. (2010). Building a corpus: What are the key considerations? In A. O'Keeffe & M. McCarthy (Eds.), *The Routledge handbook of corpus linguistics* (pp. 31–37). London and New York: Routledge.

Rhodes, N., & Pufahl, I. (2009). *Foreign language teaching in U.S. schools. Results of a national survey*. Washington, DC: Center for Applied Linguistics. Retrieved January 2, 2021, from www.cal.org/content/download/2241/29054/version/2/file/ForeignLanguageExecutiveSummary.pdf

Richards, J. C. (2006). *Communicative language teaching today*. Cambridge: Cambridge University Press.

Richards, J. C. (2015, August). Bridging the gap between receptive and productive competence. *World of Better Learning*. Retrieved from www.cambridge.org/elt/blog/2015/08/27/bridging-gap-receptive-productive-competence

Richards, J., Platt, J., & Weber, H. (1985). *Longman dictionary of applied linguistics*. London: Longman.

Richards, J. C., & Rodgers, T. (2001). *Approaches and methods in language teaching*. New York: Cambridge University Press.

Rilling, S., & Dantas-Whitney, M. (2009). *Authenticity in the language classroom and beyond: Adult learners*. Alexandria, VA: TESOL Publications.

Robinson, P. (2001a). Task complexity, task difficulty, and task production: Exploring interactions in a componential framework. *Applied Linguistics, 22*(1), 27–57.

Robinson, P. (2001b). Task complexity, cognitive resources, and syllabus design: A triadic framework for examining task influences on SLA. In P. Robinson (Ed.), *Cognition and second language instruction* (pp. 287–318). Cambridge, U.K.: Cambridge University Press.

Robinson, P. (2003). The cognition hypothesis, task design, and adult task-based language learning. *Second Language Studies, 21*(2), 45–107.

Romanova, N., & Gor, K. (2016). Processing of gender and number agreement in Russian as a second language. *Studies in Second Language Acquisition, 39*(1), 97–128. https://doi.org/10.1017/s0272263116000012

Rozental', D., Golub, I., & Telenkova, M. (Розенталь, Д., Голуб, И., Теленкова, М.). (2017). *Sovremennyj russkij jazyk: uchebnoe posobie* (15th ed.) (Современный русский язык: учебное пособие.15е изд.) [Modern Russian language: training manual. 15th ed.]. Moscow: Ajris-Press (Айрис-Пресс).

Rubinstein, G. (1995). On case errors made in oral speech by American learners of Russian. *The Slavic and East European Journal, 39*(3), 408–429.

Ruseishvili, S. (2016). *Ser russo em São Paulo. Os imigrantes russos e a reformulação de identidade após a Revolução Bolchevique de 1917* [Ph.D. Thesis, Universidade de São Paulo]. Biblioteca Digital de Teses e Dissertações da USP. Retrieved from https://teses.usp.br/teses/disponiveis/8/8132/tde-13022017-124015/pt-br.php

Russian National Corpus. (2020). *Russian National Corpus*. Retrieved from https://ruscorpora.ru/old/en/index.html

Samburskiy, D. (2014). Corpus-informed pedagogical grammar of English: Pros and cons. *Procedia-Social and Behavioral Sciences, 154*, 263–267.

Samuda, V., Van den Branden, K., & Bygate, M. (Eds.). (2018). *TBLT as a researched pedagogy*. Amsterdam and Philadelphia: John Benjamins.

Sato, M. (2013). Beliefs about peer interaction and peer corrective feedback: Efficacy of classroom intervention. *The Modern Language Journal, 97*(3), 611–633. https://doi.org/10.1111/j.1540-4781.2013.12035.x

Sato, M., & Ballinger, S. (2016). Understanding peer interaction: Research synthesis and directions. In M. Sato & S. Ballinger (Eds.), *Peer interaction and second language learning: Pedagogical potential and research agenda* (pp. 1–30). Amsterdam, The Netherlands: John Benjamins.

Sato, M., & Loewen, S. (2019). Toward evidence-based second language pedagogy: Research proposals and pedagogical recommendations. In M. Sato & S. Loewen (Eds.), *Evidence-based second language pedagogy: A collection of instructed second language acquisition studies* (pp. 1–23). New York: Routledge.

Scherr, B. (1980). Russian and English versification: Similarities, differences, analysis. *Style, 14*(4), 353–378. Retrieved January 2, 2021, from www.jstor.org/stable/42946082

Schmidt, R. (1992). Awareness and second language learning. *Annual Review of Applied Linguistics, 13,* 206–226.

Schmidt, R. (1995). Consciousness and foreign language learning: A tutorial on the role of attention and awareness in learning. In R. Schmidt (Ed.), *Attention and awareness in foreign language learning* (pp. 1–63). Honolulu, HI: University of Hawaii, Second Language Teaching & Curriculum Center.

Schmidt, R. (2001). Attention. In P. Robinson (Ed.), *Cognition and second language instruction* (pp. 3–32). Cambridge: Cambridge University Press.

Schulz, R. A. (1998). Using young adult literature in content-based German instruction: Teaching the Holocaust. *Die Unterrichtspraxis Teaching German, 31*(2), 138–147.

Schurz, A. & Coumel, M. (2020). Grammar teaching in ELT: A cross-national comparison of teacher-reported practices. *Language Teaching Research,* 1–26. Retrieved from https://journals.sagepub.com/doi/full/10.1177/1362168820964137

Sekerina, I. A. (2017). Slavic psycholinguistics in the 21st century. *Journal of Slavic Linguistics, 25*(2), 463–487. https://doi.org/10.1353/jsl.2017.0018

Shahini, G., & Riazi, A. M. (2011). A PBLT approach to teaching ESL speaking, writing, and thinking skills. *ELT Journal, 65*(2), 170–179.

Shehadeh, A. (2005). Task-based learning and teaching: Theories and applications. In C. Edwards & J. Willis (Eds.), *Teachers exploring tasks in English language teaching* (pp. 13–30). New York: Palgrave Macmillan.

Shintani, N. (2012). Input-based tasks and the acquisition of vocabulary and grammar: A process–product study. *Language Teaching Research, 16*(2), 253–279.

Shintani, N. (2016). *Input-based tasks in foreign language instruction for young learners.* Amsterdam: John Benjamins.

Shulga, M. (2017). On development of Russian morphological system. *Vestnik Volgogradskogo Gosudarstvennogo Universiteta. Serija 2. Jazykoznanije, 16*(4), 232–242. https://doi.org/10.15688/jvolsu2.2017.4.23

Shvidko, E., Evans, N. W., & Hartshorn, K. J. (2015). Factors affecting language use outside the ESL classroom: Student perspectives. *System, 51,* 11–27. https://doi.org/10.1016/j.system.2015.03.006

Sildus, T. I. (2006). The effect of a student video project on vocabulary retention of first-year secondary school German students. *Foreign Language Annals, 39*(1), 54–70.

Skehan, P. (1996). A framework for the implementation of task-based instruction. *Applied Linguistics, 17,* 38–62.

Skehan, P. (1998). *A cognitive approach to language learning.* Oxford: Oxford University Press.

Sköld, O. (2012). The effects of virtual space on learning: A literature review. *First Monday, 17*(1). Article 3496. https://doi.org/10.5210/fm.v17i1.3496

Slabakova, R. (2009). What is easy and what is hard to acquire in a second language? In M. Bowles, T. Ionin, S. Montrul, & A. Tremblay (Eds.), *Proceedings of the 10th generative approaches to second language acquisition conference* (pp. 280–294). Somerville, MA: Cascadilla Proceedings Project.

Slabakova, R. (2018). Inflectional morphology. In P. Malovrh & A. Benati (Eds.), *The handbook of advanced proficiency in second language acquisition* (pp. 381–400). Hoboken, NJ: John Wiley & Sons, Inc. https://doi.org/10.1002/9781119261650.ch20

Slabakova, R. (2019). The bottleneck hypothesis updated. In T. Ionin & M. Rispoli (Eds.), *Three Streams of generative language acquisition research* (pp. 319–345). Amsterdam: John Benjamins. https://doi.org/10.1075/lald.63.16sla

Slabakova, R., Leal, T., Dudley, A., & Stack, M. (2020). *Generative second language acquisition (Elements in second language acquisition)*. Cambridge: Cambridge University Press. https://doi.org/10.1017/9781108762380

Smart, J. (2014). The role of guided induction in paper-based data-driven learning. *ReCALL, 26*(2), 184–201.

Smirnova Henriques, A., Fontes, M. A. S., Skrelin, P. A., Kachkovskaia, T. V., Ruseishvili, S., Borrego, M. C., Zuleta, P. P. B., Ferreira, L. P., & Madureira, S. (2020). Russian immigrants in Brazil: To understand, to be understood. *Cadernos de Linguística, 1*(2), 1–18. https://doi.org/10.25189/2675-4916.2020.v1.n2.id210

Smirnova Henriques, A., & Ruseishvili, S. (2019). Migrantes russófonos no Brasil no século XXI: perfis demográficos, caminhos de inserção e projetos migratórios. *Ponto-e-Vírgula, 25*, 83–96. https://doi.org/10.23925/1982-4807.2019i25p83-96

Smirnova Henriques, A., Skrelin, P. A., Evdokimova, V. V., Kachkovskaia, T. V., Borrego, M. C., Piccolotto Ferreira, L., Zuleta, P. P. B., Ruseishvili, S., & Madureira, S. (2019). The perception of the Brazilian Portuguese open and close mid vowels by native Russian speakers. *JoSS, 8*(2), 59–84. https://doi.org/10.20396/joss.v8i2.14995

Sorace, A. (2011). Pinning down the concept of "interface" in bilingualism. *Linguistic Approaches to Bilingualism, 1*(1), 1–33.

Spada, N. (2016). Focusing on language in meaning-based and content-based instruction. *JACET International Convention Selected Papers, 4*, 3–30.

Spasova, S. (2017). Bringing in real life from the start: Scenarios in beginning Russian. *The FLTMAG*. Retrieved from https://fltmag.com/bringing-in-real-life-from-the-start/

Spencer, A. (2012). Identifying stems. *Word Structure, 5*(1), 88–108.

Staples, S., Novikov, A., Picoral, A., & Sommer-Farias, B. (2019). *Multilingual academic corpus of assignments – writing and speech* [Learner corpus]. Retrieved from https://macaws.corporaproject.org/

The State of World Language Teaching. (2020). *Results of the 2020 world language teaching survey: Language Babel, Inc.* Retrieved January 2, 2021, from www.speakinglatino.com/survey/

Stockwell, G. (2013). Technology and motivation in English-language teaching and learning. In E. Ushioda (Ed.), *International perspectives on motivation: Language learning and professional challenges* (pp. 156–175). New York: Palgrave Macmillan.

Storch, N., & Aldosari, A. (2010). Learners' use of first language (Arabic) in pair work in an EFL class. *Language Teaching Research, 14*(4), 355–375. https://doi.org/10.1177/1362168810375362

Storch, N., & Wigglesworth, G. (2003). Is there a role for the use of the L1 in an L2 setting? *TESOL Quarterly, 37*(4), 760–770.

Suzuki, Y., & DeKeyser, R. M. (2017). Effects of distributed practice on the proceduralization of morphology. *Language Teaching Research, 21*(2), 166–188.

Swaffar, J. K., & Arens, K. (2005). *Remapping the foreign language curriculum: An approach through multiple literacies*. Series Teaching Languages, Literatures, and Cultures. New York: Modern Language Association of America.

Swain, M. (1993). The output hypothesis: Just speaking and writing aren't enough. *The Canadian Modern Language Review, 50*(1), 158–164.

Swain, M. (1995). Three functions of output in second language learning. In G. Cook & B. Seidlhofer (Eds.), *Principle and practice in applied linguistics: Studies in honour of H. G. Widdowson* (pp. 125–144). Oxford: Oxford University Press.

Swain, M. (1996). Integrating language and content in immersion classrooms: Research perspectives. *Canadian Modern Language Review, 52*(4), 529–548.

Swain, M. (2000). The output hypothesis and beyond: Mediating acquisition through collaborative dialogue. In J. P. Lantolf (Ed.), *Sociocultural theory and second language learning* (pp. 97–114). Oxford: Oxford University Press.

Swain, M., Kinnear, P., & Steinman, L. (2015). *Sociocultural theory in second language education: An introduction through narratives* (2nd ed.). Bristol, Buffalo and Toronto: Multilingual Matters.

Swain, M., & Lapkin, S. (1998). Interaction and second language learning: Two adolescent French immersion students working together. *The Modern Language Journal, 82*, 320–337. https://doi.org/10.1111/j.1540-4781.1998.tb01209.x

Swain, M., & Lapkin, S. (2000). Task-based second language learning: The uses of the first language. *Language Teaching Research, 4*(3), 251–274. https://doi.org/10.1177/136216880000400304

Swan, M. (2005). Legislation by hypothesis: The case of task-based instruction. *Applied Linguistics, 26*(3), 376–401.

Taguchi, N., & Kim, Y. (2018). *Task-based approaches to teaching and assessing pragmatics*. Amsterdam and Philadelphia: John Benjamins.

Tanich, M. (Танич). Retrieved from www.culture.ru/persons/9851/mikhail-tanich

Thomas, M., & Reinders, H. (Eds.). (2021). *Contemporary task-based language teaching in Asia*. New York: Bloomsbury.

Tomlinson, B. (2018, September). *Text-driven approaches to task-based language teaching*. Retrieved from www.matsda.org/mobile/Folio_sample_1.pdf

Tremblay, P., & Gardner, R. C. (1995). Expanding the Motivation Construct in Language Learning. *Modern Language Journal, 79*(4), 505–518.

Tsalikova, I. K., Yurinova, E. A., & Pakhotina, S. V. (2016). Tekhnologiia Task Based Learning and Teaching na zaniatiiakh po inostrannomu iazyku v vuze (Технология Task Based Learning and Teaching на занятиях по иностранному языку в вузе) [Method of task based learning and teaching in teaching foreign languages in universities]. *Vysshee obrazovanie segodnia, 3*, 71–76. Retrieved from https://rucont.ru/efd/401008

Tsvetkova, N., Stoimenova, B., Tsvetanova, S., Connolly, T., Stansfield, M., Hainey, T., Cousins, I., Josephson, J., O'Donovan, A., & Ortiz, C. (2009, January 1). *Arguing for Multilingual motivation in Web 2.0: The teacher training perspective*. Paper presented at the 3rd European Conference on Games-Based Learning (ECGBL) (pp. 371–378).

Turnbull, M., & Dailey-O'Cain, J. (Eds.). (2009). *First language use in second and foreign language learning*. Bristol, Buffalo and Toronto: Multilingual Matters.

Ullman, M. T. (2005). A cognitive neuroscience perspective on second language acquisition: The declarative/procedural model. In Sanz C (Ed.), *Mind and context in second language acquisition* (pp. 141–178). Washington, DC: Georgetown University Press.

Ullman, M. T., & Lovelett, J. T. (2018). Implications of the declarative/procedural model for improving second language learning: The role of memory enhancement techniques. *Second Language Research, 34*(1), 39–65.

Unal, Z., & Unal, A. (2017). Comparison of student performance, student perception, and teacher satisfaction with traditional versus flipped classroom models. *International Journal of Instruction, 10*(4), 145–164.

Universidade de São Paulo. (2008). *Proposta Literaturas Estrangeiras Modernas – Programa Literatura e Cultura Russa 33002010184P-3*. Retrieved from http://conteudoweb.capes.gov.br/conteudoweb/VisualizadorServlet?nome=2008/33002010/041/2008_041_33002 010184P3_Proposta.pdf&aplicacao=cadernoavaliacao.

Universidade de São Paulo. (2021a, January 10). *Bacharelado em Letras – Russo*. Retrieved from http://letrasorientais.fflch.usp.br/graduacao/russo

Universidade de São Paulo. (2021b, January 10). *Pós-Graduação – LETRA*. Retrieved from http://letrasorientais.fflch.usp.br/posgraduacao/letra/

Universidade Federal de Rio de Janeiro. (2021, January 10). *Letras: Português-Russo*. Retrieved from www.portal.letras.ufrj.br/graduacao/cursos-de-graduacao/portugues-russo.html

Ushioda, E. (2008). Motivation and good language learners. In C. Griffiths (Ed.), *Lessons from good language learners* (pp. 19–34). Cambridge: Cambridge University Press.

Ushioda, E. (2014). Motivation, autonomy, and metacognition: Exploring their interactions. In D. Lasagabaster, A. Doiz, & J. M. Sierra (Eds.), *Motivation and foreign language learning: From theory to practice* (pp. 31–50). Philadelphia, PA: John Benjamins Publishing Company.

Van den Branden, K. (2009). *Task-based language teaching*. Amsterdam: John Benjamins Publishing Company.

Van Lier, L. (2001). The role of form in language learning. In M. Bax & C. Jan-Wouter Zwart (Eds.), *Reflections on language and language learning: In honour of Arthur Van Essen* (pp. 253–266). Amsterdam: John Benjamins.

Van Lier, L. (2003). A tale of two computer classrooms: The ecology of project-based language learning. In J. Leather & J. van Dam (Eds.), *Ecology of language acquisition* (pp. 49–63). New York: Kluwer Academic.

Van Lier, L. (2004). *The ecology and semiotics of language learning: A sociocultural perspective* (Vol. 3). Berlin: Springer Science & Business Media.

VanPatten, B. (1996). *Input processing and grammar instruction in second language acquisition*. Norwood, NJ: Ablex.

VanPatten, B. (2003). *From input to output: A teacher's guide to second language acquisition*. New York: McGraw-Hill.

VanPatten, B., Keating, G. D., & Wulff, S. (2020). *Theories in second language acquisition: An introduction* (3rd ed.). Second Language Acquisition Research Series. New York: Routledge.

VanPatten, B., & Sanz, C. (1995). From input to output: Processing instruction and communicative tasks. In F. R. Eckman, D. Highland, P. W. Lee, J. Mileham, & R. R. Weber (Eds.), *Second language acquisition theory and pedagogy* (pp. 169–185). Mahwah, NJ: Erlbaum.

Vorobieff, A. (2006). *Identidade e memória da comunidade russa na cidade de São Paulo* [M.S. Thesis, Universidade de São Paulo]. Biblioteca Digital de Teses e Dissertações da USP. Retrieved from https://teses.usp.br/teses/disponiveis/8/8136/tde-18062007-141410/pt-br.php

Vyatkina, N., & Boulton, A. (2017). Corpora in language learning and teaching. *Language Learning & Technology, 21*(3), 1–8.

Vysotskiy, V. (В. Высоцкий). Retrieved from www.culture.ru/poems/19515/ballada-o-borbe

Widdowson, H. G. (1998). Context, community, and authentic language. *TESOL Quarterly, 32*(4), 705–716.

Willis, D., & Willis, J. (1996). Consciousness-raising activities in the language classroom. In J. Willis & D. Willis (Eds.), *Challenge and change in language teaching* (pp. 63–76). Oxford: Heinemann.

Willis, D., & Willis, J. (2007). *Doing task-based teaching*. Oxford: Oxford University Press.

Willis, J. (1996). *A framework for task-based learning*. Harlow, U.K.: Longman.

Willis, J. (2004). Perspectives on task-based instruction: Understanding our practices acknowledging different practitioners. In B. L. Leaver & J. R. Willis (Eds.), *Task-based instruction in foreign language education: Practices and programs* (pp. 3–44). Washington, DC: Georgetown University Press.

Wulandari, M. (2019). Improving EFL learners' speaking proficiency through Instagram vlog. *LLT Journal: A Journal on Language and Language Teaching, 22*(1), 111–125.

Xiao, H., Chan, T. (2020). An analysis of governance models of research universities in selected countries: Lessons learned. *Educational Planning, 27*(1), 17–29.

Yatsenko, A. A. A., Kisselev, O. V., & Freels, S. G. (2012). Results 2012: Using flagship data to develop a Russian learner corpus of academic writing. *Russian Language Journal/Русский язык, 62*, 79–105.

Yen, P. H. (2016). Challenges of shifting to task-based language teaching: A story from a Vietnamese teacher. *Can Tho University Journal of Science, 2*(1), 37–45.

Young, E. H., & West, R. E. (2018). Speaking practice outside the classroom: A literature review of asynchronous multimedia-based oral communication in language learning. *The EUROCALL Review, 26*(1), 59–78.

Zabolotsky, J. A. (2007). *A imigração russa no Rio Grande do Sul*. Santa Rosa, Brasil: Coli Gráfica e Editora Ltda.

Zaliznyak, A. (Зализняк, А.) (1980). *Grammaticheskij slovar' russkogo jazyka.* (*Грамматический словарь русского языка*) [Grammatical dictionary of the Russian language]. Moscow: Russkij jazyk (Русский язык). Retrieved from http://zaliznyak-dict.narod.ru/c0090.gif

Бердичевский, А. Л. (2020). Преподавание грамматики РКИ. Вебинар в рамках Академической встречи "Диалоги с Россией: развитие открытого образования на русском языке." 24–25 ноября 2020.

Блик, Е. С. (2015). Использование метода коммуникативных заданий в обучении студентов английскому языку. *Педагогическое образование в России, 2*, 68–72.

Бойкова, А. С. (2013). Использование в средней школе методики обучения иностранному языку, ориентированной на выполнение задач (task-based language teaching). Курсовая работа по дисциплине "Технологии и методики обучения иностранному языку". Тульский государственный педагогический университет им. Л. Н. Толстого.

Ильин, Е. П. (1986). Умения и навыки: нерешенные вопросы. *Вопросы психологии, 2*, С. 138–147.

Леонтьев, А. Н. (1975). *Деятельность. Сознание. Личность*. Москва: Политиздат.

Насс, С. В. (2020). РКИ в современной англоязычной аудитории: к вопросу о теории и практике организации работы посредством целевого задания. В монографии "Мир без границ" (2). ПсковГУ.

Щукин, А. Н., & Азимов, Э. Г. (2010). Новый словарь методических терминов и понятий. "Икар." 253 (Shchukin, A. N., & Azimov, E. G. (2010). Novyy slovar metodicheskikh terminov i ponyatiy. *Ikar*. Retrieved September 29 2020 from http://linguistics-online.narod.ru/olderfiles/1/azimov_e_g_shukin_a_n_novyy_slovar-21338.pdf).

Index

Page locators in **bold** indicate a table

ability: learner/student 28–30, 33, 133; to meet linguistic objectives **69–70**, 88, 172, 174, 197; to read/write/speak 44, 57, 82
accounts 1, 33–34, 214
accuracy, grammatical 43, **69**, 70, 116, 188
achievement criterion 115–116, 197
acquisition: of Russian (L2) 15, 19, 21–22, 32, 58, 73; second language 17, 92, 172
action research 17, 216
activity: fill-in-the-blank 55, 57; interview activity 153, 156, 159, 161, 168; small group/jigsaw 27, 198; speaking, low stakes **58**; structure-trapping **63**, **64** see also tasks; task-based 82, 86–87, 93
advanced Russian 8, 12, 187, 190–191
affective variables 65–66, 72
Aksel, Aynur 68, 72
American Council on the Teaching of Foreign Languages (ACTFL) 7, 82–83, 86, **119**, 172, **174**, 191–192, 202, 215
Anderson, John R. 91
anxiety, minimize or reduce 62, 66, 110, 194
Appendix A: vlog instructions 75
Appendix B: vlog instructions, final 76
applied linguistics: difficulties of 5, 11; efficiency, addition of 35–36; methodology of 22, 65, 217
assessment: challenges of 206, 209, 214, 216; focus-on-form/focus-on-content 191–192, **196**, 197–198; formative 7, 9, **41**, 87, **124**, **174**; learning with tasks 4, **105**, **108–109**, **111–112**; linguistic objectives, meeting **69–70**, 84, 115–116, **159–160**; low-stakes 55, **58**, **124**, 130,
158; peer assessment 87; student self-reflection 7, 87, **156–157**; third-party 114; writing performance **52–53**
associative patterning 26, 28
attention: lack of to TBLT 78, 81, 83; learner/student 26, 49, 53, 61, 117, 161; to linguistic difficulties 89, 93, 115, 188, 193
authentic: communication 7–8, 82, 132–134, 191, 212; experiences 45, 83, 90, 200; materials/resources, use of 50, 78, 86, 89, **105**, 122–123, 125, 130–132, 160, 210–211; as meaningful 3, 6, 92; statistics/data 87, 94, 102
autonomous 82–83, 87
autonomy, of learners 1, 6, 9, 84, 128, 212
avatars 171, **174**, 178–180, 182–183, 187

Baehler, Aline 188n1
Ballinger, Susan 153, 154, 192
Basic Level Test (BLT) 114, **119**, **120**
Belinky, Tatiana 99
Benson, Phil 7, 128
bilingual learners 22, 103, 192
Blasing, Molly Thomasy 187–188
blog 193
Bolshevik Revolution 99, 189n3
Bondarenko, Maria 6, 83
Boulton, Alex 50
Bown, Jennifer 41, 44, 177, 199
Brasilia 101, 109, 114, 116
Brazilian: universities 100–101, 103
Brazil: adult learners, tasks for 102–103, **105**, 106–107, **108**, **111**, 112–113; communication skills 98, 110; cultural events, teaching 107; educational courses 100, 103–104, 116–117;

immigration to (Russian) 99; language proficiency test 113–116; university teachers/instructors 101–102, 106, 116
Brazilian: communications skills of test takers 98, 114–115; learners/students 102–104, **108**, 110, 116–117; schools 102, 104, 113–114, 117
Brezina, Vaclav 13
Brooks, Patricia J. (et al.) 32
Brown, N. Anthony (et al.) 177, 192
Bygate, Martin 4, 5, 84

California State University, Northridge USA 156
capitalize 30, 40
Castellví, Joan 5, 12–13, 20–21
Castro, T. 101
challenge: for educators 8, 10, 214; for learners (L2) 21, 23, 73, 78–79, 116–117, 201–202; task complexity 61, 126
Cho, Jacee 24
circle of literacy 84, 89
Clifford, Ray 83
CLV Way 121, 134n1
Cobb, Tom 50
Code Breakers **38**, 40–41, **41**, 44–46
Cognition Hypothesis (Robinson) 12
cognitive complexity 11, 83–84
cognitive load 12, 30–32, 84, 86
cognitive skills 77, 80–81, 83, 87, 89
cognitive tasks 199
collaborative: learning 78, 175, 193, **194**; tasks **196**, 198; virtual space **174**, 175; writing 84, **87**, 95
Comer, William 5, 9–10, 13, 44, 46n4, 184, 186, 194, 210
comfort zone 172, 177, 186
Common European Framework of Reference (CEFR) 83, 113, **119**
communication achievement 110, 115–116
communicative: activities 153, 161–162, 173; tasks 115, 152–154, 156, 160, 172, 182; teaching 9, 78, 161
communicative language teaching (CLT) 10
complexity: cognitive 11, 83–84; linguistic 12, 61, 91; morphological 13, 32, 104, 116
conceptual space 77, 79
Concordia Language Villages (CLV) 121–123
conversation: clubs 103, 117; tasks 27, 52, 73, 106, **120**, 131, 157–158, 161, 165; topics **120**

conversation task 106 *see also* peer interaction
Corin, Andrew R. 83, 126
corrective feedback 9, 49, 82, 84, 95–96, 208
Cotos, Elena 50
course tasks 198, 202
Coyle, Evette 28
Cyrillic alphabet 6, 36, 41, 44, 100
Cyrillic code, cracking 36

Data-Driven Learning (DDL): focused tasks 49–51, 53–55, **54**, **55**, **58**, **59**, 61–62
deBenedette, Lynn-Brown (et al.) 5, 10, 13
DeKeyser, Robert 84, 91
discourse, interface with 11, 13, 16, 31–32, 191, 199, 206, 209
discovery learning 7
Dolenga, Marina 101
domains 22, 114
Doughty, Catherine J. 48, 193
Dunn, William 37
Duran, Goedele 78
Dutch 4

East, Martin 191, 211
Edison, Thomas 199
elderly people 103, 117
Elementary Level Test (ELT) 114–116, **119**, **120**
Ellis, Nick C. 78
Ellis, Rod 3–5, 6, 28, 37, 39–40, 45, 47–48, 53, 78, 80–82, 87, 97n1, 123, 139, 140, 180, 190, 193, 198, 210, 214
engagement: active 45, 49; learner 173, **174**, 187; student 37, 44, 171, 173, 181, 184, 201
English as a Second Language (ESL) 4, 40, 156, 214
English as foreign language (EFL) 67
Erlam, Rosemary 37, 78, 81–82, 214
explicit: grammar instruction 66, 161–162, 186, 216; pattern building 26

feedback: corrective 9, 49, 82, 84, 95–96, 208; negative 10, 193, **194**
Feryok, Anne 28, 34
flow of information 39, 45, 81
fluency 11, 28–29, 33, 37, 68, 78, 116
focus on form(s) *see* task-based language teaching (TBLT)
Ford, Henry 196, 199–201

foreign language: learning 6, 12; teaching 3, 5, 46, 121
Foreign Languages and Translation 100
Franciosi, Stephan 187–188
French 4, 32, 58, 73, 103, 153–154

Gatbonton, Elizabeth 82, 97n1
Gilabert, Roger 5, 12–13, 20–21
Gilmore, Alex 211, 213
Glazunova, O. I. 119, 120
global competence 190–193, 197, 203
goals 26, 37, 39–41, 44–45, 73, 88, 117, 122, 180 *see also* task goals; learning goals
González-Lloret, Marta 4, 39, 73
Google Docs 198, 201
Google Maps 112, 174, 177, 182
Google Meet 101
Google Sites 171–172, 175
Google translate **52**, **54**
Gor, Kira 19, 23, 25–26, 29–30, 32
grading rubric 52, 63–64
grammatical: accuracy 70, 116; concepts 122; construction 48, 157, 175; errors **63–64**, 115; forms 23, 161, 194; gender 20–21, 32; knowledge 104, 186, 214; patterns 88, 90; structure 40, 61, 90–91, 177, 180, 214
grand simulation context 121
Greenberg, Joseph 19
Gromik, Nicolas A. 67, 72, 73
Gürman-Kahraman, Fatma 68, 72

Hacc, C.B. (Nuss, S.V.) 138
Hacking, Jane F. 66, 73
Hamilton, Arran 16
Hamilton, Heidi E. (et al.) 123, 126–127, 129
Han, ZhaoHong 28
Harmer, Jeremy 97n1
Hattie, John 16
Hayes-Harb, Rachel 66
Henriques, Smirnova 117
Henry, Kathryn 173
holistic 13, 201, 217
Housing conditions in Russia 87–88, 93

Ilf and Petrov's American Road Trip: The 1935 Travelogue of Two Soviet Writers (2007) 199
Ilf, Ilya 190, 195, 199–200
immersion: cultural 107; isolated 121–123, 127, **130**, 132, 134; language 4, 86, 129, **130**, 161, 186, 213
immigrants 98–99, 104, **124**, 196

implementation: of assignments 68, 84, 184, 201; of task based learning 8, 79, 91, 214–215
implementation of the task 84, 201
implicit: grammar instruction 25–26, 78, 186, 194, 202, 206; negative feedback 193–194, 205n1
incremental mode 1, 7–8
individual: differences 152, 154, 161; tasks 175, 185, 208; words/phrases 27, 51, 58
information gap: requires decision-making 12, 80, 82, 123; tasks/activities 10, 39, 69, 71, 184, 198
innovation 81, 201
input: based tasks 81; processing theory 11, 17–18, 21, 25–25; structured 10, 12, 28
Instructors 175
inter alia: failed functional features hypothesis 3, 23; international association with a biannual conference 3
interaction: activities 115, **120**, 135, 187–188; oral 77, 80–83, 84; outside community 7; peer *see* task-based language teaching (TBLT); purposeful 89
interactions: learner/student 153, 157, 209; negotiative **39**, 41
interface hypothesis 32
Intermediate Russian 173, **174**, 180, 182–183
International Association of Task-Based Language Teaching (IATBLT) 3–4
internet resources 11, 82, 95, 102, 106–107, 173, 175, 177
interpersonal communication 71, 82, 89, 132–133
intuition 13, 18, 33–34
Isbell, Daniel R. 153, 154, 156, 158
Italian 4, 32, 192
Iwashita, Noriko 153–154

Jing-Schmidt, Zhou 33

Kang, Eun-Young 28
Kaplan, Marsha ix, 1–2, 5, 8–9, 13, 37, 38, 46, 138, 198, 200
Kent State University, Ohio USA 156
Klimanova, Liudmila 86
Kogan, Vita 210
Kommunalka (virtual space) 171, 173, **174**, 175, 180–181, 184–185
Kramsch, Claire 125, 128

Lambert, Craig 4, 84
Lambert, Wallace E. 212
language: function 116, 185, 191;
  Germanic 79, 91; patterns 25–27, 32,
  34, 50, 55; Portuguese 51, 99, 101–104,
  106, 116–117; target 9, 37, 48, 61, **70**,
  72, 78, 81, 123, 133–134, 187, 193
language awareness 47, 49, 61–62
language learning culture, integration of
  11–12, 98–99
language mining 26, 28
language related episodes (LREs) 153–155
Lapkin, Sharon 153–155
Lazareva, Olga 115
learner corpus 47–50, 61–62
learner needs analysis 52–53, 55, 58,
  69–70, 87, 105, 108, 111–112, 124, 130,
  154–160, 174, 195
learner-centered 6–7, 37, 98, 117, 128,
  175, 209, 217
learning: goals **52, 53, 55, 58**, 187;
  hands-on 3, 129–130; task-based 3, 12,
  14, 122–123, 127–128, 132, 134, 184
Leaver, Betty Lou ix, 1–2, 5, 8–9, 13,
  36–37, 38, 46, 137, 138, 192, 198, 200
Lee, David 50
Lee, James F. 5, 38, 39, 210
Lee, Jang Ho 155
Lekant, Pavel Aleksandrovich 21, 23, 24,
  29, 30, 31
Leminen, Alina (et al.) 23, 31
Levesque, Kyle C. (et al.) 29
lexical diversity 11, 13, 32
lexical meaning 19, 24, 65
lexis (vocabulary) 58, 153
linguistic model 22, 82
Loewen, Shawn 33, 34, 153, 154, 156, 158
Long, Michael 1, 2, 3, 5, 10, 13, 19, 25–26,
  39, 47, 48, 58, 78, 80, 82, 84, 85, 89, 90,
  146, 153, 190, 193–194, 196, 198, 203,
  206, 208, 210, 214, 216
low proficiency level 77, 79–80, 84–86,
  89–90
Lyster, Roy 49, 82, 84, 192

Macaro, Ernesto 155
Mackey, Alison 3, 16, 194
Markina, Elena 5, 11–13, 104, 116, 138
Martel, Jason 83, 90
meta-analysis 4, 50
Mezhdu nami (online textbook): www.
  MezhduNami.org 10, 66, 73
Michigan State University, USA 156

Moodle 173
Morphological Complexity Index (MCI)
  13, 32, 215
morphology: compound 29, 31;
  derivational 23, 29–30, 32, 58;
  inflectional 18, 21, 23–24, 26, 29, 32;
  L2, 5, 15, 21, 23, 25–26, 29–30, 32
Morrow, Keith 210
motivation: engagement and 37, 173, 181,
  184, 187, 202; learner 49–50; student
  31, 44, 68, 74, 122, 212; teacher 8
Multilingual Academic Corpus of
  Assignments – Writing and Speech
  (MACAWS) 49, 51, 54–55, 61
Murphy-Lee, M. 44, 46n4

narrative 11–12, 28, 179, 191, 200, 206, 214
native speaker corpus 50, 82
negotiation of meaning 39, 71, 153, 183, 192
non-reciprocal tasks 81
Northern Minnesota 122–123
Norton, Bonny 125, 128
Norton Peirce, Bonny 128
noticing patterns 26, 55, **56**
novice (low mid high) 77, 80, 86,
  119, 173
novice low 40, 77, 80, 86–87, 119
Nunan, David 4, 5, 6, 9, 78, 80–81, 139,
  140, 146, 174–175, 184–186, 192,
  193, 210
Nuss, Svetlana V. 12–14

Ogilvie, Gordon 37
Oliver, Rhonda 4
One-Storied America 190, 196, 200
online aids 6, 10, 26, 55, 83, **87**, 101, 107,
  134, 182, 186–187, 202
opinion gap 67–69, 71, 80, **87**, 89, 184
oral communication 82–83, 87, 92
oral interaction 77, 80–82, 80–83, 83–84
Ortega, Lourdes 4, 73
outcome: clear 1, 6; specific 39, 44, 67;
  tangible 80, 89
output-based tasks 81

Pallotti, Gabriele 1, 2, 13, 26, 32, 215
Paran, Amos 34
participation **39**, 45, 110, 160, 198, 200
Pastushenkov, Dimitrii 153–155, 158–159
pattern recognition 7, 50, 62
Pavlenko, Olga 154, 156, 158–159, 166
pedagogic tasks 39, 41, 45–46, 190,
  194, 199

peer interaction: consensus task **156**, 156–157, 163; conversation task **157**, 157–158, 161, 165; language-related episodes (LREs) 153–155; less stressful 152–153; spot-the-difference task 153, 155, 158, **158**, 166
pelmeni (dumplings) 129–130, 134n3
Peng, Xinjia 33
performance: exercises/tasks 200; student 9, 71, 215
personal experiences 81, 123, 130
perspective 3, 17, 22–23, 38, 68, 82–83, 88, 126, 197
Peterson, Mark 187
Petrov, Evgenii 193, 195, 199–200
Philp, Jenefer 153–155
phonological: form-meaning mapping 24; patterns 45
Pinner, Richard 211, 213
planning 5, 9–10, 18, 38, 45, 58, 104, 116, 173, 184, 216
poetry 19, 108, 110, 133
post-task 84, 86, 95–96, 106–107, 109–110, 112–113, 126, 158–159, 202
post–test, immediate/delayed 50, 116
Potapova, Nina 101
Poupore, Glen 37, 39, 41
Pozner, Vladimir 191, 195, 198–200
Prabhu, N.S. 3, 5, 78, 80–81, 84, 87, 122
practice: language 17, 25, **70**, 72, 85, **108**, 109, 188; teaching 5, 15, 17, 22, 46, 79
practitioner 4, 95, 201
pragmatic 9, 87, 90
pre-task 84–85, 93, 104, 107, 109, 112, 125, 145, 157–158
Presentation-Practice-Production (PPP) 91
private: instructors 98, 101–102, 114; schools 98, 100–101, 103
proficiency: development 1, 7; levels 10, 13, 32, 77, 80, 92, 117, 132, 153, 211, 215; results, higher 8
prompts 41–42, 51, 61
psycholinguistics 22
Pylypiuk, Natalia 46

qualitative 4, 213
quantitative 67–68
quasi-separatist 125

Ramaut, Griet 78
range 4, 19, 38, 47, 78, 179–180, 183, 192, 196

rating 27, 133
real time 16, 23, 25
reason 48, 80, 107, 113, 115, 126, 154, 203
reasoning gap 80, 180, 184
recasting 82, 117
recasts 9, 193
reciprocal tasks 81
reflections: on the course 201, 206; on practice 206, 209, 213
research: empirical 194, 213–214; future 211–213, 215; individual 197, 199; peer interaction 152–153, 158
resource 3, 8, 48, 54, 178, 195
restructure **38**, 83
results 8, 11, 13, 17, 34, 45, 53, 67–68, 72, 84
Richards, Jack C. 3, 5, 78, 83, 122, 210
Rio de Janeiro 101–102, 114
Roca de Larios, Julio 28
Rodgers, Theodore S. 78
role playing games 6, 154, 156, 159, **160**, 161–162, 169
role-play 109, 116, 171, 173, 175, 180, 187–188, 201
Romanova, Natalia 23, 25
root nests 26, 28
Russia: image, mysterious 99; post war 3, 99; students in 52, 88, 102, 113, 125, 157; teachers 101
Russian alphabet (Cyrillic) 11, **38**, 40–42, 44–45
Russian as a Foreign Language (RFL): challenges of teaching 58, 209; cyclic nature 3–4; pedagogy 121; peer interaction 156; preparing teachers 100–101; research findings 15, 153; student population 58; theory of 9
Russian as a second language (L2 Russian): learner-centered approach 1, 6–7; pedagogical narrations 1; proficiency levels 1; teaching 1, 9–10, 13, 17, 34, 202, 206, 209, 213
Russian authors 99
Russian cinema 99, 123
Russian construction 26, 28
Russian culture 102, 110, 129, 159, **160**, **174**, 178, 184
Russian literary theory 100
Russian Literature and Culture 100
Russian morphology 1, 5, 10, 15, 18–19, 21–23, 35, 161, 186, 202, 209, 215
Russian Orthodox Church 99

Russian writers 99
Russophones 99, 101–102, 104, 111

Saint Petersburg State University (SPBU) 113, 114, 117
Samuda, Virginia 4, 84
São Paulo 101–102, 114, 116
Sato, Masatoshi 33, 34, 153
scaffolding 9–11, 27, 31, 45, 85–86, 123, 160, 184, 193–194, 199
Schnaiderman, Boris 99
scientific 42, 206
second language: development 41, 78, 152; learning 83, 128; proficiency 13
Second Life 173, 187–188
Segalowitz, Norman 82, 97n1
Sekerina, Irina 22
Shehadeh, Ali 38
Shintani, Natsuko 82, 84–85
Sildus, Tatiana I. 68, 72
Skehan, Peter 5, 37, 61, 80–81, 84, 103, 210
skill 5, 73, 80, 85, 91, 188, 199–200
Skill Acquisition Theory 91
skills: higher cognitive skills 80–81, 87; language 36, **52**, **55**, 68, **124**, 131, 188, 196, 203; linguistic 6, 11, 79–80, 83; real world 6, 46, 53, 123
Skype 101, **120**, 129, 159
Slabakova, Roumyana 16, 17, 21–22, 23–24
Slavic: language 46, 81; linguistics/psycholinguistics 22
Slavic Psycholinguistics in the 21st Century (Sekerina) 22
small group 27
Smirnova Henriques, Anna 6–7, 119, 212
Soviet Union 103, 191, 200
Spada, Nina 194
Spanish 4, 73, 116, 154, 192, 215
Spasova, Shannon 11, 13
speaking skills 52, **69**, **70**, 78, 81, 85, 116
STARTALK 14, 155–156, 159, 161
strategic 45, 200, 208
student centeredness 78, 80
student-centered 3, 34
students: heritage 196; Russian (L2) 30, **52**, **53**, **55**, **58**, 70, 73, 191, 206
Swain, Merrill 41, 82, 84, 153, 155, 177, 192
Swales, John 50
syllabus design 4, 11
systemic mode 1, 8

target vocabulary 117, 172, 179–181, 183
task: characteristics 193, **194**; complexity 13, 61, 83, 216; design 5–6, 11, 12–13, 45, 98, 104, 209–212, 215; implementation 84–85, 215–216; pre-task 84–85, 104, 106–107, 109–110, 112–113, 125, 147, 157–159K; repetition 4, 84, 86; sequencing 1, 7, 11–13, 129; type **41**, **87**, 111
task-based: assessment 214, 216; goals **41**, 65, **124**, **130**, 195; learning 121–123, 127–128, 132, 171, 184; lesson 9, 40
task-based language teaching (TBLT): beginner level 77–78, 80–81; characteristics 193; fluency, improving 11, 28–29, 33, 67, 78, 116; focus on form 4, 11–12, 49, **69**, **70**, 202, 209; formative assessment 9, **41**, **87**; implementing, challenges faced 11, 79, 89–90, 184, 202, 206, 210, 214; peer interaction 152–155, 160–161; vlog assignments 68
task-supported instruction (TSI) 11
task, definition of 80
tasks: analytical decision making (advanced) **156**; data interpretation/summary **87**; language skills **52**, **157**, **158**, **159**; learner engagement, university-level **174**; linguistics, professional level **124**, **130**; peer interaction **160**; real-world 6, 10, 39, 123; structure-trapping 47–48, 51, **52**, 53, **53**, **54**, 54–55, 58, 61–62; study-related verbs **53**, **55**, **58**; video/vlog making **69**, **70**
teaching methodology 10, 65, 74, 100–101
technology-mediated tasks 1, 7
Tesla, Nikola 199
Test of Russian as a Foreign Language (TORFL) 7, 98, 102–103, 113–116, **119**, **120**
theoretical concepts: focus-on-form approach 84–85, 193–194; pragmatics 4, 9, 16, 90, 216; repetitions 8, 74, 82, 84, 86, 89
time expressions 48, **70**, 76
topic 51, 68, 112, 117, 133, 158–159, 180, 192–193, 202
Tschirner, Erwin 73
TV documentary 200

undergraduate courses 4, 99–100, 214
undergraduate students 90, 99–100
Universal Grammar 25

Universidade de São Paulo (University of São Paulo), Brazil 99–100
Universidade Federal de Rio de Janeiro (Federal University of Rio de Janeiro) Brazil 100
Urgant, Ivan 195, 199

Van Lier, Leo 49, 82, 91
video project 68
Virtual Museum of Communal Living 178, 182
virtual space 6, 171, 173, **174**, 175–176, 180–185

vlog 67–68, **69**, 69–70, **70**, 71–73, 75–76
vocabulary 117; exercises 101, 161, 185, 194, 200

Whitehead Martelle, Wendy 35
Wolff, Dominik 153, 154, 156, 158
World of Warcraft 173

Yatsenko, Anna A. Alsufieva (et al.) 50

Zheltoukhova, Snezhana 6–7, 214–215

Бердичевский (Berdichevsky) 92

Printed in the United States
by Baker & Taylor Publisher Services